Converting Customer Value

Converting Customer Value

From retention to profit

Professor J.A. Murphy, Dr J. Burton,
R. Gleaves and J. Kitshoff

John Wiley & Sons, Ltd

Other Wiley Editorial Offices

John Wiley & Sons Inc., 111 River Street, Hoboken, NJ 07030, USA

Jossey-Bass, 989 Market Street, San Francisco, CA 94103-1741, USA

Wiley-VCH Verlag GmbH, Boschstr. 12, D-69469 Weinheim, Germany

John Wiley & Sons Australia Ltd, 42 McDougall Street, Milton, Queensland 4064, Australia

John Wiley & Sons (Asia) Pte Ltd, 2 Clementi Loop #02-01, Jin Xing Distripark, Singapore 129809

John Wiley & Sons Canada Ltd, 22 Worcester Road, Etobicoke, Ontario, Canada M9W 1L1

Wiley also publishes its books in a variety of electronic formats. Some content that appears in print may not be
available in electronic books.

Library of Congress Cataloging in Publication Data

Murphy, John A., 1948–
    Converting customer value : from retention to profit / John Murphy; with J. Burton,
    R. Gleaves and J. Kitshoff.
        p.   cm.
    Includes bibliographical references and index.
    ISBN 13 978-0-470-01634-3 (cloth : alk. paper)
    ISBN 10 0-470-01634-5 (cloth : alk. paper)
    1. Customer relations—Management.   2. Business planning.   3. Relationship marketing.
    I. Title.
    HF5415.5.M865 2006
    658.8'12—dc22   2005020017

British Library Cataloguing in Publication Data

A catalogue record for this book is available from the British Library

ISBN-13 978-0-470-01634-3 (HB)
ISBN-10 0-470-01634-5 (HB)

Typeset in 11/13pt Goudy by Integra Software Services Pvt. Ltd, Pondicherry, India
Printed and bound in Great Britain by TJ International Ltd, Padstow, Cornwall, UK
This book is printed on acid-free paper responsibly manufactured from sustainable forestry in which at least two
trees are planted for each one used for paper production.

To our families

Contents

Acknowledgements

Few books today result solely from the efforts of one person. In writing this book we are especially grateful to our families for their continuing, unselfish support, remarkable understanding, patience and ongoing encouragement over the years.

We are very fortunate to work in or have studied at Manchester Business School, one of Europe's largest and top business schools and we are grateful to faculty members for their inspiration and advice. Further inspiration has been derived from the doctoral research students who make up what is the largest doctoral research cohort in service quality/customer retention in Europe. Particular appreciation must be given to Jackie Fisk for her invaluable assistance. Claire Plimmer and Jo Golesworthy of John Wiley & Sons were very professional and supportive of our endeavours and we appreciate the confidence they and Wiley have displayed in our work. Special thanks must be given to Moira Smith for her professional advice and editorial skills.

Inclusion of the case studies would have been impossible without the participation and extensive input of willing organisations, truly focused on great customer management. Thanks to Alfred McAlpine Business Services who fund Professor Murphy's chair in customer management, especially John Millar (marketing and communications manager); Centrica and Andrew Reaney (head of customer experience at British Gas); Eversheds, particularly Geoff Harrison (head of client relationship management); National Blood Service, particularly

Gerard Gogarty (head of service quality); and Shell, particularly Mike Corfield, (commercial customer promise manager, Shell UK, Oil Products Limited).

Additional thanks go to all members of the Customer Management Leadership Group (www.cmlg.org) past and present, for their inspirational work in search of best business practices.

Introduction

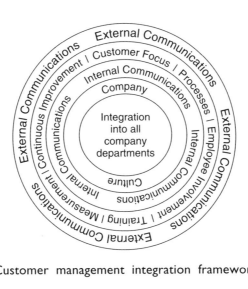

Figure 1.0 Customer management integration framework. © John A. Murphy 2005

Prior to heading a meeting of the board of directors, a stressed CEO was seated at his imposing desk, one cold day in April, reading through the annual audited accounts. This CEO felt unhappy about many of the items on the pages before his eyes. Not the least of his stress derived from the proof that his organisation showed amazing profligacy with its sales endeavours, and spent a fortune and a half on recruitment and training of new staff, who seemed to come and go like hot flushes on the cheek of a maiden aunt. As for the bottom line: that dreaded profit, double underlined; what was he to make of that, in a company with a multimillion pound turnover and such a dismal showing at the end of another year?

Suddenly, at his elbow, there appeared a stranger, who leaned over the CEO's shoulder and asked him a question.

If you could have three wishes concerning your organisation, and remember, this is not to do with your salary but it concerns the future of all your employees and customers, suppliers and middlemen, for what would you wish? Think carefully before you reply.

Of course, this is a fairy story, but the question raises certain aspects of any large, apparently thriving, organisation. These have to be addressed by the CEO, because every commercial company exists to make a profit, preferably a large enough profit to allow for expansion, to which the only opposite is contraction, followed by the black hole and either a take-over or bankruptcy. Everything else a business does is a step towards this increased profitability. Companies make profit by creating a product or service offering, usually more cheaply than they sell it on to customers. Our CEO, the one with the three wishes, needed time to reflect on the question. He represents many CEOs today, for whom the annual accounts prove harder to handle than *The Times* crossword puzzle. The clues are there but they are cryptic.

How to understand customers

If an organisation has already done everything in its power, within the scope of its knowledge of the customers it serves, to improve its products or services, logic might lead the CEO to ask for a complete understanding of his customers, in order to know how to improve his service to them. This seems, at first glance, to be sensible. However, if he looks again at the pages of accounts, he observes that the profit margin between cost of manufacture, or of direct service provision, and the income from customers is whittled away by an overwhelming set of overheads, and the net amount is nothing but a shrunken remainder.

It is not enough, merely to ask for knowledge of the company's customers. Our CEO needs to discover which customers provide most of the profit that is left. He also needs to analyse, against all his customers, a fair distribution of the overheads and look for ways in which to minimise them.

If somebody orders a wedding cake, they will not be satisfied with just any wedding cake, they want a customised cake. The baker knows what the customer wants. This is a one-to-one situation, and the baker knows his costs to serve as well as what his customer is willing to pay. The CEO, on the other hand, has a cohort of strangers to serve. Does he know whether they are happy to go on purchasing the same old products or services? How does he establish what will be required tomorrow? How does he discover those who are truly profitable? How does he find those who can and will advise on product or service development? How does he improve the company's relationship with the customers who are profitable, but only just? What does he do with those who are unprofitable? How does he persuade or threaten the middlemen, who deliver, advertise, wrap or transport his products, to think on the same lines as himself?

Where does he start to play detective?

This is a crucial item in the quest for the project of increased profitability, and, by extension, of customer retention. Retained customers cost nothing to recruit. Recruitment of new customers, by way of expensive advertising, is one of the sums that the accountant has drawn to the attention of our CEO. No matter what service or product an organisation has for sale, unless people know all about it, they will be reluctant to try it.

Who to retain and how to retain them?

Having begun to see the light with respect to customers who are loyal to the company and its offering, the CEO faces the next step: how to discover what makes them what they are, and how to bring more customers into the high profitability category. Then, there is the question of how to make certain of high-yield customers for the future, and how to retain those that are already in place. These are matters of product and service excellence. The burden of their provision falls in large measure upon the shoulders of employees. There are many approaches to cataloguing or segmenting customers, as well as understanding them, and these approaches vary from organisation to organisation. This book looks at some of the most successful of them.

What role do employees have in profitability of customers?

Thinking about customers and what they want forced our CEO to consider, too, the employees. Why is the company spending disproportionately on recruitment and training? Why is there such a huge churn? Where do disgruntled employees go next for employment and which of the organisation's secrets do they carry away with them?

No wonder that the CEO is stressed. Every step along the road brings further puzzles and uncertainties, and he begins to realise that Guy Fawkes might have had the right idea, when he attempted to blow Parliament sky high. He accepts that he, too, has to start from scratch, if he is to improve the performance of his business.

He begins to address the problem that faces every CEO at some time in his career. He needs to think what he needs to create the ideal business. He picks up a pencil and begins to sketch a little plan of how things in the organisation integrate together. He ends up with something similar to the framework with which this Introduction starts. In the centre, he has a blank. This is the space he has to fill in such a way that the rest of the company revolves around it. He pencils in the word 'culture' and in the margin, he adds the word 'pivotal'.

There is no need to be quite as drastic as Guy Fawkes. Our CEO can take his copy of the audited accounts to the board and talk them through his own considerations, receive input from fellow directors, and discuss these with shareholders. Finally, having obtained approval from all parties, it will be time to call a new tune. He warns his fellow board members to expect major changes, for which he requests their total support and active involvement, when the time is ripe. Having gone thus far, it is time to inform the rest of the people who work in the company and those outsiders who supply it with services. They will all have to play an active role in the new vision.

Identification of where the profit lies

Firstly, the chapter that follows this introduction outlines the problem of how to discover and nurture highly profitable customers, and how to exploit them for ideas, publicity and profitability in exchange for lavishing so much care and attention on them. It discusses the opportunities for bringing less profitable customers into the top group, and leaves open the question of whether to sack or nurture the remainder.

Think about overheads

Overheads, as far as company accountants are concerned, are all the costs that are not directly attributable to manufacture of product, or delivery of service. Accountants tend to divide these overheads equally between members of the customer cohort. This is incorrect, as we shall see. In fact, the very word *average* should be banned from business-speak, since it stands for an intangible and, therefore, has no useful meaning.

A regular, big-spending customer does not require advertising to lure him, or education in the use and care of the product. This customer will advertise the product to others, at no cost to the company. He will explain its use to new customers who come by way of his recommendation. If he is the ideal customer, he will offer useful advice about how to improve the product so as to meet future requirements in the market. The company accountant, if asked, cannot explain why this customer is apportioned his so-called share of overheads, when, in fact, the balance is the other way, and he contributes more than his fair share to profitability without incurring costs to serve.

What can be done with the rest of them?

Might this be one of the wishes for our CEO to consider? If he discovers that 20 per cent of customers are top of the range, about 55 per cent are not contributing anything much, once their costs to serve are correctly allocated to them, and the rest of them are making a loss, he might desire to make that 55 per cent move up the ladder and his wish would be knowledge of how to make it happen. That 25 per cent, who make a loss, might be improved, too. They should be subjected to scrutiny. If they can be improved, they should be improved. If they are incorrigible, they should be shown the door, or moved to another organisation, better geared to supply their needs. Surprisingly few CEOs realise what a small number of customers actually make the profit.

The information is on file

Most organisations hold enough data, in various forms, for a study of customer habits and preferences. What are unknown are future buying habits and requirements. This subject has been discussed many times, and there is a raft of methods whereby customer opinion might be surveyed. Each company chooses what best suits its products or services, when trawling for this type of information, some of which comes from sampling, some from direct enquiry of company records, invoices, credit notes and returned goods, not forgetting letters of complaint and compliment, focus groups, questionnaires and so on.

How does knowledge of customers affect systems and processes?

The systems and processes that lie behind production or service provision are intended to provide the best service to customers, at the lowest cost to the company. To be able to do that and know that it has been done, a company needs to know its customers intimately. The customer management integration framework shows how each section connects to all the rest by way of communication. If there is customer feedback, of a derogatory or a complimentary nature, and this is communicated throughout the organisation, systems and processes may be examined, checked and revised, and corrective measures taken. Should the finger point to something in administration, delivery, book-keeping or any other part of company activity and responsibility, this can be inspected and adjusted accordingly.

To tool up for a new product is time consuming and costly. It makes sense, therefore, to check customer hopes and expectations beforehand. Customer advice is invaluable. Back-up in the form of user manuals, easy-to-handle packaging, efficient delivery and so on all contribute to customer satisfaction, or lack of it, and form part of the systems and processes that produce and deliver the goods and services. Clearly, it pays to have good internal communication, for process enhancement; and customer-to-company communication, for an exchange of news and views. In the same way as product processes are capable of improvement in light of customer satisfaction, so are all the other processes and systems in the company.

There is a saying, 'If it isn't broken, don't fix it'. That is true, but it might be time to throw it out and buy a new one. The customer who likes to be up to date and leading edge with her purchases is susceptible to new items on the market. This customer will buy new before her old product is worn out. Think about the short shelf life of computers and mobile telephones, TV sets and automobiles, fashion and furniture. The days of passing things down through the generations is long gone. Companies have to anticipate what will be wanted, set up the processes and systems to provide it, and to go out to stimulate the demand. It takes knowledge of the customer to do all that successfully.

Is there a link between contented customers and satisfied employees?

Some CEOs think there is. It might not always be true; it might not apply to every employee; it might not apply to any employee. Those who serve customers face to face obtain instant feedback, which can be complimentary, or it can indicate dissatisfaction. With proper and well-taught complaint handling, these employees can take the information and turn it to advantage.

The annual accounts, if they indicate huge expenditure on employee recruitment and training, highlight a defect in the company's structure that needs urgent attention. It makes no sense to understand and try to retain good customers, if good employees are allowed to become dissatisfied and to defect. An organisation without employees is nothing. Only with the best, most enthusiastic, well-trained and committed employees is it possible to build a superior organisation.

There is a very firm link, then, between satisfied, loyal, highly profitable customers and satisfied, well-trained, enthusiastic employees. Part of the company's policy for creating a vision, or culture of excellence must, therefore, show equal care for employees as for customers. This entails a system of rewards for good performers. These people can be found in all areas of company activity, and even the lowliest employee deserves praise and reward for good work. Why should the best customer be the only one to receive due recognition?

Why train and develop employees?

If the annual accounts indicate inordinate expenditure on training and development of employees, directors will ask why even more should be spent. They reason that the vast sums devoted annually to this seem not to bring much in the way of reward for the company. They seldom ask whether the organisation backs up the training and development by giving employees an opportunity to demonstrate their new skills and abilities. Neither do they stop to consider why employees leave.

With a new vision to be implemented, employees also require the closest attention. When they leave, their reasons for doing so should be established and recorded. Patterns often emerge that lead to drastic changes somewhere in the organisation. Are employees' private lives taken into consideration when devising work patterns? Is there a need for child-minding facilities, for a company shop, for private medical care? Employees are not robots. They are human beings, with diverse needs and domestic situations. The more they are cosseted, the better they perform and the greater their gratitude to their employer. Why should they want to try pastures new, when they have everything they need right where they are?

Recruit the right people

Recruitment is the beginning of employee involvement in a company's vision. Square pegs do not fit in round holes. The first step in recruitment is to define exactly what role the new person is to play in the company, what skills and abilities are needed, what further training will enhance those skills, and how much the company is prepared to pay in salary and for training. Will the new person fit into the company team?

It is fashionable to think in terms of teams to manage processes and systems. The ultimate goal in team building has been achieved when the whole organisation sees itself as one united team, with a common goal and mutual trust, enhanced by open, frank and regular communication between all team members. Our CEO must make himself available to all the team members, either directly, or through managers and supervisors. Personalities must be subsumed by the company's vision. Employees, who trust their managers and supervisors to play fair with them, will feel able to communicate without fear.

Are things improving yet?

Training and development of employees, investigation of customers and their expectations, improvements to processes and systems all take up time and cost money. Breathing down the neck of the CEO and his board of directors are the shareholders, who are expecting their share of the promised profitability increase. It is asking too much of any business, to expect things to be made perfect right away. It takes time to find the weaknesses in the present system before they can be addressed, and a large organisation is an extremely complex network of people and processes. It is advisable to start with anything that is obviously in need of adjustment, and do that immediately. In its turn, it will probably highlight something else that needs to be tweaked. The domino effect will happen.

Once the minds of managers and supervisors have been brought to focus on improvements, a trickle of ideas and suggestions will make its way up to the board room and out through the company. These ideas and suggestions will probably emanate from the production line, back office, or repairs workshop, where voices used to be unheard by those who have charge of the company.

Never stop measuring, and measure everything that can be measured

The best companies, those who have found the right vision and culture to maximise customer retention and profitability, do not rest on their laurels. They know they are doing the right things because they measure everything they do, and make comparisons with the state of the thing being measured, comparing what it was before the latest improvement effort with the way it is now. If asked, the CEO of such a company would happily admit that perfection is a goal that keeps hovering, just out of reach, on the horizon. He would add, however, that he and his team are still straining to touch it.

Make measurement a trigger for action

The point of continuous measurement is to highlight weaknesses or situations that might become troublesome in future, and change them for the better. Without continuous measurement, these faults would probably remain undetected and might, in time, infect other parts of the company. It follows from this that there is as much need for continuous improvement as there is for continuous measurement. There is no time for anyone in the team to take a breather or to slacken in their endeavours.

Behind all the expenditure, the head scratching and the checking and double-checking of everything, and the improvements that are made, there is one vital requirement for the whole to work properly. Communication is that requirement.

How, what and when to communicate, and to whom?

Imagine that someone on a production line has a brilliant idea about how to speed up his part of the production process. Also imagine that he, for fear of being ignored, or laughed at, says nothing. The time he might have saved the company can be measured in terms of cash. On the other hand, he might persuade his co-workers to adopt his idea. They save time but cause a bottleneck because they have upset the rhythm of the whole production system. If the means to communicate his idea and to have it properly checked and adopted are readily available, and if he is rewarded for thinking of it, that idea will not only be incorporated into his part of the line. It will cause adjustments to be made down the line, and time might be saved in other areas because of this.

As the above example shows, communication within the organisation, from top to bottom, bottom to top, and right across all departments, refers to system improvements and also to the rewards that are given for extraordinary service to the company. Such rewards should be afforded maximum publicity, to give the employee pride in the work and to encourage others to think of improvements in their own spheres of company activity.

If the improvement also shows up in an improved product, there is a need to communicate this externally, to customers. Customers can only become experts on a company's products or services if they are given information about them.

With the idea of the whole company making a unified and harmonious team, it is wise to keep all those involved in company business informed about things that matter to them. Not everything has to be communicated to everyone. There is, though, a problem if something should be communicated to some people, is not, and employees get to know about it through the rumour mill. Management has a balancing act to perform here, when making decisions about what is told to whom.

In many areas of a company's activities, where information specific to certain tasks has to be disseminated, line managers and supervisors can handle it perfectly well. When something impinges upon everyone, the CEO should make sure how, when and to whom it is communicated. The language used to inform managerial people might be more sophisticated than that used to tell janitorial staff and groundspeople, but it must be comprehensible to all, not patronising, and it should be presented in written form.

There is a danger, too, that incomplete information, poorly understood information or late information, may lead to people talking together, inside and outside the company, and spreading false stories that can do much damage.

Definition of a culture

Having thought about customers, processes and systems, employee involvement, training and development, measurement, continuous improvements and communications, and decided what has to be done to build the vision; it is time to commit it all to paper in the form of a mission statement.

In moving an organisation forward, with all the foregoing aspects of what makes up the workplace environment, the CEO and his board have been thinking about how to describe what they want to see achieved, and they share the desire to build into it the steps necessary to keep it moving ahead. They formulate their ideas in a shorthand way that is self-explanatory.

Now, a mission statement, or company culture and values, are put down on paper. Paper usually gets filed away and forgotten. Our conscientious CEO keeps repeating the mission message, and expects his managers and supervisors to echo it. He desires that every employee will remember it, not just now and then, but every minute of every working day. How good it was, in the olden days, when great ideas were carved in tablets of stone.

From now on, all new employees are told what is expected of them. They are given a copy of the mission statement and warned that it is the law, the Gospel, the chain that binds them to the company. They are advised that they have the duty, more than the right, to show initiative in following the law, and that best efforts bring best rewards. Existing employees are given a chance to gain skills and confidence, and are encouraged to take responsibility when serving customers.

After the mighty machine has run itself in and people are comfortable with their new roles and the new systems and processes, and when continuous measurement informs about continuous improvement, employees begin to feel happy, excited, stimulated and eager. This communicates itself to customers, who often share in the general joy of connecting to the company. This has a knock-on effect, slight in some companies, tremendous in others.

At the end of a year, maybe after two years, the accountants add up their figures, check them, and shake their heads. Something has happened: an earthquake has shaken the company to its foundations. Overheads are down, profits are up; the customer portfolio has expanded. Many of the middle ranking customers have stopped buying from all and sundry and have decided to stay loyal to this one. Some of the poor performers have melted away; others have increased their purchasing activities. New customers are clamouring to come aboard. That crucial bottom line of profit looks very healthy.

What next?

With more profit, the company can spend more on improvements. That elusive goal of perfection keeps moving and growing smaller, but it remains visible. Customers, those who stay long enough, become lazy about looking for pastures on the other side of the hill. As long as they can be satisfied, they remain locked in to the company. Employees can receive larger salaries and derive more job satisfaction from their tasks. In their turn, like customers, these employees know a good thing when they experience it, and they no longer scan the Situations Vacant columns. Overheads no longer loom ominously over the company; they are shrinking in inverse proportion to the expansion of profitability and customer retention, and to employees staying in post.

To come back to the harassed CEO and his chance to have three wishes; what does he now think he needs? He has a revitalised company, his customers are content with what is on offer, the R&D people are bubbling with new ideas, for the implementation of which, amazingly, finance is available, there is backing from the board of directors, and the employees are always smiling.

In his position, his three wishes might be along the lines of:

- Strength and determination to keep moving ahead, and to stay on track.
- To retain the support and team spirit of everyone within the organisation, including suppliers and the middlemen who contribute to delivery of the goods or services.
- To keep a long jump ahead of competitors and have contented shareholders.

The stranger will shake his head and remind the CEO that he has solved his own problems and has no need of magic to continue as he is going. Our CEO is a shepherd: his flock of sheep comprises customers and employees; the wolves are competitors; the danger point comes when the shepherd forgets to be vigilant.

The framework that features in this book might be seen as the sheepfold, with its safety arrangements in place in the form of carefully chosen, well-guarded customers, perfected processes and systems, total employee involvement, comprehensive training and development, continuous measurement, leading to continuous improvement, harmonised by efficient communication, all revolving around a culture of excellence, which has the aim of maximising customer retention and profitability.

Let the wolves starve.

I

The Customer Profit Conundrum

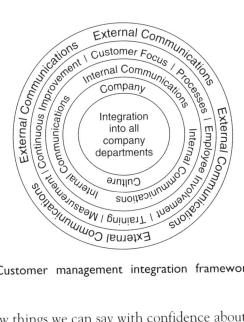

Figure 1.0 Customer management integration framework. © John A. Murphy 2005

One of the few things we can say with confidence about any company is that it will have customers. These customers do business with suppliers because they receive value and not because they want their suppliers to make a profit. The key question that needs to be answered is: 'Are all customers profitable?' Perhaps, even the question is wrong and it should really be: 'Are you making a profit from all of your customers?' The customer profit conundrum is the fact that very few companies are able to measure individual customer profitability and so these questions cannot be answered.

Customer profitability is one of the most poorly understood concepts in business. Despite revived interest in the measurement of individual customer profitability, after a history of sporadic application and academic interest, there are no clear and robust methods commonly available for companies to follow. There is also confusion between customer profitability, customer lifetime value and customer economic profit, and the term 'customer equity' is sometimes applied indiscriminately between them.

The growth in customer relationship management (CRM) should have brought the customer profitability issue to the fore. There is little purpose in striving for stronger relationships with customers if they are actually unprofitable. Yet this point keeps getting missed from the agenda. Much has been written about recognising the lifetime value of customers, especially through the concepts of customer loyalty and customer equity. Most books and articles fail to recognise adequately the fundamental issue of true customer profitability, and many ignore this vital issue altogether.

Every organisation needs to decide who manages profits. Often, the day-to-day goals of departments, to increase output, reduce costs and keep customers satisfied, are only obliquely linked to profitability and do not allow action to be focused where it is actually needed.

The analysis of *individual* customer profitability opens a door on a new way of thinking about business. It provides routes to a clear strategy for profitable growth, which have previously been unavailable. This chapter outlines the key elements of customer profitability before providing a detailed technical methodology including a discussion of the management issues and with specific real examples of its use. It also highlights the fact that, for most companies, a large proportion of customers will be unprofitable.

Common misperceptions about customer profitability

Ask a company if it has unprofitable customers and you will usually get one of two responses: 'No, we don't have unprofitable customers', or,

'Ah, yes, 80% of our profit comes from 20% of our customers'. Even when a company acknowledges that it does have, or might have, unprofitable customers, it cannot readily identify which they are. The other misperception is that companies think that nothing can be done about unprofitable customers.

Challenging these misperceptions is the first hurdle in tackling the complex, yet critical, issue of customer profitability.

One of the most common rules of thumb in business is the 80:20 rule (otherwise known as Pareto's rule or law). This rule derived from Vilfredo Pareto's analysis of wealth distribution in nineteenth-century Italy, where he found that 80% of land was in the hands of 20% of landowners. Since then, it has been applied effectively in many contexts. For example, 80% of customer complaints come from 20% of reasons, 80% of production defects come from 20% of causes, and even 80% of revenues typically come from 20% of customers. Pareto is effective in so many situations that his formula has become accepted as an almost universal truth.

In the matter of profits, the rule does not necessarily apply. Using it, one might argue that, if 80% of profits come from 20% of customers, then 20% of profits come from the remaining 80% of customers, on the basis that all customers must be profitable.

Consider the most extreme example of a loss-making company. This will still typically have a range of customer revenues, which may well approximate to a Pareto-type distribution, but all of its customers are unprofitable, on average, since it is still making a loss overall. This is because of the nature of profit, where, although it is not possible to own a negative amount of land, it is possible to have a negative profit, i.e. a loss.

The flaw of averages

For a profit-making company, the common assumption is that all customers are profitable. In order to test this hypothesis further it is useful to introduce portfolios.

The idea of a portfolio is useful when dealing with a range of similar yet distinct profit-making assets; for example, a portfolio of shares, or a portfolio of business units. Figures 1.1(a) and (b) show the range of returns for a portfolio of business units and a portfolio of shares.

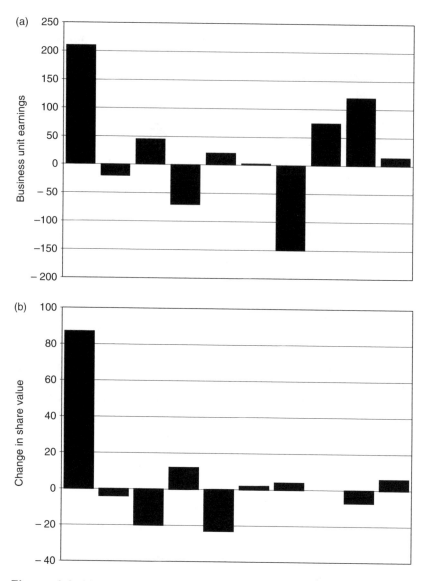

Figure 1.1 (a) Business unit portfolio returns (£M). (b) Share portfolio returns (%)

It is easy to comprehend that there can be losses within a portfolio, despite an overall gain from it. However, it would be meaningless to state that in Figure 1.1(a) the average return on each business unit is £5.7 million, or in Figure 1.1(b) the average return on each share is 24.9%. Using average returns does not allow changes to be made to improve overall profitability, nor does it assist with the selection of future new business units or shares. Yet this is precisely how most businesses deal with their customer base. By failing to recognise the issue of customer profitability, companies fail to recognise that, despite a healthy bottom line, there can be a considerable number of unprofitable customers within their customer portfolio. This is the flaw of averages.

The analysis of individual customer profitability will typically reveal that a company is servicing a proportion of unprofitable customers. This proportion can be significant, in many cases over 50% of the customer base. This leads to some startling results, which are contrary to Pareto's formula, and seem to challenge basic mathematics. For example, it is common to find that 20% of customers actually provide well over 100% of profits, with the remaining 80% causing a loss. So, where 20% of customers provide 200% of potential profits (a not uncommon finding), the remaining 80% of customers provide minus 100% of profits, in other words, a loss equal to 100% of the profits. This finding should have profound consequences on the way that a business is run and yet it often gets overlooked.

Misperceptions about Pareto and the use of flawed averages mean that companies fail to understand the spread of customer profitability. When customer profitability distribution is properly calculated, we enter the world of hyper-Pareto, where levels of profit concentration are even higher than 80:20.

Customer profitability analysis (CPA) should become a core discipline for all firms.

A definition of customer profitability analysis: the allocation of costs and revenues to specific customers over a specific period with the aim of measuring individual customer profitability.

There are other definitions in use, including that of the Chartered Institute of Management Accounting (CIMA), which defines customer profitability analysis as the 'analysis of the revenue streams and service costs associated with specific customers or customer groups'.

Customer profitability analysis enables a company to gain an understanding of the drivers of individual customer profit, and to take practical and focused steps to improve overall profitability performance.

An overview of customer profitability analysis

The measurement of customer profitability requires a combination of accounting and marketing skills that is often lacking within a firm, due to compartmentalisation of the business.

The relevance of management accounting to strategic decision making has been covered in other books, however, before discussing customer profitability, it is important to understand why most commonly used management accounting conventions do not provide the right information to allow individual customer profitability to be measured.

According to Johnson and Kaplan (1991) it was recognised almost 100 years ago that indirect costs could represent more than direct costs, and so, costing systems that primarily involved direct costs would be inaccurate at best and misleading at worst. Indirect costs have continued to increase for most businesses over the last 50 years, especially service businesses, making this discrepancy even more relevant.

Modern management accounting has been heavily influenced by the requirements of financial reporting, and this has led to an excessive emphasis on product costing, especially for the purpose of valuing stocks and work in progress. This does not allow companies to put together a clear picture of customer profitability. The power of modern information systems enables the analysis to be carried out more easily.

How to measure profit

Profit is typically measured using a Profit and Loss (P&L) statement (or income statement). The P&L represents one of the key annual financial reports, and consists of several parts, each reflecting a different aspect of profit for a business, for example gross profit, trading profit, profit before interest and tax, profit for the financial year.

Basically, a P&L covers the following:

Total	**revenue, turnover** or **income**
Less	cost of sales (cost of goods sold)
Equals	**gross profit**

Total	**gross profit**
Less	other expenses (operating expenses)
Equals	**trading profit** or **net income**

The cost of sales (cost of goods sold) typically contains only direct costs, and so, for a retailer, this would be the actual wholesale cost of the goods sold. The costs in other expenses comprise a range of costs with different characteristics. These include direct and indirect (or overhead) costs such as lighting, insurance etc., which can represent fixed or variable costs, together with some non-cash costs. Depreciation is the main non-cash cost, in that it is a way of accounting for capital consumption over the lifetime of an asset. These costs are drawn together into the other expenses category for the purpose of reporting overall financial performance in the trading profit.

Behind these financial statements there will be management accounting systems to assist with the day-to-day running of the business and decision making about its future. However, management accounting systems have evolved in a way that often masks information about individual customer profitability.

Model financial statements, such as those from Deloitte Touche, break down other expenses into the following categories:

- distribution costs;
- administrative expenses;
- other operating expenses.

There are no clear distinctions between these groups, which are often referred to as sales, general and administration, or even sales, marketing, distribution and administration (SMDA) costs. There are no generally recognised definitions for these categories, and the only proviso for financial reporting is that a company must be consistent in its definition of 'administrative expenses', 'cost of sales' and 'distribution costs'.

Since many of the below-the-line costs relate to customer relationships by way of sales, marketing, distribution and administration, customer profitability becomes a key strategic factor for organisations to consider. The proportion of these costs to individual customers is difficult to extract from financial statements and from management accounting systems. The allocation of these so-called other expenses to customers is, however, the key part of the calculation of individual customer profitability.

The nature of customer costs

If all customer costs were variable and varied in direct proportion to sales, it might be argued that all customers could be profitable. However, there are fixed costs and costs that are independent of the level of sales in every company. When these are taken into consideration, the question of individual customer profitability becomes even more important, and yet it seems even more opaque.

Many companies find that some customer-related costs are actually super-variable, that is, they increase at a faster rate than sales. This can have a dramatic impact on customer profitability and underlines the need to measure customer profitability.

The accurate allocation of SMDA costs directly to individual customers is key for the calculation of individual customer profitability.

Operationally, all businesses have a hierarchy of customer-related costs:

- product costs (usually direct and often called cost of goods);
- selling costs;
- servicing costs;
- relationship costs;
- business-sustaining costs.

These are shown in Table 1.1 together with some examples.

Table 1.1 The customer cost hierarchy

Product costs	Selling costs	Servicing costs	Relationship costs	Business-sustaining costs
Cost of goods	Sales and marketing	Distribution, administration	Sales and marketing, administration	Administration
Direct costs of product e.g. materials, packaging	Customer acquisition cost, Advertising	Cost-to-serve Order processing, shipping etc.	Account management, administration, hospitality, CRM systems	Senior management, premises, R&D

Usually, only the product (or service) cost is considered in the measurement of gross profit. All of the other costs are lumped together below gross profit, to allow the measurement of trading profit. Clearly, many of these costs are linked to the servicing of individual customers, and yet there is no formal mechanism to measure individual customer profitability.

To illustrate this, consider a range of typical customer-related costs for a consumer product. First, there are customer acquisition costs; these include the costs of marketing campaigns in their widest sense: market research, advertising, promotion and channel costs (including incentives and discounts).

Secondly, there are the costs to serve the customer, including order taking, order processing, inventory management and customer-order fulfilment costs. Customer-order fulfilment includes product storage, picking, packaging and distribution. Behind this there will also be the cost of processing the financial aspects of the transaction: collecting and banking payment. Post-sales customer service might also include technical support, returns and complaint handling.

Thirdly, there are relationship costs: examples of which include running user groups, newsletters, web chat-rooms, CRM systems and so on.

Finally, there are business-sustaining costs, which often represent the entry-level for the business: head office, investor relations, human resources management, finance, insurance costs and so on.

In each case mentioned above the behaviour of the company and of the customer can influence the real level of individual customer profitability.

Before going into the detailed method for CPA a consideration of some basic information that can be gleaned from a P&L statement (Figure 1.2) will help to illustrate the reasons for doing a detailed analysis.

Figure 1.2 represents a 6.36% return on sales revenue. The key question is does every pound of revenue yield just over 6 pence of profit?

The revenue figure shown is in fact the sum of revenues from each customer. The costs of goods sold will often be in direct proportion to the revenue from each customer. The key question is how to apportion indirect costs and overheads. This has troubled accountants since the earliest days of commerce.

Having accepted that it is difficult to discover how to apportion these costs to individual customers, it is possible to utilise some basic facts that can be extracted from the P&L if we know the total number of customers, in order to question assumptions about the profitability of customers.

Using Figure 1.2, and assuming that there are 250 customers, we can do some very basic analysis.

Revenue

The average revenue per customer is £22,229. However, looking at the detailed breakdown of revenues from the customer base, the highest

Revenue	5,557,291
Costs of goods sold	2,111,771
Gross profit	3,445,520
Other expenses	3,083,389
Operating profit	362,131

Figure 1.2 Example of a profit and loss (P&L) statement

customer revenue is £210,724 and the lowest is just £16. In fact, when we look at the customer revenue data, we find that 80% of revenue comes from approximately 40% of customers.

Gross profit

The average gross profit per customer reveals an interesting 'flaw of averages'. The average gross profit per customer is £13,782. Since it was established that the smallest customer generates just £16 revenue, the flaw is immediately obvious. It is also important to recognise that 187 customers (out of the 250 in this case) actually generated revenue of less than the average gross profit.

Overheads

In allocating overheads to customers, the most common method used is to allocate the overhead in proportion to each customer's revenue, as a percentage of total revenue. This means that the largest customer, who contributes 3.89% of revenues, will also attract 3.89% of overheads. This is equivalent to £119,944 whereas the smallest customer, with revenue of just £16 or 0.0000028% of revenues, attracts just £8.63 in overheads.

The question to be asked is what are the reasons for the overhead being incurred? Is it reasonable for just £8.63 to be the cost of serving the smallest customer? The average overhead per customer is actually £12,334 and is probably nearer the true cost to serve each and every customer.

Customer profitability analysis (CPA) and activity-based costing (ABC)

Customer profitability analysis is often confused with activity-based costing because they are based on the same basic concept, identifying the drivers of cost. However, the fundamental frame of reference for each is different. Both approaches trace or apportion overheads to a cost-driver, but for ABC these costs are typically product-related, and for CPA these costs are customer-related.

With ABC, it is common to find that a high percentage of products, when fully costed, are being sold at a loss. Efforts can then be made to reduce this loss, or to cease production of certain products. This assumes that all products can be sold at a profit, and fails to take the needs of customers into account.

There have been cases where companies have shed unprofitable parts of their product portfolio, only to find that their customers leave. This is because customers want to purchase a related range of goods, not just the few that the supplier thinks can be sold profitably. A commonly encountered analogy is that of a supermarket, where staple goods, such as milk and bread, are often sold at a loss to provide an incentive for the purchase of a more comprehensive basket of goods. The supermarkets aim to make a profit on the customer, not on each product. If a supermarket carried out a product-focused profitability analysis and, on finding these products unprofitable, decided to withdraw milk and bread, it would soon find itself failing to meet the needs of its customers. This can be true for all businesses, not just supermarkets.

Activity-based costing has also been the traditional domain of manufacturing companies, and it has not always recognised the needs of service businesses, where a far greater proportion of costs is indirect. New time-based methods for ABC make this easier.

It is interesting, when considering ABC and CPA, to examine the influences on individual product or customer profitability. For ABC and products, the reference is often what the company does, whereas for CPA and customers the reference is often how the customer behaves. By examining customer needs and behaviour, it becomes possible to develop a wider and more sustainable understanding of how to grow the business profitably.

So, although the methods used for ABC and CPA have many similarities, there are critical and fundamental differences in their application.

Where is CPA appropriate?

CPA is relevant to all businesses as a strategic issue. There are, however, several factors that will influence the approach taken to measuring it. These factors include the:

- availability of customer information;
- number of customers served;
- variation in customer spend.

Availability of customer information means having the ability to recognise individual customers and their attendant revenues. This is seldom a problem in the business-to-business (B2B) context, and there are also many business-to-consumer (B2C) companies that have access to specific, individualised customer data, including airlines, telecommunications providers, banks and insurance companies. Having access to individual data, and assuming it can be scaled up from transactions to get a total customer view, is the key to making a detailed customer profitability analysis.

Where there is no individual customer data, it will still be possible to carry out a basic CPA, using customer modelling around behavioural analysis. The rise of loyalty cards has been one of the main ways in which companies have tried to get more information about their customers.

Similarly, the number of customers served can affect the approach taken to CPA. With up to 5000 customers it is possible to use a basic spreadsheet to do the analysis, and most cost categories can be analysed to an individual level. Above this level, companies often tend to use agglomerations of customers to enable the reporting of results in decile or quintile blocks.

Finally, the level of variation in revenues from customers also makes a difference. Where customer revenues are very similar, it might be perceived that there is very little use for CPA. This might be true, but experience shows that it is always worth examining customer profitability. Single-sized pricing generally means that some customers will be underserved, and an opportunity is being missed, while others will be being overserved, receiving services that they do not need, want or value.

These factors might influence the way in which the analysis is carried out, or the way the results are used, but CPA is relevant for B2B and B2C companies, with high or low growth, mature or start-up, and regardless of the number of customers.

Online versus off-line analysis

Historical data for the previous year, so-called off-line data, normally forms the basis for the analysis. Most companies use this as a starting point for their CPA. A year is a normal analysis period, smoothing any seasonal fluctuation, but where this is not a factor, smaller periods, like six or three months, could also be analysed.

The alternative approach is to develop an online model, whereby cost elements are allocated to customers on a per activity basis, as incurred, to give a current picture of customer profitability. This data, although current, can only be of real use if it is summarised for a relevant period, however, and this is usually an accounting year.

Companies should begin with off-line analysis of historical data because it takes time to be comfortable with the approach used and historical data is readily available. Once the benefits and power of CPA have been recognised, it will be possible to move to a live, online system. There are vendors of online analytical tools for the measurement of customer profitability; they do not always measure the true level of individual customer profit, but often focus on gross profit.

How to measure individual customer profitability

There are no standard recognised methods for CPA. While the basic concept is simple: to subtract customer costs from customer revenues in order to identify customer profitability, complexity arises because there are many types of costs: direct, indirect, fixed, variable and so on.

Companies often evolve their own approaches in practice, but the fact that different approaches provide very different results should be of concern to anyone trying to measure genuine customer profitability.

The different CPA methods used in practice

CPA methods range from broad and simple methods based on using percentages of sales to allocate costs, through to intricate allocation methods based on those actual activities that incurred the costs. We have encountered a variety of methodologies, including:

- gross profit contribution;
- partial overhead allocation (some overheads allocated in proportion to revenue, or even activity);
- customer-related cost allocation (bringing sales costs and relationship costs, for example);
- full allocation (even tracing) of customer costs.

There are also industry-specific approximation methods, such as Federal Reserve Board functional cost analysis figures as used in the US banking industry.

However, these methods all give very different results, and care should be taken about the appropriateness of each method, especially when the conclusion is to sack some customers. It is important that the more detailed methods are used because, when it comes to migrating unprofitable customers, it is essential to understand the reasons for the lack of profitability. This cannot be done effectively if only the gross margin contribution is known. A key point raised with regard to costs at the basic level is that, for large customers, overhead costs are generally overallocated, and for smaller customers they are generally underallocated.

However, whichever method is used for the analysis, the process and discipline of carrying out CPA will stimulate a customer profitability mindset, which can lead to positive results being achieved. This would suggest that the specific method is less important than the fact of actually carrying it out.

The customer profitability paradigm usually represents a revolution in thinking for most companies and, therefore, it is difficult to accommodate this by simply evolving current systems.

A step-by-step approach to measuring customer profitability

The basic equation for customer profitability analysis is:

Customer profitability = Customer revenue − Customer-related cost

Within the customer-related cost lie several levels of cost, and these will be broken down in the following sections. Before discussing costs, it is actually necessary to begin with a discussion of the measurement of individual customer revenues.

Individual customer revenues

Identifying individual customer revenues is the most straightforward part of customer profitability measurement. Customer transaction data should be readily available in the sales ledger, and need to be combined at the individual customer level. There are some issues commonly encountered here, including the problem of duplicate data, the issue of multiple sites for the same customer, and adjustments to revenue from the use of credit notes, for example. Finally, since CPA can be completed for a company, division or subsidiary, regional business unit, or specific channel, care should be taken to ensure a complete view of the customer, what the customer spent, and its strategic significance for other divisions of the company. What could be an unprofitable customer for one department could be a highly profitable customer for another.

Duplicate data will typically affect a very small percentage of customer records but should not be ignored. Customers can be included more than once into a database for a range of reasons, even due to the name of the person placing the order. Data cleansing to remove duplicates should be carried out in order to minimise the impact of this.

The issue of multiple sites potentially within the control of the same customer can pose a more serious problem. For example, a single customer with small expenditure at multiple sites could represent a significant amount of revenue overall. The best approach is to treat transactions individually to begin with and then to combine them, as appropriate. This is because there are transaction level costs, so it might be important to recognise the number of transactions that each customer has undertaken.

It is also important to reconcile the total customer revenue with any credit notes, discounts or rebates, especially if applied retrospectively, based on volume, for example.

Individual customer gross profit

Having identified the revenues from customers, the next step is to calculate the customer gross profit. The starting point is to determine the direct costs of the different types of products or services the company has purchased. Some of this detail is obtainable from a company's stock purchase orders or invoices. The more complex the company's product or service basket the more time will need to be spent collating the data. Although this may be time-consuming, it is easily done. It might also be necessary to begin the process of CPA with a consideration of the accuracy of product costs. These are the costs of products or services that can be attributed directly to products, and could include materials and packaging, for example.

Customer gross profit = Customer revenue – Cost of goods sold

The starting point for profitability analysis should be to gain a clear understanding of product or service costs; particularly important when a company has a wide range of products. Activity-based costing can be used to assign the costs of activities and resources to those products that incur them. Incorrect cost allocation leads to ineffective pricing, where some products might be being sold at a loss.

Whichever method is used, the aim is to get a value for the gross profit on each customer's revenues.

Allocating other expenses to individual customers

The complex part of individual CPA is usually in understanding and measuring all the other expenses cost-related to individual customers. These costs are in many layers, like an onionskin. The term DACCs, or directly attributable customer costs, is sometimes used to describe these costs.

The full customer cost-to-serve model should include:

- selling costs; (customer acquisition costs)
- servicing or processing costs;
- relationship costs (essentially customer retention costs);
- business-sustaining costs (costs of being in business but not doing business).

Examples of each of these are given in Table 1.2, followed by a detailed discussion of each of the items together with the approaches used to measure them.

Selling costs

If a business has been operating for a long period, the majority of its customers will not have been acquired in the year under consideration. Typical customer acquisition rates, as a percentage of the existing customer base, are often between 2 and 10%, except for very high growth companies. Selling costs can therefore be considered to be zero

Table 1.2 Directly attributable customer costs

Selling costs	Servicing costs	Relationship costs	Business-sustaining costs
Advertising, sales force, promotions	Order processing, shipping, installation etc.	Account management, administration, hospitality, CRM systems etc.	Offices, senior management, insurance, audit, R&D, premises etc.

for the majority of customers. This is not to say that costs from the sales and marketing functions, such as key account management etc., will not have been incurred but simply recognises that these costs are actually part of the relationship cost. The selling costs associated with sales and marketing activities, including advertising, usually only apply to the acquisition of new customers.

The problem lies in the fact that companies seldom measure the different categories of customer very well. Some companies have no idea how many customers they have for each product or service they offer. This is because there are different types of customer:

- customers served in the last 12 months (this time scale is arbitrary since a relationship could have a longer natural period than 12 months, for example a 3-year capital expenditure cycle);
- customers who have lapsed after making a purchase;
- prospective customers;
- target customers.

CPA is usually only concerned with the number of customers served in the last 12 months, and within this group it is important to recognise the actual number of customers that have been acquired in the period.

Companies often do not dare to measure the total selling cost, nor do they compare it against the number of customers acquired in the same period. This is usually because of fears of low measurable impact.

When the number of new customers acquired in a period is measured, it can be a pitifully low figure. Many promotional offers that were aimed at acquiring new customers fail to win new customers and give a discount to existing customers instead. At the height of the dotcom bubble, many companies' customer acquisition economics were so flawed that it was costing them more to acquire a customer than the expected lifetime value of the customer.

Where do selling costs go?

It was John Wannamaker who first said, 'I know half the money I spend on advertising is wasted, but I can never find out which half.' This is still true for most organisations, and is one of the biggest obstacles to CPA. Of course, it is essential to recognise the complex nature of advertising and the fact that it is not always designed to generate sales. It is also possible to develop the brand through advertising, or even to provide additional value to existing customers who bask in the glow of the brand value. But, the majority of advertising is about getting customers to buy. It might start with awareness, interest and desire, but it should end with action.

The other complicating factor is that it is hard to recognise the actual reason for a customer making a purchase. The real reason is likely to be a complicated cocktail of needs, adverts, word-of-mouth recommendation, previous experience and budget. However, if a company has managed to attract 1000 new customers and the total marketing and advertising budget was £1 million, then, however you dress it up, the net effect is an average spend of £1000 per customer.

There is also the matter of timing of customer acquisition and allowing for prospects that are just around the corner. For financial reporting, all costs incurred in the period have to be allocated to that period, regardless of whether they constitute an investment with a view to future cash flows. For simplicity, the same approach should be followed with selling costs.

However, it is possible to split selling costs into two categories: successful, that is linked to the acquisition of a customer, and unsuccessful, that is all other expenditure that could be considered to be a business-sustaining cost. The likely magnitude of this expenditure will cause questions to be asked about the effectiveness of the sales conversion process. It is not just advertising costs, there is also the question of sales-force costs. These can be quite large, and examples of selling costs for a field sales force are:

- salaries and commission;
- car;
- laptop and communications;
- travel expenses;
- occupancy;
- home office allowance;
- medical and other insurance;
- taxes and national insurance;
- pension.

Since all of these costs are incurred to acquire new customers, they should be defrayed against those same customers. The issue of unprofitable customers will be dealt with later, but it is worth noting that many customers will be unprofitable in their first year of a relationship with a company due to their high costs of acquisition.

Other costs of acquisition include the costs of promotions and deals (for example, buy one get one free), which might represent reduced revenue together with any incurred costs for items such as a telephone handset or free gifts. Whichever costs are included in selling costs, the aim is to quantify the cost of acquisition of new customers in the period under analysis.

Servicing costs

The next level of costs is servicing costs which include the costs of key activities derived from customer requests – essentially customer fulfilment costs. They might include order processing, special packaging requirements and shipping costs. Examples of some typical servicing costs are shown in Figure 1.3.

Some companies evaluate a sample of customers to see the way in which servicing costs vary. Approximate costs per activity can then be allocated on a customer level. The majority of these will have two key cost drivers: the number of transactions and some customer-specific data, such as location of the customer.

• Balance and payment enquiries	• Order delivery and product collection/return
• Change account details	• Price enquiry
• Change/Create price	
• Copies of invoices and proof of delivery (POD)	• Proactive price notification
	• Product safety and technical data sheet request
• Debt management	
• Delivery status	• Product price quotation – spot
• General feedback and issues	• Product returns
• Invoice enquiries	• Require promotional material/product
	• Technical and product enquiries

Figure 1.3 Examples of typical customer servicing costs

There is a range of possible costs for the servicing cost that will depend on the product or service being offered. Key questions to ask at this stage are how does customer behaviour affect the level of servicing cost, are some customers over-served, getting more value than they need and how could company systems be changed to manage this more effectively?

Relationship costs

Relationship costs are those costs incurred while managing and developing the customer relationship. Often these costs are incurred at the discretion of the company rather than the customer, although individuals on a sales force might have the final discretion.

There is a wide range of activities that can be put into this category, including:

- management review of the customer account;
- face-to-face negotiations;
- joint promotions;
- industry forums;
- regular calls;

- industry newsletter update;
- price notification.

And it can involve a range of people, including key account managers, field sales staff and office-based staff, including telemarketers.

Sampling of data: sampled average versus total data

The key question that arises for relationship costs is whether to measure or analyse data for all customers with, for example, interviews with the entire sales force about their activities, or whether to take a sample. In addition, averages can be used for some smaller, attributable costs.

Sampling and the use of averages reduce the accuracy of the data but take less time and are perhaps more repeatable for future measurement. As with all management information, there is a trade-off between the cost to get the data and the benefit that will be provided from knowing it.

Business-sustaining costs

Business-sustaining costs are those incurred to keep the business running. Despite many of them not being able to be directly linked to individual customers, these costs must be covered by the overall net customer profit remaining after allowing for the cost to serve.

There is extensive debate over whether *all* overheads can or should be allocated to individual customers. The costs of IT, R&D and senior management are all incurred in trying to serve existing customers, or to acquire new customers, and yet many companies are reluctant to allocate them.

The arguments against allocation are often that the costs are fixed, or that they fit into the 'rule of one' that was developed as a rule of thumb for activity-based costing. This states that if there is only one managing director, for example, you shouldn't allocate his/her cost between different customers because, even if you reduced the number of customers, you will still need one managing director.

However, an analogy from voyage accounting for mercantile shipping is relevant here. After each voyage, all costs related to the voyage were deemed to have been incurred to fulfil the import of goods, and so all expenses were offset against the income generated by the goods. In a similar way it can be argued that all costs in the last year have been incurred either to acquire or to serve the existing customer base. There may be reasons why this is not reasonable: for example, with R&D for future product development, but some allowance of the cost has to be made in the current profit and loss.

The assumption is sometimes made that reducing the number of customers is the main action resulting from the analysis of customer profitability, and so fixed costs should not be included in the analysis since they will remain after customers have been sacked. As we shall discuss later, whilst sacking customers is a viable strategy after CPA, it is not its prime goal.

Final integration of cost data

The final stage in CPA is to combine the customer-related costs and to subtract these from the individual customer revenue in order to measure the individual customer profit, as shown below:

> Customer profitability = Customer revenue − (Cost of goods + Cost to sell + Cost to serve + Relationship cost + Business-sustaining cost)

Getting started with customer profitability analysis

The method outlined in this chapter is necessarily detailed and perhaps daunting to anyone setting out to measure customer profitability for the first time. There are some short cuts that can be taken to give an overview of the customer profitability issue.

1. Recognise that it is an issue. The company about to undertake CPA must be convinced that customer profitability is relevant. When a company is profitable, the commonly held belief is that all customers are profitable.

2. Use available data to create a simple model. This is best done by developing a simple process flow of customer interaction, to see where costs are incurred. The key data you will need are:

   – total revenue by customer (to include discounts/rebates and credit notes);
   – total business unit costs, especially overheads;
   – for each cost group (sales force, call centre, etc.) identify the drivers of costs.

3. For each customer, subtract from their total revenue their direct product or service costs (cost of goods sold/cost of sales) to obtain a customer gross margin. If you have a good understanding of your basic gross margin, for example, if prices are set to give a 45% gross profit, you can apply this to get a quick recognition of the customer gross profit contribution.

4. The key stage is to subtract other expenses or overhead costs. This can be done relatively quickly by:

   – focusing on significant activities and costs, allocating costs that can easily be identified and that are directly traceable to specific company/customer interactions, such as customer acquisition, servicing and retention costs. Tackle more ambiguous costs later;
   – use estimates where possible. They will not be 100% accurate but will provide a starting point. If it is apparent that the figure might have a significant impact on customer profitability, more accurate measurement can be made through the collection of additional data;
   – try to apply costs at the lowest possible activity level, to maintain maximum analytical flexibility, such as per transaction rather than per customer, to begin with. That way, they can be rolled up in many different ways;
   – determining customer profitability is not an exact science but a process. There will never be one correct number for a customer's profitability. Thus, the chief concern is not

pursuing the most precise measurement, but consistency in the application of cost-assignment methods.

5. Sort the customers in order of the net profitability and draw a cumulative profitability curve.

6. Before considering what to do with the unprofitable or less profitable customers, consider the company's reliance on key customers; see if there is anything in place to secure their future spend, and consider what can be done to ensure the continued relationship. This is essential and sounds logical but it is often overlooked.

7. Understand the reasons for unprofitable customers and consider whether anything can be done to increase their value to the company, before you decide to 'sack' them. Link the results to other applicable metrics, like life-time value, strategic significance etc. This is to ensure that you incorporate other factors, which call for the retention of unprofitable customers.

For those companies who, due to a variety of products or services and a wide range of homogeneous customers, feel that focusing on individual customers is impractical, there is an alternative. Customers with similar buying habits can be dealt with as groups. Careful segmentation of the customer base is a prerequisite of this approach. There is debate whether CPA should be done first, ignoring a company's current segmentation; or whether segmentation should be accepted as is and a CPA done on each particular segment. The argument for segmenting first is that a company's cost structure and processes will be very similar for particular segments, and it is easier to allocate costs in this way. In addition, for companies with a large number of customers, the amount of data that needs to be available and analysed in respect of individual customers makes the alternative approach impractical.

However, there are good reasons why CPA should be carried out before segmentation, as follows:

1. Each customer's behaviour may be different, even in similar segments, and the allocation of costs on a broad base (average allocation) provides a result that does not clearly show the associated cost impact per customer.

2. The fact that costs are averaged makes it difficult to identify which customers' behaviour to modify; it is difficult to achieve when a company works with customer groups as opposed to individuals.

If the barrier to analysis is the sheer number of customers, sample groups of customers can be selected, but cost allocation must still be done at the individual level. An alternative method to consider is that proposed by Peppers and Rogers (1997). They promote the use of life-time value (LTV) to determine the ranking by profitability of customers, and suggest customer value tiered into groups such as quin-tiles. They propose identifying three different types of customer: most valuable customers (MVCs); second tier customers (STCs) and below-zero customers (BZs). They then recommend different strategic actions for each of these groups, including sacking of BZs.

Common barriers to customer profitability analysis

Many of the barriers and pitfalls to face when undertaking CPA can be avoided if they are anticipated.

There has been little clear guidance on the subject before now. One of the main barriers is a widespread lack of understanding of the methods used for CPA. It has prevented diffusion of knowledge from the CRM and customer management specialists. This leads to extensive denial of the fact that any customer could be unprofitable. This is often linked to a perceived lack of relevance to the organisation, since it is profitable overall.

Who actually manages profit? Surprisingly, it is the case that there is no one managing it directly, and this means that there is not always a clear leader for the analysis. The true cost to serve the customer is often regarded as just another shared overhead. There is reluctance to rock the boat on cost allocation, and this is especially true where it might also affect performance incentives.

Senior management buy-in is essential for any major project. Since CPA is a very broad analysis, it demands a high-level champion because it will require finance and marketing to talk to each other effectively. Also, resources will need to be made available for doing the initial analysis.

The perceived availability and accuracy of data and management information is another barrier to beginning CPA. However, most organisations will quickly discover that they have ample data to begin with in a range of different systems outside the main MIS. For example, sales force automation, customer contract systems, help desk and other systems. In fact, one barrier can actually be too much information. This can lead to paralysis by analysis. The lack of a clear methodology can lead some organisations to spend too much time chasing minute detail rather than getting an actionable ballpark figure.

Finally, a barrier for all new projects is 'initiative fatigue'. Companies are already swamped by other initiatives, such as six sigma, balanced scorecard, business excellence etc. Most of these actually have a specific customer dimension, which should be leveraged to ensure take-up. For example, where these initiatives talk about the voice of the customer, this could be replaced by the voice of the *profitable* customer.

Running a CPA project

The overarching context for carrying out CPA is to improve customer profitability in the short to medium term in a sustainable fashion. This can be done as part of a recovery strategy, or as an enhancement to current performance. It might also be part of a CRM system implementation project.

The commitment of senior management is critical to the success of any major project. This is especially true for CPA, since the nature of the changes that must follow is widespread, involving finance, marketing and sales personnel, and will often be of a strategic nature for the business.

It is essential to create a clear mandate for CPA with emphasis on *profit* not just revenue growth.

Whether or not external consultants are used to drive the process, it will usually be necessary to create a cross-functional team to implement the results. A team of people might need to be taken out of their day jobs and specifically dedicated to the project for its duration, to work alongside the consultants, if used. This team should comprise people from the finance and marketing sides of the business.

CPA can be seen as a dry and analytical subject, and many companies choose to brand the process, to make it more accessible to staff and customers alike. It is good to choose a name with a positive connotation; rather than referring to it in terms of customer profitability, give it a working title, like Valuing Customers, for example.

One way of starting the CPA exercise is to carry out interviews at many levels within the organisation, to define the business case and to state the case for change. The case should be communicated face to face with all staff, with strong industry-specific metaphors being used by the senior manager, when stressing the need for swift and effective action to improve profits.

A brief session with a selection of sales, marketing and customer relations staff will also be of use and should provide some sound-bites that can be used to stimulate the project. The successes of the project should also be communicated widely within the company. Customers will get the message when the effects of CPA trickle through the company, and most companies do not communicate the nature and scope of the CPA exercise to their customers. What happens with CPA inside the company is not usually of much concern to the customer. If the project has significant potential to change the way customers are managed, it might be appropriate to inform customers about the project at some point. The message to customers should then be that the company is aiming to improve its customer fulfilment process.

During the initial CPA research, many companies will find that customers are receiving poor customer service when they are passed around the business, seeking resolution to problems and enquiries. This is time-consuming and expensive for the company, while being frustrating and offering poor service to the customer. One of the key lessons is to ensure that the service re-engineering process is effectively linked to a detailed service investigation, to ensure that service is enhanced where possible. Customers are generally positive and receptive to any efforts to improve service, providing service actually improves, and improvement is not just promised for some time in the future.

No specialist software package is necessary for CPA as a one-off exercise. The basic tools used are accounting systems (e.g. SAP or Sage), CRM systems, the Excel spreadsheet and the Access database. There are software systems that claim to run customer profitability, but they are often based on gross margin only, or on very limited and often averaged cost information. Others offer online analytical systems, but these should be used with caution, as the concept of 'real-time' profitability is highly nebulous. The paucity of clear and structured approaches to

CPA is one of the reasons for the lack of effective software. This book aims to provide, instead, a robust, yet customisable approach to the measurement of CPA.

It can take three to six months to gather and analyse customer profitability information. If CPA is to be used on an ongoing basis it is clear that there needs to be a transition from the initial analysis stage to the changed day-to-day management of the company.

The process of implementing changes as a result of CPA is a medium- to long-term one. The real benefits from changing the customer management process as a result of CPA will be achieved over a time-scale of approximately 12 months. This is because there are many areas that will need to be involved, including customer contact centres, the sales force and internal processes.

However, CPA does provide sufficient detailed information to allow quick wins to be identified, especially in relation to the targeted acquisition of new customers. Recognition of profitable customer types provides additional segmentation opportunities for the targeting of new customers relatively early in the analysis process. Migration of existing customers to profitability might require some investment but there will be a clear financial case for it.

It is advisable to create a team to develop ways of making the CPA approach part of the longer term culture of the company. In addition, the analysis could be carried out more frequently, such as on a monthly basis, with additional data being provided directly from sales force automation software and other CRM software. Relative profit values, not absolute values, are often used, for the ongoing measurement of profitability.

Post-CPA, there could still be some limitations to changing the customer response, due to the lack of detailed information being made available to front-line contact centre staff. Specific data requirements should be used to develop a blueprint for future CRM and financial systems.

The results of CPA

It is probably fair to say that every company has unprofitable customers. The results of CPA are often astonishing, and it is common to find initial widespread disbelief at the results. The initial reaction is to doubt the figures and question the methodology.

There are documented cases of companies where:

- 33% of customers give 125% of profits (with 67% of customers giving −25% of profits);
- 18% of customers give 600% of profits;
- 22% of customers give 250% of profits;
- 50% of customers give 150% of profits;
- 10% of customers give 320% of profits.

Without a detailed CPA, it is likely that any company will divert resources into unprofitable customer relationships and run the risk of disappointing a highly profitable customer.

Tools used to present results of CPA

There are two key diagrams used to display the results of CPA. These are the 'see-saw' as shown in Figure 1.4 and the 'whale curve' shown in Figure 1.5. Both diagrams display the profitability of customers from the most profitable to the least profitable. The see-saw displays individual customer profitability, from most profitable to least profitable, while the whale curve shows the cumulative profitability.

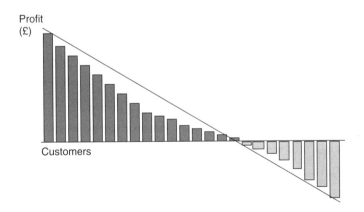

Figure 1.4 Presenting CPA results – the see-saw

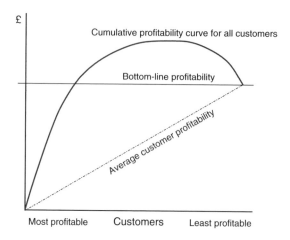

Figure 1.5 Presenting CPA results – the whale curve

The whale curve is useful to demonstrate graphically the varying profitability of individual clients, as it provides additional information of key relevance to the company.

First, since the graph is cumulative, it ends on the actual bottom-line profit figure. This provides a 'check and balance' to the analysis as well as giving a fixed point around which to consider the rest of the results.

Secondly, it is easy to see the impact of average profitability per customer as shown on the straight line from the origin to the final profit point. The following points can be deduced from Figure 1.5.

- 60% of customers are profitable overall, 40% are unprofitable (60% profit-makers, 40% profit-takers).
- The 60% provide some 140% of profits, and the unprofitable 40% provide –40% of profits.

Why do companies have unprofitable customers?

Why do companies have unprofitable customers, since they clearly do not set out to acquire them? Instead of simply stating the apparent reasons for customers' lack of profitability:, small, unpredictable orders, high distribution costs etc., it is important to recognise the organisational context in place for customer management. Companies have unprofitable customers because they fail to measure individual customer profitability, and as a consequence, they are unable to manage customer profitability.

The organisational context for customer management provides a variety of reasons for why and how companies acquire unprofitable customers. These are discussed below.

1. The sales force is continuously under pressure to close deals within a pricing range given to assist negotiations. They often chase volume, since this is how they are incentivised.

2. Pricing errors due to incorrect estimation of resource times, especially where job costing is applicable, because of a lack of recognition of the extent or complexity of the problem.

3. Companies put systems, structures and people in place that incorporate a 'one size fits all' approach, usually driven by economies of scale. Often, customers are unprofitable because they receive the same level of service and support as a more highly profitable customer, when their own level of business does not justify this. For example, same-day shipping on a small item, when the customer is not significant to the business.

4. Some companies provide products or services at cost or below, initially, with the intention to recover the initial costs and make more profit over the whole product life cycle. Sometimes profit does not materialise because customers switch, or anticipated long-term volumes do not materialise

5. Customer behaviour changes over time. Initial pricing of products and services does not allow for changes in customer behaviour. Usually, pricing is the competitive issue for negotiations. Companies will price initially based on expected average behaviour, and are unable to anticipate changes to individual customer behaviour. It can be that originally anticipated behaviour changes over time but these changes are not monitored and often become the norm. Changes in behaviour may result in substantial resource consumption through back-office activities, like order quantities, specific delivery and packaging requests, payment recovery etc. This change in customer behaviour is not usually followed by associated price increases.

These factors result in a disconnection between the customer revenue and the actual resources consumed. To remedy this situation, companies have to focus on restoring the connection between customers and costs. CPA is a key tool to help companies do this.

The actual reasons why customers can be unprofitable are manifold, and some of the main ones were listed by Robert S. Kaplan and Robin Cooper in their book *Cost and Effect*, Harvard Business School. Exhibit 10–4, p. 191. See Table 1.3.

Improving customer profitability

There are many specific actions with a clear benefit to the bottom line that can be developed as a result of completing CPA. These are typically wide ranging and involve cost savings, profit improvement,

Table 1.3 Why customers are unprofitable

High cost-to-serve customers	Low cost-to-serve customers
Order custom products	Order standard products
Small order quantities	High order quantities
Unpredictable order arrivals	Predictable order arrivals
Customised delivery	Standard delivery
Change delivery requirements	No changes in delivery requirements
Manual processing	Electronic processing (EDI)
Large amounts of pre-sales support (marketing, technical and sales resources)	Little to no pre-sales support (standard pricing and ordering)
Large amounts of post-sales support (installation, training, warranty, field service)	No post-sales support
Require company to hold inventory	Replenish as produced
Pay slowly (high accounts receivable)	Pay on time

performance improvement, better customer management and performance management etc. CPA provides a level of understanding about the business that other methods do not provide.

There is a misconception that the main outcome of CPA is the sacking of customers. This mindset perhaps arises from ABC, where many examples exist of companies reducing the number of products on offer as a result. However, sacking customers is the last resort and should only be considered when all else has failed. A customer in the hand is certainly worth two in the marketplace.

The first thought when confronted with a small proportion of highly profitable customers and a larger proportion of unprofitable ones should not be sacking. This is like looking through a telescope the wrong way. The wise company thinks about how to ensure that it can retain those highly profitable customers. It also seeks to improve the profitability of most of the rest.

Building on this, there are three core strategies that will be extensively influenced by the measurement of customer profitability. These are:

- customer acquisition;
- customer retention;
- customer development.

There are five levers that can be used to improve company profitability based on the results of CPA, which are part of the three core strategies. See Figure 1.6.

The first level is to reduce the cost to acquire new customers. This is done by using the most effective channels in terms of conversion efficiency and cost

The second lever is effective cross- and up-selling of products to your customer base. Cross-selling is one of the most powerful ways to improve profits. For a wide range of companies with tens of different product categories, the typical cross-product holding ratio is often just over 1–1.1 to 1.3 – showing that there is ample scope to improve.

The third lever is increasing the lifetime of your customer relationships by having effective customer retention plans in place.

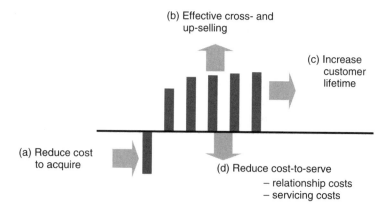

Figure 1.6 The basic levers of customer profitability. © KitshoffGleaves 2004

The fourth lever is to examine the costs to serve customers – both servicing costs and the costs of ongoing relationships.

The final lever is one that is not available unless CPA has been carried out and that is the targeting of profitable-type customers in the first place.

Using these levers, it is possible to migrate customers to more effective cost-to-serve channels appropriate to each customer's actual profitability. In addition, some customers might have to be sacked. However, sacking is usually the last resort and it should be recognised that there are many good reasons why a company should have unprofitable customers (See Chapter 2 – Strategically Significant Customers). Sacking should be carried out in a diplomatic and structured fashion, and usually begins by raising prices for those customers or reducing benefits, e.g. free shipping. Customers should be targeted with changes made around the specific levers identified, and only if they are unwilling to accommodate the changes should they be sacked. Some of those sacked might be passed to smaller distributors that are also customers of the company. Others might come back as customers under the new terms after being sacked.

Customer segmentation recognises the key factors in relation to cost to serve and CPA develops a structured approach to customer segmentation, and hence service offering, driven by customer profit-ability banding and strategic importance. The concept of MASP (most appropriate service provider) can be used to ensure that segmentation leads to enhanced customer profitability. Examples of how this works may be found in the case studies at the end of this book.

The customer response

In the case of companies where extensive customer migration and change have taken place as a result of the findings from CPA, customers were generally happy with the results, since the project had successfully aimed to enhance their experience and satisfaction.

Comments from customers included words to the effect that:

We wondered how long it would take you to notice that our credit terms were so generous.

I'm glad you don't send out a rep anymore. I don't have the time to see him.

Where customers were sacked, the process was handled in a consistent and planned fashion, and the majority of customers were either willing to change the way they did business, or to be moved to other channels. Some who left eventually came back under the new terms.

What could have been a painful process was handled in such a way as to keep the majority of customers satisfied.

Management barriers to making changes as a result of CPA

There are many barriers to making changes as a result of CPA and some of these can come from internal inertia and resistance.

- Sales force resistance – selling is considered to be a 'black art'.
- The sales force often has a different mindset – real value versus volume – and one ends up fighting against typical macho goals for the sales force.

- If we don't understand the method, we won't use the results. Lack of trust in results – cynicism – history doesn't repeat itself, for LTV calculations especially.
- Perverse incentives – based on rewarding behaviour that doesn't lead to additional profit.
- It is fine having a post-CPA strategy but operations can't use the information due to the current IT configuration.
- Clashing targets and strategy disjoint.
- 'The customer is always right' – need to challenge this assumption and ask if the customer is always profitable.

Conclusion

Customer profitability is a relatively poorly understood issue, which can have massive implications for the profitable growth of any organisation.

CPA can be a complicated process but it is grounded in a series of steps that are essentially intuitive. Most organisations currently do not have in place systems that are suitable for the measurement or management of individual customer profitability. This includes information systems, reporting systems, customer management systems and rewards systems.

Remember the five levels of cost, when considering customer profitability:

- cost of goods;
- cost of selling;
- cost to serve;
- relationship costs;
- business-sustaining costs.

Some advanced customer profitability concepts

The method of conducting CPA outlined in this chapter is robust and will provide usable data on individual levels of customer profitability.

There is more, however, to the story when we consider not just profit but also the timing of the cash flows, and the whole concept of economic profit and shareholder value.

Cash flow

The method outlined in this chapter is limited to a consideration of customer profitability, a key goal for organisations. However, 'cash is king', and for many organisations, especially smaller ones, the actual cash flow for each customer relationship could also be taken into consideration.

Some companies consider the impact on working capital or net working capital, which is defined simply as stocks + debtors – creditors, as part of a customer profitability process. There is a cost in extending credit to customers, and some allowance can be made for this.

Customer capital/equity

Accounting profit, discussed already in this chapter, is a very basic way to consider profit. The term economic profit is used to describe any profits over and above the opportunity cost of capital. A similar concept is economic value added (EVA™).

The same concepts will be true for customer value added (CVA). Customers, whether nominally *profitable* or not, will provide a spread of returns above and below the line of effective EVA return. This is shown in Figure 1.7.

Similarly, and while not the focus of this book, there is something to be said about customer capital in the context of intellectual capital and human capital. The excess value of a firm over its net assets is often ascribed to intellectual capital, and increasingly to human capital. However, the value of the firm is perhaps most accurately described as the sum of future profits from customers, discounted to a present value. In cases where a major customer defects from a business, the share price will drop to reflect this loss, despite the firm retaining the same intellectual and human capital. The really important message

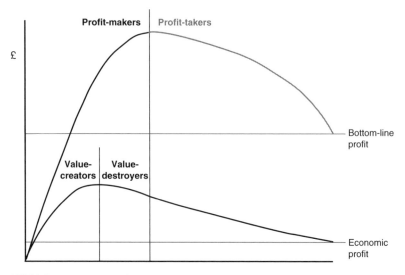

NB This figure assumes that the company is making a bottom-line profit and that it is also making an economic profit. Economic profit is always less than bottom-line profit and even customers contributing to bottom-line profit will not necessarily return an economic profit.

Figure 1.7 Profit-makers and profit-takers

from this book is that the future value of a firm could actually be dependent on the profit generated by a small percentage of the customer base. So, in reality, there will be two whale curves for every business; one based on profitability alone and another, with even fewer profitable customers, if economic profit is taken into consideration.

The customer as a real option

When a customer completes a transaction, the supplier has an opportunity to make a profit on the transaction. Whether that opportunity is seized or squandered is dependent on the systems that are in place for managing customers. For example, if pricing is lower than the true cost to serve, the customer relationship will not be profitable to the company.

In fact, a series of options are built into all customer relationships. First, there is the option to make profit from the transaction or series of transactions comprising the relationship. The longevity of this option depends on the company's ability to retain the customer. If the customer is retained, another option arises, that of selling more to that customer through cross- and up-selling. Finally, there is also the option to develop the relationship into one that is even more profitable for you, but which can also provide superior value to your customers, through careful management of the modes and channels of interaction with the customer. Very few companies recognise these options clearly, and even fewer exploit them effectively. It might be possible to measure the value of customers using the options-pricing theory.

2

Segmentation

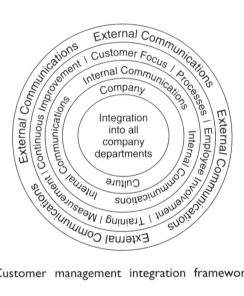

Figure 2.0 Customer management integration framework. © John A. Murphy 2005

This chapter provides a framework for segmenting customers based on profitability analysis. It also provides practical guidance on how to use the results of customer profitability to make operational changes. Underlying this framework is the essential, but often overlooked, linkage between the two different disciplines of finance (accounting) and sales and marketing.

After completion of customer profitability analysis (CPA) it is immediately possible to segment customers into two groups: the profitable and the unprofitable.

For profitable customers, the first questions to arise are:

1. Who are the customers the company needs to strive to retain?
2. What retention activities are in place for these customers?
3. What have these customers got in common?
4. How did the company acquire them?
5. How can the company acquire more of them?
6. Do frontline staff know who the profitable customers are?
7. Are the marketing and sales force activities focused on acquiring more of them?
8. Is advertising focused on acquiring more of them?
9. Are marketing and advertising focused on the most successful channels?

For the unprofitable customers, questions to be answered include:

1. Why are they unprofitable?
2. What have they got in common?
3. How did the company acquire them?
4. Do frontline staff know that they are unprofitable?
5. What systems and procedures are in place to prevent the acquisition of more unprofitable customers?
6. What can we do to make them profitable?

Many companies are unaware of the advantages of CPA, and use segmentation methods and methodologies based on the assumption that all customers are profitable. They continue to market and sell to segments, or customer groups, that are essentially destroying profits. In addition to this waste of resources, companies, who do not segment with customer profitability at the core, miss an opportunity to align their pricing and service offerings with actual customer behaviour and associated costs.

Although two distinct customer segments are immediately identified with CPA, markets, market dynamics, customer behaviour and customer relationships are more complex. It is not sufficient for a company to think simply in terms of profitable and unprofitable customers. CPA can be utilised to take account of this complexity, and application of the results will influence a company's strategic thinking about the markets it operates in and its operational customer management.

There is no consensus of opinion about the role of segmentation in companies and how to define segmentation.

Kotler (1978) states that segmentation is the subdivision of a market into distinct subsets of customers, where any subset may conceivably be selected as a target market to be reached with a distinct marketing mix. He regards segmentation as an analytical tool used to research markets in a meaningful way, and suggests the use of target marketing to evaluate, select and concentrate on those segments that the organisation is capable of serving.

The method outlined in this chapter is for segmentation that builds in a range of factors and allows a company to concentrate its resources on profitable customers. It is a generic approach, which enables a company to choose the factors most relevant to its market and its customers. The focus on profitable customers acknowledges that not all customers are equal, and that resources should only be expended on the customers or customer groups that contribute to the overall profit of the company. There are other, currently unprofitable, customers whose profitability can be enhanced, and these are also identified as a result of CPA.

Accounting systems do not clearly show the costs that a company incurs as a result of individual customers' behaviour. CPA as suggested below provides that visibility of information and allows companies to act on facts rather than opinions. Using this method will allow companies to:

- answer key strategic questions about their customers and the markets in which they operate;
- understand customer behaviour and the effect that this behaviour has on costs and overall profitability;
- focus on operationally aligning their offerings to customers' behaviour, or to focus on influencing customers' behaviour;
- increase profits by eliminating inefficiencies in their customer management processes.

The generic approach is a six-step process, which is shown in Figure 2.1.

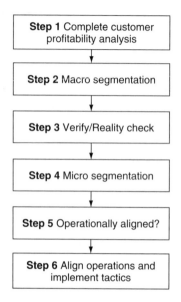

Figure 2.1 Six-step framework

Some key concepts are discussed in this chapter, to facilitate understanding of the six-step approach. These concepts are:

- customer life cycle;
- life-time value (LTV);
- strategically significant customers;
- customer portfolio analysis.

The answer to the question: 'Which approach is best for me?' has been complicated in the past by the fact that more research was devoted to developing new models and approaches, rather than testing existing methods in real-life contexts.

This chapter does not attempt to highlight all the segmentation methodologies available; many are covered in marketing textbooks. It does not generally distinguish between business-to-business (B2B) and business-to-consumer (B2C) markets, either, but the generic model is flexible enough to incorporate both.

Segmentation incorporating profitability

The following approach is equally appropriate to mature and fast-growing companies, for services or products, in the B2B and B2C marketplace, or both. No two companies are identical and the key is to pick which parts are most appropriate to you.

The methodology proposed here has six key steps:

1. Completion of customer profitability analysis
2. Macro segmentation.
3. Verify/Reality check.
4. Micro segmentation.
5. Investigate if operations are aligned.
6. Align operations and implement tactics.

This is also shown in Figure 2.1.

Step 1: Completion of customer profitability analysis

Customer profitability analysis underpins the approach to the suggested segmentation approach. Practically, it is advisable to ignore current company segmentation, when taking this step. Customers are not grouped together at this stage, although it may be feasible to do this later, in order to be able to allocate costs in environments of:

- complex product and service mixes;
- complex channels and partnering arrangements;
- lack of data on the indirect cost to serve.

The 'whale curve' discussed in Chapter 1 immediately identifies customers that are profitable and unprofitable, thus identifying two distinct customer segments. Other terms can be used for these groups: value adders and value destroyers; or one might call them flowers and weeds, or friends and foes.

The two customer groups are shown in Figure 2.2.

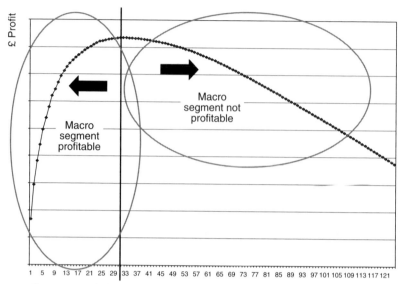

Customer profit (ranked most profitable to least profitable customer)

Figure 2.2 Two distinct macro customer segments
Source: KitshoffGleaves, 2003

Step 2: Macro segmentation

These two macro customer groups are directly associated with three generic customer management activities, namely, *acquisition, retention* and *development* (Figure 2.3). Customers are the lifeblood of any company, and before they can be retained and developed, they must be acquired. Functionally, this is the role of sales and marketing. Retention signifies holding on to customers, after they have been acquired. Customer development is normally associated with activities of both cross- and up-selling, but, from a profitability perspective, the term is used for the migration of unprofitable customers to profitability. Based on the 'whale curve', the generic strategies of acquisition and retention are associated with the profitable segment and development with the unprofitable segment.

The customers on the left-hand side of the curve are crucial for the financial well-being of a company, and specific retention strategies can

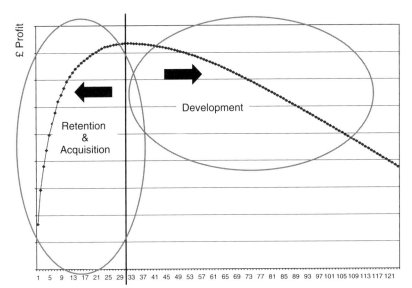

£ Profit

Development

Retention
&
Acquisition

Customer profit (ranked most profitable to least profitable customer)

Figure 2.3 Three generic customer strategies
Source: KitshoffGleaves, 2003

be aimed at those customers who truly represent 80% of the company's profits. The company that has identified its most profitable customers will be in a position to consider what it is doing, operationally, tactically and strategically, to ensure that these profitable customers will still be customers tomorrow. The retention segment also represents the type of customer the company wants to acquire, and it could act as a reference against which to focus sales and marketing personnel for acquisition activities.

Identification of the individual customers in these two distinct groups forms step 2. It has been shown that, in some cases, this step is enough for an analysis on which to base meaningful decisions. As an example, macro segmentation of a fast-growing company, with an active customer base of 200, was seen by both the managing director and external consultants to be meaningful enough for the company's board to make a key decision and realign the company's marketing spend. CPA can be used, with broad macro segmentation alone, to influence a company's thinking about strategies for future profitability.

Step 3: Verification/Reality check

Customer profitability analysis only measures a customer's current profitability. Current profitability is not the only criterion on which a customer's potential value should be based. Under some business models, all acquired customers will be unprofitable in year one and even year two, and so to screen on profitability alone is woefully inadequate.

Many companies will have a strategy of subsidising customers, for example:

- Packaging machinery making money on the packaging materials.
- Vending machines making money on the items sold.
- Mobile phone service providers subsidising handsets, to get call and rental revenues.

Not all customers will initially be profitable in these cases. The hope is that the customer will have a positive life-time value, providing profits in years to come. It is helpful to use an additional screening process, to assess customers for their strategic significance. In addition, there are some valid reasons why a company has to continue relationships with unprofitable customers. Companies should scrutinise all customers, and consider the following:

1. customer life cycle;
2. life-time value;
3. strategically significant customers.

Customer life cycle

The customer life-cycle concept was originally introduced by Cunningham and Homse (1982), building upon the concepts of the product life cycle.

These authors discussed customer life cycle with regard to four groups of customers, namely:

- Tomorrow's customers (customers the company is trying to gain, regain).
- Today's special customers (customers purchasing large quantities and the company is engaged in development work with them).
- Today's regular customers (also large customers, but the relationships are old-established and development takes place intermittently).
- Yesterday's customers (numerous but small volume and little or no development).

With these four customer groups in mind, these authors suggest a customer classification that is similar to a decision matrix, and recommend the use of another dimension of analysis, which is multivariate and involves sales volume, age of relationship and so on.

Some companies use this approach, but, with customer profitability as the goal, emphasis should be placed on identifying recently acquired customers who are unprofitable at the moment, due to acquisition costs not yet being recovered, but who may become profitable. These customers need to be identified as part of the reality check. Examples of this customer type are contract customers at the early stage of a contract, where volumes have not yet materialised, or customers of the mobile telephone industry, where handsets are often subsidised, and call volumes and profits may not yet have exceeded the initial cost of the handset. These customers can often be identified by members of the sales force, or by examination of data from the customer's account history, if it is available.

Companies should also consider how the duration of their relationship with customers impacts on company profit. The impact on company profits as a result of the length of the relationship with customers was identified by Bain & Company in six key categories. These six are as follows:

1. Customer acquisition cost – this is an important part of overall customer profitability and should not be ignored when assessing the value of customers. In a graphic example of one new customer, Bain demonstrates that the acquisition cost is of the same order

as the year one base profit, meaning that this customer would not show a clear profit until year two.

2. Base profit – the assumption in the same graphical example is that the customer is actually profitable on a base case. If you have identified unprofitable customers, the benefits, as identified by Bain, are not applicable to them.

3. Profit from increased spend – it is not always a given that a customer will do more business with you. This is almost certainly the case if you do not seek to develop them by cross- and up-selling.

4. Profit from reduced operating costs – by knowing its customers, a company will be able to deal with them more effectively, but it requires knowledge of customer behaviour and careful management of the customer, coupled, if necessary, with incentives for their *good* behaviour.

5. Profit from referrals – this depends on the nature of the industry in question and on the level of satisfaction that customers have with your service. Word of mouth is one of the strongest forms of marketing, but it needs to be encouraged and rewarded in order to be effective.

6. Profit from price premium – most companies (particularly B2B) find that they can command less of a premium, the longer a customer stays with them. There might be a small group of price-insensitive customers, who will not shop around, but, on the whole, some pressure will always be on price. Smart customers will also know that their 'loyalty' and consequent avoidance of acquisition cost should be worth something to you.

In conclusion, it is important to recognise that it is not a universal rule that customer relationships become more profitable over time. There are many instances where it is certainly not the case.

Strategically significant customers

It is worth considering whether unprofitable customers are strategically significant customers. Strategically significant customers are those with whom the company has to deal as part of its long-term survival or development, regardless of whether or not they are profitable. Customers can be of strategic significance for a number of reasons. There are cost, strategic and marketing perspectives that need to be considered, as well as the life-time value of the customer.

From a cost perspective, the customers who are major overhead absorbers also need to be identified. Major fixed overhead absorbers can be at the production level (plant or production capacity) or at the service level. Often overlooked are infrastructure costs and processes that are in place to meet specific customer requirements. Firing or sacking of customers is the last resort, but the consequence of firing one of these customers can lead to a downward spiral of profitability. Your profitable customers now absorb more of the fixed overhead, which results in other customers, previously profitable, becoming less profitable or unprofitable.

From a strategic perspective, a company may want to accept unprofitable customers if:

- It runs a loss leader strategy for a product or service, and relies on this to obtain other sales within the same company.
- It runs a break-even strategy for a product or service, and relies on this to obtain other sales within the industry. This often happens in concentrated industries, where suppliers need to be seen as active in order to be asked for profitable 'spot' orders.
- Customers who have helped the company to come up with innovative ideas that have led to new service and/or product development.
- Customers who are willing to participate in research and development of new products and services.
- Customers who can influence the decision making when a company is thinking of moving into new markets or customer segments.

From a marketing perspective, use of customers for reference purposes is often the reason why a company may regard them as unprofitable customers. These are customers who are:

- Quoted and referred to as existing product or service users, as part of a company's marketing and sales literature.

- Customers who have a dominant market position, or strong brand, with whom the company wants to be seen to be associated (prestige value).
- Customers who allow site visits for prospective new customers to see products and services used operationally.

It is also important to determine the amount of profit a company can earn from a customer over the years, or periods, during which it deals with a customer. This is referred to as life-time value (LTV) or customer life-time value (CLTV). Its use in industry as a valid and useful tool is gaining wider acceptance, and some companies already use it to determine retention spend, or potential discount incentives, if the customer communicates that he/she intends to do business elsewhere.

Most companies calculate LTV based on customer or account turnover, or cash flows, as opposed to profits. It is very accurate and reliable if the expected life-time of the customer's relationship to the company is linked to a contract period. If not linked to contracts, customers can always defect or switch to a competitor, and, at best, these calculations present potential life-time values. At this stage of the analysis it is time to see if a currently unprofitable customer can become profitable in a year or two, and LTV calculations are used to establish this. This is the same as looking at the account's future potential, and acquisition cost is included in the LTV calculation in order to determine this. After completing calculations, customers can be ranked from lowest to highest LTV.

Although some strategically significant factors may be subjective, it is important to identify these customers in the analysis, and once they are identified, they can be grouped as highly strategically significant, non-strategically significant or of low strategic significance. This grouping of customers can be found in both of the two macro segments identified and is shown in Figure 2.4.

Some authors recommend using CPA to develop key customer strategies at this stage of the analysis. As an example, Gordon (1998)

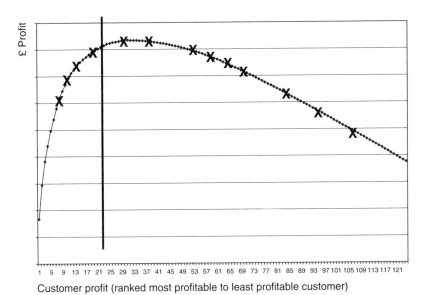

Customer profit (ranked most profitable to least profitable customer)

Figure 2.4 Strategically significant customers
Source: KitshoffGleaves, 2003

divides customers into four segments, with associated strategies implied by their profitability status. They are:

1. reward and invest;
2. manage;
3. discipline;
4. fire.

His suggested customer portfolio is shown in Figure 2.5.

Reward and invest

These are customers who are profitable today and look likely to be profitable in the future. They need to be rewarded with special treatment, and key decision makers must be entertained. Investment can be in the form of time spent with them, assignment of the best staff to

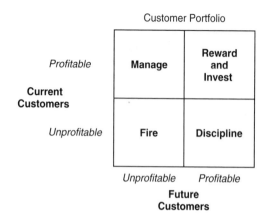

Figure 2.5 A customer portfolio matrix and strategies according to Gordon (1998)
Source: Gordon, I.H. (1998) *Relationship Marketing*. Ontario, John Wiley & Sons, Inc.

deal with their needs, or special systems or processes to provide tailored product or service.

Manage

These are customers who are currently profitable but who may become less profitable or even unprofitable in the future. These customers have a year-on-year history of reduced purchases, are investing in cheaper substitutes, or may be operating in a market segment where the outlook for the whole segment is unfavourable.

Discipline

Gordon (1998) recommends two main ways of implementing this strategy. One is to change and/or cost-reduce the processes employed by the company to market, sell, serve, support and manage these accounts. He also suggests charging customers in this category a fee for not conforming to the company's 'rules of engagement' as 'best customer'.

Fire

Getting rid of customers is also an option. Companies need to evaluate which customers merit investment in relationships. There is no reason why companies should continue to serve customers who are unprofitable now and have no likelihood of contributing to future profit. Gordon suggests that they become someone else's problem or opportunity.

The concept of firing a customer is not new. Most companies have screening processes in place (ability to pay, credit records etc.) to ensure that they do not deal with customers at a loss. However, nobody can predict how behaviour will change over time. This is the challenge for companies, and firing customers is, in effect, a culling process for those who have slipped through the pre-screening process, or whose behaviour has changed, affecting the cost to serve.

There are other customer portfolio models proposed in the literature. The models are constructed using different variables, but very few are underpinned by customer profitability. It is assumed that companies only want to deal with profitable customers. Some models propose customer strategies, without covering all the options available to companies.

A next step is for all customers to be further analysed in a process of micro segmentation. The aim is to group customers together, to discover if there are differences in profitability between customers in the same SIC group or location. This immediately identifies benchmark opportunities for development, and also provides companies with peace of mind when they see that the potential sacking of a customer is based on a systematic analysis of present and future profitability prospects, and after consideration of all other opportunities explored.

Step 4: Micro segmentation

At this stage we already know which of our customers are profitable and which are not. In addition, we know who the strategically significant customers are.

It is at this stage when companies are able to look for similarities between the two distinct groups of profitable and unprofitable customers. These similarities can be broadly classified as general factors and cost factors. Evaluating the general factors allows a company to make strategic decisions, and evaluating the cost factors allows a company to pinpoint current cost inefficiencies, resulting from the way in which customers are served. General factors to be considered include:

- industry type;
- use;
- location;
- contract and non-contract customers;
- product and service mix;
- channel.

Cost factors to consider should be those that absorb the most resource time and include:

- marketing and sales time;
- special service or information requirements;
- technical assistance;
- referral fees;
- number of invoices;
- legal fees;
- discounts;
- rebates.

The selection of these factors will depend on a company's specific circumstances.

Next, it is useful to analyse the similarities and differences in the cost-to-serve drivers between the profitable and unprofitable customers. This provides real insight into individual customers' behaviour and the way they are served, and it also starts to show what particular customer development is needed in order to 'migrate' an unprofitable customer to profitability by aligning operations to customer behaviour. If two companies (one profitable, the other not) are in the same location and industry, both companies should be evaluated to identify which cost factors differentiate the two.

For example, if a customer is unprofitable because of recurring, time-consuming contract negotiations and legal fees, it might be helpful to the situation to extend the contract period. The profitable set of customers becomes a benchmark for the non-profitable customers, with similar general factors, and the trick is discovering how to align company actions and customer behaviour to get similar cost patterns. This micro segmentation allows companies to understand their cost structure and their cost to serve, and by comparing and contrasting profitable and unprofitable customers, they will have identified the key issues to be addressed.

Step 5: Investigate if strategies and operations are aligned

Once companies have a thorough understanding of the reasons for profitability, or otherwise, they can decide upon individual customer strategies, and investigate whether they are operationally aligned with the three generic strategies of retention, acquisition and development.

Retention

Companies can boost profits by almost 100% by retaining just 5% more of their customers (Reichheld and Sasser, Jr. 1990).

Despite startling figures such as those quoted above, companies often demonstrate little obvious effort to retain customers. One study estimated that, on average, US corporations lose 50% of their customers every five years. An interesting point is that, despite it usually costing more to acquire a new customer than to serve an existing one, marketing spend is not clearly or effectively targeted at customer retention. Companies even offer incentives to new customers, at better terms than to existing customers – this encourages defection and rewards the 'promiscuous' customer.

If acquisition is analogous to hunting, the analogy for retention is farming. The question is: how can organisations manage these two very different approaches, especially within a common framework of incentives? In addition, how can the two approaches be reconciled with marketing spend?

Customer retention is only relevant where there is an ongoing purchasing relationship. Many companies seek ways of generating ongoing revenue streams from customers, rather than one-off revenues, by moving from products towards services. Many companies' retention strategies are weak, poorly conceived or non-existent, and there are no sales and/or marketing activities or incentives focused on customer retention.

Many companies accept the inevitable customer churn, and work harder to acquire new customers rather than adopting a balanced approach to all their existing customers. Questions about retention should be asked in respect of all the customer management activities. Are the departments or staff responsible for complaints handling aware that certain customers are a priority for retention, and do they prioritise their activities, responses and service recovery effort based on this? It is simply a matter of working through a list of customers' complaints (and compliments), and questioning staff to determine if strategies and operations are aligned.

Conscious customer retention includes a wide range of activities aimed at adding value for the customer from its relationship with the company. Mechanisms to increase customer retention are sometimes referred to as 'lock-ins', although many people, including customers, dislike this term and prefer to consider it as additional value within the relationship. Examples of specific customer retention methods include:

- Pricing – the use of retrospective volume discounts can encourage retention.
- Payment methods – the use of direct debit, for example, has two benefits: it smoothes the cost impact for the customer and promotes retention, since the customer has to actively cancel payment.
- Account management, including corporate hospitality activities – this is where the hunter/farmer approach can be in conflict.
- Extranets and other systems to provide effective data interchange with customers.

- Equipment loan – systems such as vending machines or fridges are supplied to customers for use with other paid-for products from the company.
- Vendor-managed inventory is another example, where the vendor provides not just the material but the management of it for the customer.
- Newsletters and other customer bulletins.
- Loyalty schemes – whether based on points for the individual or other benefits for the customer, these are also targeted at retention.
- Contractual lock-ins e.g. penalty clauses.

Lock-ins can normally be categorised into two types – structural or emotional. Structural lock-ins are often more rigorous than emotional ones. Emotional lock-ins usually relate to the promotion of an emotional tie with the customer. The distinction is blurred in some cases. Economists include lock-ins as a type of switching cost for the customer – a cost in terms of money, time or emotion.

Customer retention activities will usually have a cost implication – the key questions for any organisation are: 'Do the methods work?' and 'Are they cost effective?'

Customer profitability analysis has revealed cases where customers are being retained in very expensive ways without commensurate levels of spend. This can be due to historically higher levels of spend, or just tradition.

Managing clients for loyalty does not necessarily equate to managing them for profitability. The level of profitability will depend on the nature of the service being provided. The results of CPA help to identify the most important customers to retain and, by extension, should help to identify those at whom loyalty activity and programmes should be targeted. Knowledge of a customer's profitability provides an understanding of the effectiveness of the available budget for loyalty schemes. A loyalty scheme that costs more than the benefits it generates does not add value to the business operating it.

Customer profitability analysis helps to identify the customers to retain, and the information it provides can be used to target win-back activities. However, why spend time trying to win-back unprofitable customers? Defections or churn can be positive if it is of unprofitable, non-strategic customers.

Across-the-board averages of customer satisfaction, such as 90% satisfied or very satisfied, are of little use if just 10% of customers provide 50% of profits! CPA can help a company to target those customers to be used for customer satisfaction surveys. If you know which of your customers are most profitable, it should be possible to target them as a priority for response with a 'crash team' or immediate response service team, if the need arises.

Acquisition

Companies must ask questions around their current marketing mix and acquisition efforts. It is crucial to explore methods and procedures to improve pre-screening of customers, to prevent the acquisition of potentially unprofitable customers. The analysis in step 4 allows a company to identify the most profitable segments, locations, product mixes and most cost-effective methods or channels by which to acquire new customers. Is the company's marketing and sales effort focused on acquiring more of the profitable customers? Is the marketing spend aligned with the channels where these customers are acquired? Are the sales-force incentives aligned with profitable types of customers in mind?

Development

The greatest untapped source of profit lies within the existing customer base, and this profit can only be realised through effective customer development. Customer development is a term that usually refers to two key areas of activity:

1. Up-selling: selling more to the same customers, increasing 'share of wallet'.
2. Cross-selling: selling other products to the existing customer base.

However, CPA allows a third type of customer development, one that that is clearly linked to improving overall profitability: realigning customers to the right level of service.

Up-selling

Up-selling is about maximising the value of the sale to the company. It is especially important where fixed costs or potentially perishable items (like holidays, flights etc.) are concerned. If it is possible to sell a customer a more expensive option (even if it is marginally priced), this will increase profits. This is about increasing the company's share of the customer's wallet. A seldom-heard concept in relation to customer development is that of down-selling. This can be used as a retention tool, when a customer is about to defect. Sometimes customers will not appreciate that a competitor's lower price is due to a lower level of service or product specification, and so it is possible to match the price by matching the product quality. This is called down-selling. Overall, a combination of up- and down-selling should, perhaps, be called right-selling: selling the customer the product or service that is right for them and for the company.

Cross-selling

On paper, cross-selling is the least expensive type of selling. Providing the quality of the relationship is good, it will always be easier to develop an existing relationship further, rather than to begin a new one. However, most organisations seem to place more emphasis on acquiring new customers than retaining or developing existing ones. Cross-selling is a much talked about, yet underused, marketing approach for many companies. As an illustration of this, the almost ubiquitous figure of between 1.1 and 1.3 is, for many companies, the average cross-product holding. This is very much independent of the type of company and even the number of products on offer. So, if six different products are on offer and the cross-product holding is still less than 1.5, versus the ideal 6, this highlights the extent of the missed opportunity. However, with six different products, there are actually 63 different permutations of single or multiple products. (N.B. an understanding of the motives for certain types of cross-product holding can aid segmentation; e.g. a dishwasher with extended warranty might be the typical cross-product holding for a mature consumer.)

The barriers to cross-selling are many, including:

1. Data availability. The availability of suitable data between product divisions is often a barrier against understanding and hence of improving the process of cross-selling. Indeed, data protection legislation is often cited as a barrier to the sharing of customer information between companies under the same parent group.
2. Incentives also play an important part in cross-selling. If individuals have sales targets for their own areas or products that do not allow recognition of cross-selling efforts, individuals will tend to focus almost exclusively on meeting their own targets. Allocation of credit for cross-selling can also be a very complex process. An initial introduction might lead to a successful piece of work being completed, which in turn leads to further work for another area of the business. Deciding who gets the credit for these follow-on sales can be very difficult and acts as a barrier.
3. The psychology of cross-selling is also important. The sales team may simply avoid revealing customer and prospect details, in order to retain a bank of future prospects. Also, the degree of personal relationships, in service organisations particularly, means that cross-selling is actually very difficult to do.

Companies should investigate what can possibly be done for each unprofitable customer, to ensure that the customer contributes to the bottom line.

Customer development

Once a company uses CPA to identify unprofitable customers or customer groups, these can become targets for a third category of customer development – the migration of customers from unprofitable to profitable. This migration is a complex process, with many possible actions for each customer or group of customers. This process includes:

- Sacking customers (although this should be a last resort).
- Increasing prices.

- Reducing the cost-to-serve by insisting on certain channels being used for no/low profit transactions such as web-enabled, self-service for low cost transactions such as consumables.
- Offering alternative 'no-frills' products.
- Charging for additional services that historically have been part of the overhead – moving to menu pricing based on a clear price/service trade-off.
- Negotiations to influence the customers' behaviour.

Practical examples where customers modify their behaviour include customers willing to modify their order quantities, extend contract durations, and payment methods or terms. These are some of the main ways to migrate customers to profitability, or to improve their level of profitability. This category of customer development actions *cannot* be accurately targeted without carrying out CPA.

Step 6: Align operations and implement tactics

Aligning operations is equivalent to introducing a major cultural change process into an operation. It is underpinned by new thinking and a different focus. For companies who have always believed that 'all customers are equal' this can be quite difficult to achieve. All staff, customer-facing or not, need to be made aware of the major issues. As well as the need to focus marketing and sales on the profitable segments, the administrative department must be made aware that they are often the first to know if customer behaviour has changed (late payments, reduced account activity etc.). Procedures should be put in place so that the organisation can react if a customer's behaviour changes. The key point is that operational alignment will affect all the customer management activities. Companies should set clear targets for each generic strategy, to assist them with this transformation, and align incentives accordingly. They often have adequate mechanisms and incentives for customer acquisition, but not for the retention and development strategies.

Tactically, when they implement changes, companies should be very sensitive towards customers. For example, if it is decided that an unprofitable customer should no longer get invitations to special entertainment events, it is better to reduce the invitations over a period, rather than give an abrupt notification of the change. In concentrated industries this is even more important. Handled badly, it could damage the company's reputation. Companies should also investigate the reasons why customers defect, and implement changes to their systems or offerings accordingly.

For acquisition, the key to success is aligning incentives to reflect the new focus. If the incentives are aligned it is easier to influence sales-force behaviour. Patience is required by companies; change will not occur overnight, and it will take time for personnel to adapt to changes. As an example, moving from a target number of sales visits per week to a target of balanced retention visits, and to have a target number of sales based on profitable segments, looks easy on paper, but it alters salespeople's routines and convenience visits, as well.

Kaplan and Narayanan (2001) make the following points:

Following CPA, CRI, a market research company, has established strict policies for screening new clients. Before, it took any client who came in through the door (or over the phone), using standard hourly pricing rules. Now, all initial inquiries are routed to a single manager, who screens new customer leads using the responses to six standard questions. She now rejects those she estimates will fall short of CRI's profitability goals. Typically, only 10% of inquiries pass this initial screen.

A second manager then does in-depth research on the potential clients. Those that pass this screen are welcomed to CRI's 'freshman class' and assigned to an existing account team. The account team – charged with growing the business from all existing accounts – works closely with the freshman client to migrate it to a higher level of business.

After a year, the account teams determine which of the 'freshmen' are promoted to 'sophomores'. Those not promoted are let go; it's either up or out. A sophomore is expected to show real growth in sales and profits by year two. Sophomores are expected to double sales in the second year. Clients who graduate from the sophomore class get the royal treatment.

Within 4–5 years of launching this approach, CRI had reduced its *number* of customers by 50%, yet *revenue* had increased by 60%, and operating *profits* were more than 300% higher. CRI could devote intensive attention to its established client base, knowing that the revenues per customer more than compensated them for the extensive research and support provided.

Customer development is tactically the most challenging task facing modern management. Successful companies systematically work through the unprofitable customer group and, as a first step, identify if any cross-selling or up-selling potential exists. If opportunities are identified, targets are set and a programme implemented to attempt to migrate customers. If there are no opportunities identified, the next step is to establish whether customer behaviour can be influenced, or if services to these customers can be slowly withdrawn, or if any process inside the company can be altered so that the revenue yield exceeds the associated costs.

There will be customers who can only be moved to profitability if the price is increased. These customers are essentially given the choice of whether they want to continue using the product and services. There is some evidence that if this is done with proper communication, customers who choose to switch to another supplier often return as a customer before very long.

Figure 2.6 shows how customer portfolio analysis provides a more actionable breakdown of customers than profitability analysis. The percentages shown are based on detailed analysis with one company, and will vary from company to company. The most striking fact is that there are more customers in the re-engineer category than any other. If these customers can be successfully re-engineered to more appropriate

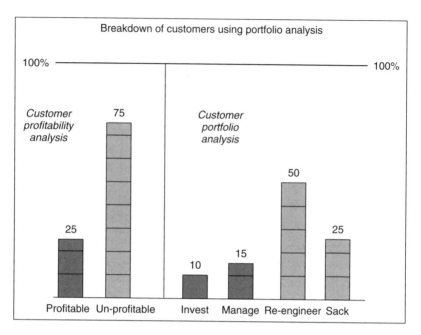

Figure 2.6 Customer profitability and portfolio analysis
Source: KitshoffGleaves, 2004

cost-to-serve processes, the overall profitability of the company can be increased dramatically.

Conclusion

Customer profitability analysis provides an analysis of those customers that are currently profitable and unprofitable. This is a relatively narrow view of profitability, since it does not consider the longer term potential of customers. Hence, the recommendation that customer profitability is followed by customer portfolio analysis, which allows for the strategic significance of customers, including life-time value. Based on the customer portfolio, strategies for specific customer segments can now be implemented.

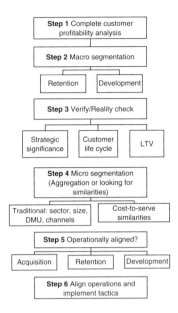

Figure 2.7 Steps to make customer profitability analysis and segmentation work
Source: KitshoffGleaves, 2003

Retention, acquisition and development are three generic management strategies and crucial for effective customer management. To implement these strategies effectively and focus on customers contributing to a company's profitability, companies must understand the cost to serve individual customers. This understanding will allow them to develop unprofitable customers in a structured way.

The sacking of unprofitable customers must always be the last resort, and companies should implement better pre-screening of potential customers, to prevent the acquisition of unprofitable ones.

The six-step approach outlined above allows companies to answer the following questions:

1. Who are the profitable customers it wants to retain?
2. What particular retention activities should be developed and where should they focus?

Customer acquisition KPI	Number of prospects converted into customers
	Per customer acquisition cost
	Customer net present value
	Relative success rate of acquisition channels
	Conversion rate
Customer retention KPI	Raw customer retention rate
	Raw customer retention rate by customer segment
	Sales-adjusted retention rate
	Profit-adjusted retention rate
	Sales and profit-adjusted retention rates by customer segment
	Share of wallet of retained customers
	Customer defection rate per channel
	Cost effectiveness of retention tactics
Customer Development KPI	Cross-product holding ratio
	Number of customers migrated to new terms or products

Figure 2.8 The customer scorecard
Source: Buttle, F. & Cox, J with KitshoffGleaves (2004) *Mid-market CRM Customer Relationship Excellence in Mid-size Enterprises*. White Label Publishing

3. What pre-screening activities can be developed to avoid acquisition of unprofitable customers?
4. Where should the marketing and salesforce activities focus on in order to acquire more profitable customers?
5. Where should advertising spend be focused in order to acquire more of the profitable customers?
6. Who are the unprofitable customers it needs to develop?
7. Why are they unprofitable and where should the company focus its resources in order to change this?

Figure 2.7 summarises how the six-step approach and key concepts are integrated, to segment customers based on their profitability.

To help companies achieve and implement these tactical changes, they might use a customer scorecard and relevant key performance indicators (KPIs). An example that may be useful to companies at the macro customer level is shown in Figure 2.8.

3

Customer Focus

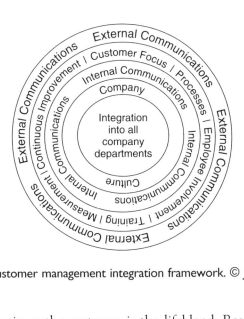

Figure 3.0 Customer management integration framework. © John A. Murphy 2005

For modern business the customer is the lifeblood. Responsibility for the way in which an organisation focuses on its customers lies with the sales/marketing director. It is by consideration of customers' needs and expectations that a company ensures the development of new products and new ways of giving service. Managers and employees need to combine their efforts into new channels, to let that lifeblood flow freely. This chapter concerns itself with internal and external customers;

developing and fostering a service culture and commitment to best practice initiatives; customer acquisition; listening to customers; recognition and reward of loyal customers; logical customer-relationship development and management; service recovery and how to deal with complaints and compliments; and the importance of trust.

Customer acquisition is a changing technique. Customers ebb away from organisations for a number of reasons, not always because of dissatisfaction or competitor appeal, and they need to be replaced. If it is possible, the reason for customer defection needs to be discovered. Insurance companies and credit card organisations, for example, are discovering that customers can be lured away by offers of gifts and special discounts from rival companies. As these tempting inducements are only for new customers, the purchaser will change his provider annually, in pursuit of more such offers. These customers will never become loyal. The question remains, is it worth trying to attract them short term?

Marketing was once aimed at the masses, with mass production, mass distribution and mass advertising. Today, there are many more ways in which people shop. Advertising, once described as 'shouting at the masses', is becoming more complex, in line with the growing variety of shopping opportunities. There is no longer a mass market. In its place are a number of smaller segments of consumers, divided by a number of criteria. These segments are being recognised and certain segments specifically targeted by modern organisations. New segments reveal themselves daily.

Consumers who can be segmented according to any of the criteria used today, nevertheless, differ somewhat in their individual needs, perceptions and buying behaviour. Organisations that discover what makes their offerings attractive, and to which segments of customers they are likely to appeal most, can concentrate their efforts on those customers. The art of marketing for specific segments of customers lies in the way in which the segmentation bands are detected and understood. The groups or segments must be similar enough to appreciate the offering, large enough to make the offering profitable, and potentially loyal enough to make the marketing effort pay off.

Niche marketing is aimed at segments of the market for which no other organisation specifically caters. The customers for niche marketing are fewer and they are often prepared to pay more for something that exactly meets their needs.

Segment and niche marketers tailor their offers and marketing programmes to meet the needs of various market segments. They do not customise their offers to each individual customer. Thus, segment and niche marketing fall between the extremes of mass marketing and micro-marketing.

Micro-marketing is the practice of tailoring products and marketing programmes to suit the tastes of individuals and locations. Micro-marketing includes local marketing and individual marketing.

Local marketing involves tailoring brands and products to the needs and wants of local customer groups, cities, neighbourhoods and even specific stores. It can drive up prices by reduction in economy of scale. It meets the needs of the company's first-line customers, retailers, who prefer finetuned product assortments for their neighbourhoods.

Individual marketing has always existed. Tailors, cobblers, cabinet-makers and thatchers are examples of one-to-one marketing that have slowly declined. New technologies are allowing this type of specialist marketing to return.

Not all customers are individual shoppers. The greatest value turnover of goods and services is between business and business. Business markets can also be segmented and specific segments effectively targeted.

Segmenting business markets

Consumer and business marketers use many of the same variables to segment their markets. Business buyers segment geographically, or by benefits sought, user status, usage rate, loyalty status, readiness state and attitudes. Business marketers also use some additional variables, which include business customer:

- demographics;
- operating characteristics;
- buying approaches;
- situational factors;
- personal characteristics.

Businesses can, by going after segments rather than the whole market, have a much better chance to deliver value to consumers and to receive maximum rewards for close attention to consumer needs.

Segmenting international markets

With the whole world from which to choose customers, businesses that trade in the international marketplace cannot serve every one of the 170 and more countries that might yield customers. Even the largest producing organisations limit their activities to about half the potential outlets. One common segment is geographic, where it might be assumed that countries in close proximity share certain common traits and behaviour. Other segments might be countries within a region such as Europe or South America. The segments are decided by the offering, and must vary from organisation to organisation and the degree to which products must be customised.

Oil and petrol, obtained in many parts of the world, and processed either at source or after distribution, do not require much customisation. Books and clothing, on the other hand, require a great deal. To market these types of products requires a certain level of affluence and education on the part of customers. Thus, a segment of Third-World countries might not wish to or be able to buy books and clothing. The populations of poor nations are more self-sufficient than those in richer nations. Their needs are common, but their purchasing power is restricted.

Once a company decides on the attractive market segments it would like to make its own, it has to start the wooing process. Wooing, whether of an individual or a customer segment, requires tact, understanding, and persistence. There has also to be a mutual and lasting attraction if the courtship is to be successful. Organisations should follow the same guidelines for finding their perfect and enduring partnerships with customers.

Forrester Research analysts suggest that as many of half of all customers now shop for information in one channel, then shop elsewhere when it comes time for money to change hands. These customers have taken advantage of the first channel before escaping to a rival. Initial attraction has been superseded and the relationship destroyed.

Each customer wants to be treated as an individual

Long-term customers of a business see a business as *belonging to them*. In the same way, they want business organisations to treat them as if they belong to the organisation and are important to it. Like the blushing bride, the newly acquired customer wants certain things from the partner: *understanding, empathising, avoidance of complacency*. If the bond is to endure, there must be no cessation of these courtship routines. They build trust and provide stability in business–customer partnerships. Divorce is messy and expensive, for couples and for businesses that lose their most valued customers.

In-depth knowledge of customers creates a strategic advantage, by stimulating a process of mutually desired and agreed exchange of information. With this, new and different value can be created. A bi-directional relationship treats customers as human beings. This bi-directional exchange maximises the advantages of treating customers as individuals.

Choosing customers

Organisations need to discover what they must do to make themselves more attractive than their rivals to the customers they want to acquire or retain. Every business offers something to someone. Almost every business has competitors who would like to take its customers. Most businesses offer something different from the competition that appeals to a segment of its customers. It is possible for a business to be *all things to some people*. It is essential to discover what you offer that is more attractive than the offering of the competitor most likely to acquire your customers or intended customers.

There might be exploitable segments of your market area as yet unexplored. If you should discover any, and they seem worth effort and time to acquire, the decision about whether to try and acquire them is simply decided. If the competition is weak, the accessibility good and the chance of achieving quick success in demonstrating new capabilities is there, it is worth pursuing.

The practical advantage of choosing customers by segmentation, when seeking to meet expected service by perceived service, is that it identifies in advance their basic needs and expectations. Only when these are understood can steps be taken to meet them. The gap between expected service and perceived service, if it exists, requires five key service attributes to be put in place. The customer has to meet with reliability, responsiveness, assurance, empathy and tangibles. (Tangibles are the outward signs of a company's appearance. Tidily dressed staff, a wholesome and clean environment, etc.) Segmentation of customers facilitates best use of limited resources.

Management should determine, when reviewing its service quality initiatives, how far it is separated from customers, and by what means it is separated. What customers feel about the service received from a business might be completely at odds with what management thinks customers feel. Reconciliation and mutual understanding are the keys to discovering the customer's view of the business.

Referrals are good for everyone. Staying connected with customers increases customer satisfaction, which can mean additional business. Long-term customers can be a company's best sales force. Some organisations are not shy about using their best customers in just that capacity and rewarding their 'sales' efforts.

Relationship management is essential, because not every customer will be worth cultivating. Organisations need to think seriously about which customers they want to get and keep. The door should remain open, though, just in case these unprofitable customers become profitable in the future. In the meantime, organisational resources should be shifted from serving unprofitable customers towards developing relationships with profitable customers.

Defining and delivering excellent customer experience relates to and determines the level of satisfaction the customer receives while interacting with the organisation. Some firms define customer experience in terms of 'touch points' between the company and customer, such as installation, change of service, or discontinuation.

Companies that provide a venue, for example, restaurants, retail stores and places of entertainment, define the experience as specific occasions. A useful way to think about the relationship is to identify whether a given attribute is a *dissatisfier*, or a *satisfier*, in the mind of the customer.

'Dissatisfiers' are aspects of the customer experience that represent basic minimum performance in the product category. If these are inadequate or absent, customers become dissatisfied, but high levels do not necessarily lead to high satisfaction. 'Satisfiers' are aspects of the customer experience that motivate or energise customer attitudes and behaviour. What constitutes a satisfier, or dissatisfier, varies by customer, due to both differing customer expectations and differing needs.

Sampling

- Their experience won't necessarily be represented properly by sampling the different touch points they happen to encounter. In sampling these interactions, it's more important to know how they collectively affected the high-value customers than how each individual touch point performed across all interactions. Research effort should be allocated disproportionately to sampling these types of customers and measuring the full range of their experiences, even at high cost.

Managing the total customer experience

Managing the total customer experience begins with an 'experience audit', whereby a company recognises the clues it is sending to its customers. Anything that can be perceived, or sensed, or recognised by its absence, is an experience clue. Thus, the product or service for sale gives off one set of clues, the physical setting offers more clues, and the employees, through their gestures, comments, dress and tones of voice provide still more clues. Each clue carries a message, suggesting something to the customer. The composite of all the clues makes up the customer's total experience.

Leading the customer experience

Business strategies centred on the holistic design and delivery of total customer experiences consistently create superior customer value. Total experience has been defined as the feelings customers take away from their interactions with a firm's goods, services, and 'atmospheric' stimuli.

The clues that make up a customer experience fall into two categories:

- *Mechanics* = clues emitted by things.
- *Humanics* = clues emitted by people.

The first concerns the actual functioning of the goods or service. The second category concerns the emotions and includes the smells, sounds, sights, tastes and textures of the goods or service, as well as the environment in which it is offered. Organisations must manage the emotional component of experiences.

In an article entitled 'How to lead the customer', Haeckel *et al.* (2003) suggest the following approach to managing the total customer experience:

Three principles of managing the total customer experience:

Principle 1: Fuse experiential breadth and depth. Congruence, or fusion, of clues within and among experience stages is critical. For instance, guests at a hotel don't live in the lobby. However, if lobby clues fuse with guestroom clues, then one part of the experience reinforces another.

Principle 2: Use mechanics and humanics to improve function. Mechanics and humanics must be addressed simultaneously and blended with the functional clues of the offering into reciprocally supported experience clues.

Principle 3: Connect emotionally. Managing customers' experiences requires awareness of all their senses throughout the experience. Sight, motion, sound, smell, taste, and touch are direct pathways to customers' emotions. Connecting with customers in a sensory way is crucial to managing positive emotional elements of the experience.

Managing the impact of delays

Before the delay, customers are believed to rely most heavily upon personal sources when forming their pre-purchase expectations about service quality and choosing a provider. During the delay, poor attitude, carelessness or slow service can significantly diminish customer satisfaction, even when the technical aspect (the outcome) is acceptable. After the delay, an apology is the least the employee can offer, to show empathy toward the customer. Many organisations train their employees to apologise for inconveniencing customers. There are times when an apology is not enough.

Sarel and Marmorstein (1999) propose a four-part strategy for managing the impact of delays:

1. Segmented solutions.
   Not all customers are equally affected. Customers who had experienced frequent service delays in the past are *far angrier* when they encounter another service failure. Their problems must be given priority and eliminated.

2. Customer-specific information systems.
   Firms ought to move towards information systems that capture the differential experience of individuals, or at least key segments.

> 3. Fix the chronic problems first.
> It is more important to tackle the chronic problems that cause frequent delays than be concerned with the impact of the occasional delay.
>
> 4. Just managing expectations is not enough.
> Customers who had experienced many delays in the past and, therefore, were not surprised by the current delay, were the most dissatisfied segment. Obviously, just minimising surprise is not enough.
>
> Republished with permission, Emerald Group Publishing Limited: http://www.emeraldinsight.com/ijbm.htm.

Improving employee performance is an essential element in dealing effectively with delays. This must cover:

- Employee training.
  Employees need to be made aware of the impact of their behaviour on customers. Training should be directed at raising employee awareness levels of the significance of these issues.
- Delivery process improvement.
  Processes and procedures need to be re-examined, to ensure that they do not hinder employee effort to serve.
- Customer education and information.
  Customers need to understand why employees behave in a certain way, and these situations provide opportunities to inform and educate customers about what employees are doing. By this means, some customer apprehension may be reduced, the wait may become less uncertain, and customers will know what to expect during the wait.
- Effective apologies.

Employees connect to the customer

Employees can be the key to competitive strategy. Therefore, employee satisfaction has come to be considered as a prerequisite for good customer experience, leading to customer satisfaction. If you have mismanaged your internal customers – your staff – you are unlikely to be very successful with servicing your customers. It is the experience and attitudes of individuals in closest contact with customers that are most likely to affect whether or not customers are satisfied and willing to return to the company. It is also the people who are in direct contact with customers who determine who the retained and satisfied customers are, and their experience determines how they treat the customers (see Figure 3.1).

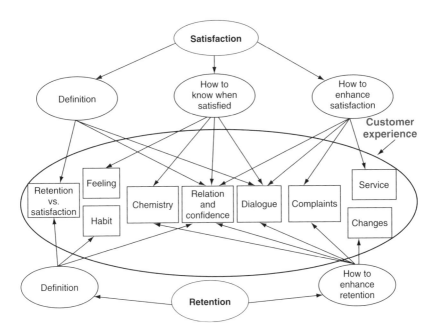

Figure 3.1 The link between customer experience, satisfaction and retention
Source: Hansemark O.C. and Albinsson M. (2004) Customer satisfaction and retention: the experiences of individual employees. *Managing Service Quality*, 14(1): 40–57. Republished with permission, Emerald Group Publishing Limited

Customer retention

Customer retention occurs with the customers' liking, identification, commitment, trust, willingness to recommend, and repurchase intentions, with the first four being emotional and the last two being behavioural intentions.

Employees view customer experience to be enhanced by having good relationships and high levels of trust. Managers should be concerned when employee understanding of key concepts differs within the organisation, and differs also from management's understanding. The totality that customers experience is called the service experience of customers with respect to a service operations system. It is essential, therefore, for employees and management to work to the same ends. Organisations setting out to win customers, deliver good service and survive vigorous competition have to engage in continuous improvement.

What if customers charged the organisation for their time?

The company's behaviour would change drastically, and for the better. When the wait could not be further reduced, they would try to add value to the experience. Consequently, reducing customer non-value-added (NVA) time is a new source of competitive advantage, ripe for innovation. NVA time has long been a focus of companies' productivity enhancements.

Tackle delays by first mapping the time customers spend engaged with the company or product. Focus on finding the *points of impatience*, when a little bit of a customer's time wasted causes disproportionate irritation. Consider what a customer's highest expectations are at any given moment during an engagement with the organisation.

Customers' complaints should be explored carefully, so that similar complaints do not become ingrained, and yet, in spite of the seriousness of this area of business, many companies make mistakes when they try to discover root causes of dissatisfaction.

Clark (2003) explores the matter in a piece entitled 'Bad examples'. He lists nine common mistakes in approach to experience measurement and complaints handling.

Experience measurement – Common mistakes

1. Asking only about your product.
2. Asking only about your company.
3. Asking only about satisfaction.
4. Not asking about price.
5. Asking only your current customers.
6. Letting your salespeople or distributors administer the survey.
7. Focusing on mean scores and 'top two boxes'.
8. Not letting customers talk.
9. Using only one method.

The same author has some suggested alternatives to the foregoing.

The antidote to the mistakes:

1. Remember that customers increasingly make their choices based on supplemental benefits above and beyond the core. Ask about important elements of the total experience customers have with your organisation.
2. Ask about satisfaction with other companies as well as your own, and report results in terms of satisfaction relative to key competitors.
3. Ask specifically about loyalty. For example: 'How motivated are you to find an alternative to the product you are now using?'
4. If you ask a customer, 'Would you like X?' they will tend to say yes. If you ask, 'Would you pay £10 for X?', you get an answer that is more likely to resemble reality.
5. Seek out samples of competitors' customers and former customers, to counter the positive bias.
6. Use HQ staff or an external agency to administer your customer satisfaction research.

7. In many competitive markets, it appears that the real benefit from satisfaction comes from moving customers from 4 (satisfied) to 5 (very satisfied) on a typical five-point scale. This finding has been a driver behind the movement to 'delight' the customer. Mere satisfaction is not enough, and only extraordinary experiences guarantee loyalty. A case study in *Customer is King*, by Robert Craven, features Jim McPherson, a training programme designer, who felt that something different was needed in a marketplace of similar products. He designed his questionnaire on three definitions of satisfaction level: SAME – BETTER – WOW, and the responses spurred him on to initiate changes to put at least a third into the WOW column. Using the five-point satisfaction scale anchored with 'very dissatisfied' and 'very satisfied', consider how many customers fall into each group. What characterises each set of customers in terms of segmentation variables (e.g., demographics) and purchase behaviour? How valuable are these customers to the firm?

8. Every survey or interview should end with one open-ended question that allows the customer to express whatever is on his or her mind. Save time at the end of the survey to listen to their comments. Ask about their experience with your company, or their current supplier. Ask whether there are any issues not covered during the interview.

9. Supplement, review and refresh the primary method. Market leaders in customer satisfaction measurement use multiple methods of assessment. If your approach has been primarily quantitative, then qualitative approaches such as focus groups, depth interviews or customer visits can provide new insights.

In addition to discovering customers needs, hopes, desires, requirements and reasons for dealing with the organisation, data about the customer's purchasing behaviour and capability is required, and how well or badly the customers' expectations are currently being met, or could be better met in future. The success or otherwise of service quality initiatives can only be viewed from the customers' perspective.

Data collection

Data collection should identify customers' anticipated standards and reveal the factors that might disappoint or alienate the customer, were some of these standards to fall below a certain level. So-called moments of truth occur at every contact point between customer and supplier, when the customer draws conclusions about the supplier's overall service quality. These conclusions will vary from one individual to another, but there are many similarities. It should also be possible to determine what aspects of competitors' offerings attract or repel your own customers.

Data collection should be the means to an end, not an end in itself. First, the motives behind any form of data collection should be clearly defined. Valuable data, often overlooked by top managers, are letters of complaint, and the rarer letter of compliment. These are powerful tools for service improvement.

Data collection should help an organisation to:

- identify the moments of truth in the company's organisation;
- discover what are the values customers seek at each of these moments of truth;
- identify the chain of internal customers and the values that must be transmitted up that chain to achieve the satisfactory result at the moment of truth;
- start the quest for a mission statement;
- establish what are the positive and negative aspects of the company's culture.

The definition of quality starts and ends with customers. Exactly how customers define the service quality of an organisation's offering should be established from the data gathered.

As to the questions actually asked and the way in which they are asked, there are many options. All data requires skilled analysis, but when levels of satisfaction have been explored, it should be remembered that only those customers who say they are very satisfied, or who describe the goods or services purchased as excellent, can be regarded as loyal.

Questionnaires should be tailored to the product or service and the type of user. As well as matters pertaining to service and product quality, variables to be measured might include:

- Flexibility – how fast is the company in changing and adapting to new requirements?
- Accuracy – lack of mistakes and defects, precise corrections.
- Time – minutes, hours, on time, overtime, time saved.
- Quantity – over-budget, under-budget, profit, loss, break-even.
- Quality – type of material, finish and durability.

Having formulated the questions, the size of the poll must be calculated. The sample should be sufficiently large for the margin of error in the results to be as low as possible. There will always be a margin of error in any survey, but the larger the sample, the smaller the margin.

Next, the way in which the survey is conducted is important. Postal surveys do not produce the response of those where the questionnaire is handed to the customer by an employee, or where there is an incentive to complete. Either way, with self-completion questionnaires, the customer must be told the benefits of completion and be able to understand the objectives. It should be easy to complete. The questions should be short. There should be space for further comments. The form should be easy to return. Busy customers often take away questionnaires to complete later, when they are less busy.

Focus groups are more expensive and provide smaller samples, but they are sometimes rich in information and provide different types of information from questionnaires. One economist, Stanley A. Brown, is of the opinion that for every market segment to be researched, two sets of focus groups should be conducted.

Questionnaires focus on hard facts, as do telephone surveys, postal surveys, mystery shopping and third-party surveys. Focus groups explore opinions and soft issues. Similarly, so do face-to-face interviews, videos, free-phone and suggestion schemes.

The accuracy and appropriateness of the methods by which an organisation conducts a survey determine the reliability of the results.

Internal customer surveys, focus groups in particular, are run by outside consultants. It is essential to preserve confidentiality, whichever method is used to survey staff, if they are to express their views freely and frankly. Employee attitude surveys are necessary before a service quality improvement programme can be put in place. It is advisable to explore issues via a loosely structured interview or focus group before developing a structured survey format.

Benchmarking is another way in which companies listen to customers. It enables companies to compare themselves to the best organisations in the same category, to identify differences in performance, to document why these exist. Steps can then be taken to meet and surpass these best organisations by developing a set of standards and an action plan to bring about the desired improvements.

The more direct *feedback* an organisation receives from its customers, the better it is able to develop its relationship with them. Research should be used as the first step of a programme to establish the needs of internal and external customers, and to act as a benchmark against which to measure the effectiveness of the programme.

If the feedback process is seen as an essential link with service excellence provision, the objectives and the way in which it is set up become clear. First, it must be highly visible and accessible, and should actively facilitate the involvement of employees and customers. Secondly, it should have corporate-wide solutions such as that provided by Charter Continuum for managing all forms of feedback in one integrated and centralised system. Such a system incorporates a flexible diary management process and call-logging wizard for the effective management of customer intelligence, feedback data capture and analytics. If customers are to have faith in the feedback system, they should be able to see that it is being used effectively by the organisation. Central to maximizing customer satisfaction is the ability to maximise trust.

Action plan

Managers need to be facilitators, staff need to be implementers. Unless this relationship is understood, staff cannot be expected to conform to the company's excellence culture and managers are evidently not fully aware of what that culture requires them to do. To achieve excellence, therefore, managers need to know what is necessary to enable feedback between employees and managers, to facilitate an exchange of knowledge about what customers expect and desire, and to provide the tools and skills training for the job. Their other role is to ensure that the right people are in place and that they are performing to the best of their ability. There is a linking relationship from the top to the bottom, and its strength is tested at every interface. Customers will pay more for what they see as higher quality, or more reliable service.

Rather than theorise about this, it might be advisable to offer an action plan to help companies to get to practical grips with the steps to be taken towards implementation of a culture change to achieve service excellence. In simple terms, it can be expressed in the following format:

Strategy formalisation

Step 1   Communication to all employees
Step 2   Qualitative research
Step 3   Quantitative research
Step 4   Analysis of findings
Step 5   Creating the quality philosophy
Step 6   Appointment of factor owners
Step 7   Communications
Step 8   Culture change
Step 9   Finalisation of strategy document
Step 10   Roll out schedule

Everyone concerned in any way with a transaction is part of the chain and a measure of its strength. Working with other companies, changing the nature and style of products and services, provision of after-sales service and customer follow-ups are undertaken in response to what customers ask for.

Employees, from management down, are internal customers. They should think of themselves and their colleagues, as well as the external customer, in this context. They all have a role to play in forming and developing internal and external customer relationships, and should be asked to address the following:

- Every employee should be able to define exactly who their customers are – both internal and external.

The key issues to be faced when developing customer relationships, then, are frequency of contact, communications, listening and responding.

When the director of a successful company makes suggestions on how to attract the attention of customers, the advice offered is worth consideration. Brian Plowman, director of Develin & Partners, Harefield, Middlesex, wrote a lengthy and considered article, which he headed: *Creating a differentiating customer proposition* (DCP). The choice of words, he emphasises, is important.

- Differentiating: not running with the herd, but being noticed by customers and potential customers. Not being different for the sake of it, but providing a total service that puts the business ahead of the competition.
- Customer: changing the emphasis away from the business managing its prime financial ratios through forcing staff to sell, often against the best interests of customers.
- Proposition: the DCP has to be something the customer would propose to others (advocacy), rather than the business exhorting staff to sell and forcing customers to buy. When a company gets it right for the customer, then the financials follow.

The first ingredient

The DCP must lead to customer retention and customer advocacy, providing a total service where being a customer is to value the relationship. The relationship creates a delight factor that has a value to customers greater than the sum of the traditional constituent parts of the products and services. Building a partnership relationship is thus the challenge and will require a different way of treating the customer. The retention of the customer and their advocacy more than outweighs a poor sale in the current financial year that eventually leads to permanently lost customers.

The second ingredient

The DCP must include the dimension of accessibility; access determined by customers, convenient to them, locking out competitors.

The third ingredient

The DCP must encompass the internal framework of the entire business and all its processes; a lowest unit cost business within which it is also a pleasure to work.

Listening to customers

Listening to customers is a technique that can be learnt. Cementing relationships comes about when people listen to one another. All employees have a role to play in this and frontline employees more so than most. Listening to customers is the most efficient and least expensive method of data collection an organisation can deploy. It is a continuous window onto what customers think about organisations, it is accessible to all levels of staff, from top management to the most junior employee.

Feedback will not always be critical. It can also highlight where things are being done well. Organisations who take listening seriously will make it easy for customers to make comments, treat complaints as a learning opportunity and go out of their way to listen and respond to customers, even if this means major changes in work practices.

When feedback is not as complimentary as an organisation hopes it will be, there is a silver lining to the cloud, if the correct actions are taken. TMI National Complaints Culture Survey, 2003, concluded that complaints can be beneficial. The survey indicated that 90% of satisfied complainants will repurchase, and 60% of customers will pay 5% more for a better level of service.

The same survey reported the way in which customer expectations have become more demanding. Survey results, in respect of *Complaint management: customer expectations*, show that 65% of customers now expect complaints in person to be dealt with immediately, or on the same day. Virtually all customers want their written complaints to be acknowledged, and nearly one-third expects this acknowledgement within two days; 43% of customers also expect written complaints to be resolved within one week. Over half of all customers expect their telephone complaints to be resolved immediately, or on the same day.

Complaint management: customer satisfaction

Table 3.1, which is an extract from the *Customer Care Alliance Report*, 2004, reveals the alarming damage done to companies who fail to make a satisfactory response to customer complaints. Mollified customers are, nevertheless, capable and too often willing to tell

Table 3.1 Complaint management: satisfaction level impact

	Satisfaction with action taken	Satisfaction with organisation	Willingness to recommend	Word of mouth*
Satisfied	11%	76%	60%	6.5%
Modified	39%	22%	17%	9.3%
Dissatisfied	51%	4%	4%	13.4%

*Word of mouth – The number of people told about a good/bad response.

Table 3.2 Complaint management: customer expectations

Expectation	Looking for	Received
An apology	48%	30%
An explanation	45%	23%
Product repaired/Service fixed	28%	15%
All of money back	19%	8%
An assurance that problem would not be repeated	32%	7%
Some of money back	16%	7%
Free product or service in the future	8%	4%
Financial compensation for lost time/inconvenience	14%	3%
Just to express anger, tell their side of the story	12%	2%
Revenge/Make them pay for hassle/inconvenience	3%	0%
Other	7%	8%

others about their lack of total satisfaction with an organisation that does not meet expectations, and the less satisfaction the customer receives, the more damaging his/her word-of-mouth comments to friends, family, neighbours and competitors.

In March 2003, the *Customer Care Alliance Report* dealt with *Customer expectations and what they actually received*. Table 3.2 *shows the results*.

In her practical book, *The Art of Giving Quality Service*, Gober (2003) Mary Gober proposes 10 appropriate steps to take in complaint management.

Complaint management in 10 steps

1. Listen without interrupting.
2. Don't get defensive.
3. Respond with: glad, sure, sorry.
4. Express empathy.

5. Ask questions to understand the problem.
6. Find out what the customer wants.
7. Explain what you can do.
8. Discuss alternatives and agree on action.
9. Take action immediately.
10. Follow up to ensure satisfaction.

Due to its importance to the way in which an organisation uses customer feedback to maintain its service quality objectives, a formal, ongoing system should be installed that can bring in feedback regularly. This formal system will make it clear to customers that you want to listen, and this will encourage them to talk.

A formal listening system, that includes staff as well as customers, turns staff into channels for customers' comments and complaints. This involvement encourages staff to make suggestions of their own for improvements in services. Staff are often far more aware of the matters exercising the minds of customers than are managers. Use of the word 'feedback', rather than 'complaints', projects a more positive image of the system.

If the listening process is seen as an essential link with service quality provision, the objectives and the way in which it is set up become clear. First, it must be highly visible and accessible, and should actively facilitate the involvement of customers. Secondly, it must be based on listening. This must be backed up by proper training in how to listen. Finally, it must be treated like any other process and be updated regularly. If customers are to have faith in the listening system, they should be able to see that it is being used by the organisation. The more open and visible the system, the more likely it is that customers see it is valuable and will use it.

Suggestion boxes are an obvious option, but some people do not find it easy to express their thoughts in writing. This is particularly the case in districts with multi-ethnic populations. Telephone hot lines, with interpreters where needed, are another option. Some organisations have a front desk, where management members can meet the customers face to face and learn how they feel about the organisation.

It is useful for members of staff to talk about the service to a proportion of customers, face to face, each week. Training is important and it can help to change the culture of the organisation. Staff who are trained and empowered to deal with customer comments and complaints build an organisation with listening as part of its make-up. This will become an inherent element of its organisational and service cultures.

To summarise why organisations should listen, the following points must be considered. Listening is valuable, and feedback is more than complaints. Listening is a reliable guide to what an organisation does well and where it has room for improvement. Customers should be made aware that their feedback, comments and complaints are appreciated. Once the facts are known, action can be taken where needed. Once action has been taken, customers should be made aware of what has been done.

Measures influence behaviour toward (or away from) the DCP

What gets measured gets done. Old measures will have been successful at delivering the old strategies. If the new strategy is to deliver the DCP then new measures are required to deliver the new strategy. There always appears to be a reluctance to drop many of the old measures that have served the company well in the past. The wrong measures, or the right measures misused, are the strongest influence on employee behaviour.

Staff react to those measures that are linked to appraisals, money, advancement and the avoidance of 'poor performance' against the measure. The measures on staff are often in conflict with meeting the needs of customers, let alone building a DCP, but without empowerment and in an environment where management is not readily questioned, staff will meet the needs of their immediate customer (their manager) and ignore the needs of the external customer.

If managers never realise the long-term damage an inappropriate measure is doing to the business, then can we blame them for driving wrong behaviour? It is interesting to note that often the measures placed on staff are a combination of the staff member's output, competence and performance, whereas the manager is measured purely on the degree to which output targets are achieved by staff. The competence and performance of a manager should include an understanding of how measures determine behaviour. If this were the case, many staff (victims) would be freed from the conflicts they are subjected to at the customer interfaces.

The ladder of loyalty

When people first access a company, they are prospects, the first rung of the ladder. After a purchase, they are customers. If nothing much upsets them, they may become supporters.

The next vital step in the relationship is to make them advocates. These are customers who tell other members of their family, their friends or other businesses, that the company is the best. Advocates stay, which is far cheaper than having to replace customers who have left. The final step is for both parties to see each other as partners. This is something different from selling them products. It is all about understanding, even predicting, a client's needs in an environment of total trust. This state is very fragile and likely to be eroded if the company is still using any questionable practices.

Recognise and reward loyal customers

Everything already covered in this chapter inevitably leads to one simple question: how do we recognise and reward loyal customers?

There are three basic types of external customer who remain loyal over the longer term.

1. The people who simply prefer stable, long-term relationships. They are loyal, no matter what company they patronise.
2. Those customers who spend more than others, pay their bills promptly and require less service.
3. Those who find your products and services more valuable than those of your competitors.

The better a company is at attracting customers who belong to any, or all of these categories, the better the rewards they reap. It has to be understood, however, that some types of customer are innately loyal. Others would defect for a small discount.

Referrals are the most cost-effective form of acquisition. Customers acquired through referral are potentially more loyal. Car Phone Warehouse maintains that 90% of its new customers are acquired through referrals, and it retains 65% of these. Xerox discovered that customers who are very satisfied are six times more likely to be loyal than those who are merely satisfied. The goal, therefore, is to ensure that their customers are very satisfied. They do this through offering service excellence.

Robert Pavich (2003) reveals that, over the past five years, many banks have invested substantial capital in Internet and wireless initiatives to try to improve customer service. Charter One Bank's alerting service, called FYI, delivers its retail and small business customers information regarding recent transactions, low balances, new e-bill arrivals and more, via telephone, email, wireless text and fax, and secure inbox.

With new thinking on the subject of customer loyalty and its influence on profitability, managers and CEOs are coming to realise that culture is not just one aspect of the game; it *is* the game. At the end of the day, an organisation is nothing more than the collective capacity of its people to create value. Corporate values, as described by Enron, are

- communication;
- respect;
- integrity;
- excellence.

As the story of this unhappy organisation teaches, these values are commendable, on paper, but worse than useless unless the company delivers them.

Gauging customer loyalty

The two most effective questions, across industries, that can be asked when gauging customer loyalty are:

- How likely is it that you would recommend the company?
- How strongly do you agree that the company deserves your loyalty?

Customer satisfaction is only the beginning of the loyalty continuum, so it should not be the goal. After all, over 65% of satisfied customers are not necessarily loyal.

Micro-marketing is the ultimate in customer service provision

The possibilities for this type of mass micro-marketing are almost endless, and will soon be available universally. The benefits to the customer of making purchases via the Internet, for example, are obvious and clearly appreciated. The scope for making an organisation indispensable to the customer is vast but, as with all good ideas, every business is looking to exploit the new opportunities.

It is not the end of competition. If anything, it widens the scope to every organisation to exploit the armchair customer base. It is not yet the end of conventional shopping, but the time will come when customers will prefer and expect it. Organisations that anticipate change and prepare to meet it will have the edge, but they must work to keep ahead.

There are ways in which internal customers (employees) can be rewarded for helping to make the new ideas successful. As organisations move away from labour-intensive marketing and service provision, return on capital grows. A system of rewards for extra effort by staff might be introduced by management, to encourage employees to try harder. Bonuses are one possibility, or election of 'Employee of the Month', for example, who might be nominated by customers, other staff, or by management. Good effort should be celebrated and if this is done spontaneously, it can be very effective. It should ideally reflect the way in which customers receive the employee's efforts, and such a scheme needs to be high profile, if customer feedback is sought. Most people take employment because they need to earn money. Financial rewards are, therefore, generally the most appreciated.

Some of the dividends from modern technological innovations should be ploughed back in improved training for and recruitment of higher quality staff and in better salary structures. The future ideal, then, is to operate as a corporation but offer micro marketing to individual customers, by taking goods to them, rather than bringing them to the goods.

This service should be supported by knowledgeable and trained employees, who would be able to demonstrate the products and arrange for them to be delivered, and who would be able to recognise the opportunities for making further sales on the basis of current and recent purchases. Such employees must also be able to listen to customers and utilise what they are told. They should also provide information to customers, to create a dialogue between the organisation and those whom it serves.

Monitoring performance

There is good reason for organisations to monitor the steps they have implemented in the battle for overall service quality. It concentrates the minds of all employees as well as managers on the objectives to which they have all agreed. It identifies weaknesses in all important areas, if these exist. Management should continue to monitor, participate in and support the organisation's performance targets and strategies. Survey results should be widely disseminated among employees, to focus their interest on the company's success. Decisions should be made swiftly and all feedback should lead to action. Improving customer satisfaction has been described as more a journey than a destination. It is advisable to keep one's eye fixed on the road.

In a perfect world, customers would receive perfect service from an organisation whose employees and management share an ideal, customer-orientated, common goal. Customers and organisation would work in perfect harmony and every customer would be completely satisfied at all times and be content for things to go along as they are forever. The organisation would comprise superhuman people who are devoted to its ideals, and who never entertain the thought of resignation.

Things in the real world are not always like this. Customers and employees can become disenchanted and look for pastures new. We recognise that loyalty has to be earned and does not come cheap. The more highly trained our employees and managers, the more expensive it is to recruit and train replacements for them. The same is true of customers, who take time and money to acquire and train before they are profitable.

Everything we have said in this chapter is intended as a guide to building the one element without which a company and its customers cannot relate, and that is trust.

In the public forum there are data that can be readily obtained and used by marketers to target specific segments of potential customers. Registry offices, courts, licences for cars, television sets, rental contracts, subscriptions, mail order purchasing and many other avenues exist for obtaining information about the public. The proposed new identity cards will undoubtedly open up new avenues for exploitation. Such data can be and often are abused. When unwanted mail, faxes or telephone calls intrude into our lives, we feel that our privacy has been violated. Organisations that use these intrusive methods of attracting our attention often achieve the opposite to what they expect.

Is the customer responsible for the avalanche of junk mail? How often do we read the small print on a mail order form, where we are invited to tick a box if we do not wish the data on us to be disseminated? How often do we tick the box, assuming we spot the opportunity to do so? Telephone calls are all logged against the databank the telephone company uses when invoicing customers. If we use the telephone to order goods or services, we are giving away data about ourselves to the telephone company and the firm from whom we are purchasing something. We do the same sort of thing when we pay by credit card or cheque. The Internet is just one more point through which information about us leaks into the public domain.

The problem with data is that it can be gathered, copied and distributed, so that the consumer has no way of discovering its source. Sometimes, too, people find among the junk mail an advertisement for something they actually require, and they proceed to order it. This encourages companies to continue the practice. Where mass marketing was once all that organisations considered necessary, segmentation has led to a new approach. It is segmented mass marketing, using databases to define the segments.

The European Parliament has considered various ways in which intrusions into our privacy might be controlled by legislation. The proposals were countered by the suggestion that legislation to protect privacy might actually generate more junk mail, since specific targets would subsequently be harder to isolate. Every household has a dustbin, into which most unsolicited mail is unceremoniously dropped. Magazine and television advertising can be ignored. The telephone call from a double-glazing salesperson, or holiday company, is more aggravating. People find it difficult to terminate the conversation in a way that does not leave them feeling uncomfortable. There is now one avenue open to them to ban unwanted telephone and fax messages, should they happen to learn about it.

Organisations should understand customers' need for privacy and exhibit the fact that they are aware of this need. Many customers come to an organisation as a result of referral, which implies that certain facts will be known to each about the other. Some customers, not quite in this category, can be obtained indirectly, by means of other organisations, but it is essential not to hand control of the relationship with your customer to someone else. This means – do not allow anyone else outside your organisation to have access to your database.

Be honest with your customers, if you want to gain their trust; and tell them what you intend to do with data they provide. If you want customer cooperation with questionnaires, or on any other collaborative effort, the promise you give them about the results is an explicit bargain with the customer. Organisations have been formed to use fax and email to offer a service that benefits customers and marketers by using data gathered by one means or another but within a closed system. The data is not disseminated beyond the user group and customers often find the type of marketing shot they get by this means is valuable.

Another aspect of trust is the way in which the organisation is run. Managers must train and then trust employees to do their work properly. There must be openness in marketing and in dealing with prices, complaints, mistakes, servicing and personnel, as well as with the customers' data. People and processes subjected to too much checking and supervision tend to stultify. To bestow responsibility breeds responsible behaviour; and organisations can find considerable cost savings as well as enhanced levels of employee and customer satisfaction when trust replaces control.

Trust building should be part of service and organisational culture, and employees should be trained in its relevance to customer retention. In taking a lateral glance at the matter; a possible alternative might be to allow customers to post their personal shopping requirements on the organisation's bulletin board, and allow the organisation to respond, or not. The advantages of this are obvious: cheapness, individualised response, and the opportunity to offer other products or services when the goods are delivered.

Why it is vital to build trust

New technology allows massive scope for innovation in marketing, but it requires careful deployment. Invasion of privacy is an unpardonable offence. The days of mass micro marketing are here. Regulation will follow abuse. Success and profits will accrue to organisations who have prepared to face the challenge. Organisations who behave fairly and honestly at all times will be trusted and will keep their internal and external customers loyal and contented.

Organisations who violate trust and intrude into customers' privacy might well make extra sales, but only the once. Ongoing, valuable customer relationships are not for them. Yet, as we have seen, it is the ongoing, long-term relationships that count most. They cannot be valued highly enough, and are not worth risking on a one-off flash in the pan.

Summary

In the examination of what constitutes customer focus, we saw that it begins with the company culture of service excellence. Its implementation is initiated by the sales/marketing director and requires participation by all employees. The reason for giving this subject maximum attention and concomitant resources is the impact it has on profitability, or otherwise. When the company sets out to offer service excellence, it defines its most profitable customers, as we saw in the preceding chapters.

This is done by accumulation of data gathered by various types of market research, not the least of which comes from complaints and compliments, often via frontline employees. It is these profitable customers upon whom future efforts will be focused. They are selected and sorted into useful segments, sufficiently large for the business to serve profitably, diverse enough to provide a fair and accurate sample, and offer useful feedback that can be used for future innovation of product and service.

Well-selected segments, properly served, contain customers from whom most of an organisation's future business will come. This will be from an increase in portfolio and frequency of purchases. It will also grow by way of referrals. The loyal customer begins to act as a super salesperson, unpaid, for the company. It is this customer, who would not think of looking elsewhere for the kinds of goods and services provided, that is most cost-effective, requiring little in the way of advertising, and whose requirements and expectations are already being met.

To build a worthwhile customer relationship, it is necessary to connect with customers. Part of this process is observation of customer behaviour and the way in which competitors relate to their own customers. It means that time has to be set aside to listen to customers, in order to know what they need and expect from the organisation. Having established contact, the relationship needs to be nurtured and broadened. A dialogue should grow from the contact. Companies should listen to customers and encourage customers to listen to them. In this way, customers feel as if they are being treated as individuals, and this flatters them.

Relationships grow on a basis of mutual trust. This should be fostered, not left to appear from thin air. When two people are mutually attracted, they take time to study one another, find ways to please, look for common ground. Business relationships can last longer than many marriages. They can be equally important to the happiness of the people concerned. We have mentioned ways in which trust might be broken, and how to correct the situation early.

One way in which trust can be helped to develop is the way in which customers' complaints and compliments are handled. Complaints are opportunities for improvement. They should, therefore, be given the most careful attention, and are the ultimate responsibility of top management. Well handled, complaints can substantially increase the depth of loyalty a customer feels for the company. If the situation is successfully recovered, the complainant will feel deeper attachment to the company. See Chapter 4 – Processes and Systems.

The customer management integration framework shows how *customer focus* is bounded by the two-way communication between company and customer and sits alongside all the other activities that take place within the company.

In focusing on customers, managers and chief executives need to know how employees listen to and respond to customers' needs and expectations. Action must be taken to ensure that there is a good system through which information can be gathered and distributed. Every employee/customer interface is a source of information, from the customer and about the company and its products. Managers must know what promises are given to customers and how well these promises are kept. Again, at every interface between staff and customers, promises are made, and this includes any advertising material. A broken promise makes for a disgruntled customer.

The thinking behind all customer focus initiatives is, unequivocally, the profits they generate and the costs they incur; the one to be balanced against the other.

A company management should be able to state what its customers think of the service given and should be able to pass this information on, in meaningful terms, to all employees. Employees need to be positively encouraged to pass back to managers all customers' comments, especially adverse comments, and there needs to be a way in which these can be processed to make further improvements to service quality.

The DCP approach, as advocated by Brian Plowman of Develin & Partners, recommends moving away from the old-style management emphasis on forcing staff to sell, and adopting instead the view that it is more sensible to serve customers in such a way as to generate their loyalty and trust, since this is the route to profit. This means provision of product and service quality and excellence that matches and exceeds customer expectations.

In 2004, Dr John A. Murphy carried out a survey of 1000 customers, and a series of focus group meetings were held to identify the top eroders of satisfaction/trust. The customers were asked, 'What is it that makes you irritated or dissatisfied as a customer in terms of the service you receive from companies?' From the responses, it was possible to compile a ranking, in order of importance, of these eroders.

Eroders of satisfaction

- Waiting for call to be answered/telephone queues.
- Poorly trained staff.
- Not caring/lack of empathy.
- Menu-driven/touch-tone/automated/voice-activated telephone systems.
- Unavailability of staff to take calls/answer queries.
- Insensitivity to problems/complaints.

While all of the above are important, it is significant to point out that in the technology-related issues (telephone), customers in the age range 55–64 were adversely affected by 3–4 times that in the age range 18–25. On the issue of caring/empathy, females were 1.5 times more affected than their male counterparts.

Eroders of trust

- Failure to keep promises.
- Receiving wrong advice/information.
- Non-return of calls/emails/letters.
- Insincerity.
- Overcharging/hidden charges.
- Being told lies/untruths.

While all of the above are important, it is significant to observe that males were twice as concerned about receiving wrong advice/information as their female counterparts. On the issue of non-return of calls/emails/letters, customers in the age range 65–9 were up to three times more reactive than those in younger age groups and up to five times more reactive to overcharging/hidden costs.

In addressing the critical issues implicit in the above research, one cannot but observe the dominant influence of the people factor: the impact made by employees who know what to do right, and who do it. While some companies already recognise and do something about this, and others aspire to be the so-called 'employers of choice', the reality is that most businesses pay lip service to the fact that employees are their greatest asset. A recent government report encouraged large companies to include information on human capital management in the operating and financial review (OFR) of their annual reports. This makes eminent sense, as the OFR is meant to analyse the main factors likely to affect a company's performance, and people policies are most certainly one of those. The report, referred to as the *Kingsmill Report*, suggests a broad framework for companies. This includes spelling out their thinking on the link between human capital management and strategy as well as relevant information on employee training, development and retention.

The value of all customer focus initiatives will definitely be revealed in the end-of-year audited accounts.

4

Processes and Systems

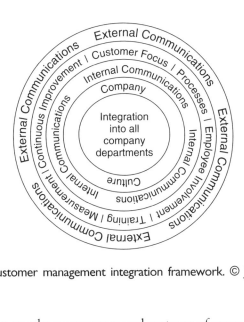

Figure 4.0 Customer management integration framework. © John A. Murphy 2005

Every business employs processes and systems of some sort, in order to provide products and/or services. The way in which these processes and systems are constructed, monitored and continuously improved is vital to their success. Some processes are more critical than others. All contribute to the overall quality of the company's offering. They can be devised to cover every aspect of an organisation's activities.

In a research report based on the experiences of customer-facing staff in five outstanding organisations identified in Service excellence= Reputation=Profit, for Warwick Business School (January 2003) and published by The Institute of Customer Service, Professor Robert Johnston conducted interviews with five frontline employees in each of five major organisations. The interviews were structured round seven simple questions. The interviewees were first asked to say something about their job, and whether they enjoyed it and why. Then, they were asked what 'Excellent service' means to their customers. The next question was how do they personally contribute to their organisation's reputation for excellence, and how do they deal with the situation when things go wrong and customers complain. They were then asked what difficulties they found in delivering this great service day to day. The last question was why they chose to work for their organisation.

From the sometimes lengthy replies, it was possible to make useful deductions and to highlight what makes good practice across companies and organisations. The reasons why people enjoyed the job were, in essence, the job itself, the support received and the outcomes. Professor Johnston's report covers all aspects of service quality and illustrates the areas where processes and systems are not only beneficial but also essential, especially those that affect frontline people.

He makes the point that senior managers who walk the job and talk in a friendly and encouraging way to employees, asking for comments and opinions, and who take the time to listen to what people have to say, can learn more about the organisation than they can by any other method, and they can, if they are responsive, also discover what steps are necessary to remedy defects. This form of information exchange can be included in a process review; and it often indicates areas requiring attention.

In this chapter, we define and explain processes and systems; demonstrate the benefit of process reviews and improvements; look at how to identify critical processes; process re-engineering; quality systems and systemisation; and give guidelines on how to establish a telephone charter. Processes are a logical requirement in ensuring consistent delivery of services to maximise customer focus objectives. Overall responsibility for processes and systems could, in the context of the customer management integration framework, rest with the operations or technical director.

Definition: A process is a series of interrelated transactions that convert inputs into outputs (results) that offer value to the customer by way of satisfied key expectations.

Processes include administrative processes. Processes consume resources and require standards and documentation *for repeatable results*. ISO 9001:2000 Quality management systems – Requirements, section 7, provides a definition of process management and is now the basis for most nationally accepted standards. The document says:

> *Any activity or operation which receives inputs and converts them to outputs can be considered as a process. Almost all product and/or service activities and operations are processes.*

A process is very often more clearly understood when represented pictorially, using basic flowcharting symbols (see Figure 4.1).

> *For organisations to function, they have to define and manage numerous interlinked processes. Often the output from one process will directly form the input into the next process. The systematic identification and management of the various processes employed within an organisation, and particularly the interactions between such processes, may be referred to as the 'process approach' to management.*

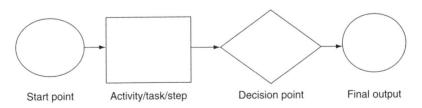

| Start point | Activity/task/step | Decision point | Final output |

Figure 4.1 Process mapping
Source: Quest Worldwide (1999) *The Lean Toolbox: Tools for Lean Operating*. Quest Worldwide Education Limited. Reprinted with permission of Quest Worldwide

The ISO continues,

> *...customers and other relevant parties play a significant role during the process of defining input requirements. Process management is then implemented for all the processes required to realise the product and/or service and the process outputs are verified. Customer satisfaction measurements, and satisfaction measurements of other relevant interested parties are used as feedback to evaluate and validate whether customer requirements have been achieved.*

As defined in the EFQM excellence model, criterion 5,

> *Processes are the way in which an organisation designs, manages and improves its processes in order to support its policy and strategy and fully satisfy, and generate increasing value for, its customers and other stakeholders.*

It recommends that processes are systematically designed and managed; processes are improved, as needed, using innovation in order to fully satisfy and generate increasing value for customers and other stakeholders; products and services are designed and developed based on customer needs and expectations. It offers advice on how products and services are delivered and serviced; and how customer relationships are managed and enhanced.

The input side of a process consists of suppliers who furnish materials, methods, machines, people and environment, which are deployed to add value, which is output to customers as product, service or data.

Process reviews/Process improvement

Once an organisation starts to look at processes, it becomes more aware of how many separate steps go into making a given product or providing a service, and how they dovetail to form a work process. Employees appreciate exactly how their work relates to the rest of the organisation. Management learns how to quantify aspects of work in ways that demonstrate whether it is meeting the expectations of customers. It becomes evident that many work-related problems are caused by flaws in the work process themselves, and not by people.

All work is completed in phases, or by key processes. They are basically of four types:

1. Provision of information about the products or services offered to customers.
2. Acceptance of the order
3. Provision for the service or delivering the service.
4. Billing and collecting charges for the service.

For each of these there should be a written procedure that is derived from the overall service blueprint. This is the company service quality mission, to which we shall revert later. The written procedure for each key process or phase should answer the following questions:

- What resources are required to perform the phase (staff, skills, equipment)?
- What inputs (quantity and quality) are required from internal and external suppliers?
- To what internal or external customer need(s) does this phase relate?
- How will we know if the needs are met?
- What health, environmental, safety or other legal requirements must be addressed in meeting the needs?
- What connections must be made with internal and external customers to complete the task?
- What records show its completion?

Any procedure that answers these seven questions will meet the requirements of the ISO 9001:2000 standard. The ISO guidelines state that 'quality control should be designed as an integral part of the service processes: marketing, design and service delivery'.

A well-designed and implemented service quality information system makes it probable that a company will invest service improvement money in ways that actually improve service. The rewards are far in excess of expenditure. The outcome is information to be shared by all employees about the organisation, its aims and the way in which those aims are to be achieved. It is beneficial when decision-makers use it. All employees are decision-makers. Therefore, it benefits and motivates all employees when they use it.

The aim of a service quality information system should be the establishment of a 'service logic' to drive and unite the activity of all organisational functions. In practical terms, if service quality is scored monthly, each department will be eager to discover how well it has done. Employees respond positively to this type of motivation. It helps to develop a team spirit within departments as well as loyalty to the company.

When process reviews are undertaken for the first time, it is advisable to start with modest goals in view. Assemble the knowledge and views of as many people as possible who are involved in the specific work process with which you intend to start. Be prepared for defensiveness from employees. No one wants change. It intimidates and can alienate. Remind them that they are all customers in the chain of input and output, and the exercise in hand is intended for their benefit as much as for the external customer.

Customer research provides the logical basis for internal processes. Processes that are necessary to realise the required product and/or service and their sequence and interaction shall be determined, planned and implemented, and the organisation shall consider the outputs from quality planning. That is the theoretical outline of the procedure. The exercise should enable the organisation to:

- Develop a comprehensive system to ensure that customer requirements are translated into specifications for new products and services.
- Ensure that suppliers are aware of the company's quality requirements.
- Identify critical processes and establish key performance indicators.
- Facilitate process design and change.
- Streamline service delivery.
- Facilitate the introduction of formal quality systems.
- Develop a charter and guidelines for telephone and voicemail operations.

Customer requirements

When customers are surveyed for their perceptions of quality and levels of satisfaction, the data are often of very limited value. Customer data should be collected so that they can be used as a starting point for quality improvement. Quality improvement should be an ongoing process, to ensure that customer requirements are translated into specifications for new products and services.

Formal quality systems should be introduced to cover every stage in delivery of product or service, and should be enshrined in quality standards. First, however, key processes should be examined, to determine where improvements in the system as a whole would be most beneficial to the customer. Such customer-orientated improvements will be equally beneficial to the organisation, in terms of staff satisfaction and improved profitability.

Identification of key processes

Every company has a number of processes in its product or service provision. Some of these are key processes. They are those processes that have a significant influence on the specified service. Until they are identified and examined as steps in a process from input to output, it is difficult to appreciate how each step relates to the next. In the sense that internal customers are as important as external customers, each step in a process should meet the expectations of the next customer (processor) in the line.

It is the key expectations of each customer that have to be met, if the key process is to work efficiently.

Levels of contact prescribe the environment required for customers. Contact with customers varies between organisations and necessitates specific approaches to process management. Where customers do not have direct contact with the process, it can be streamlined for organisation and method (O&M) efficiency criteria. The more contact the customer has with the process, the more allowances must be made for customer requirements. Customer-orientated space and its integration with O&M, is an aspect of a quality initiative that should be examined early on.

O&M is a process that can be used to focus on customer-relevant service. It has even been suggested that marketing functions might best be handled by people throughout a firm. This is in preference to having a formal marketing department. If all organisation and method studies are to become customer-focused, their aims and outcomes are redefined in terms of marketing.

Key activities need to be analysed to select those characteristics whose measurement and control will ensure service quality. Methods for evaluating the selected characteristics must be defined. The means to influence or control the characteristics within specified limits must be established.

This approach to work processes highlights flaws in the system, which are very often the cause of work-related problems. It becomes possible to streamline workflow to improve the quality of output (product or service) for the benefit of the customer. It is often possible, at the same time, to alter the process so that it is easier to follow, or saves time, money and effort.

It follows from this that the customer, internal and external, has to identify what is required and advise the provider what is expected, to enable expectations to be met all down the line.

Where service delivery and customer expectations are not identical, five major causes of discrepancy have been identified. These are spoken of as the five gaps model (Servqual).

1. The first is between customers' expectation and management understanding.
2. The second is between service quality specifications and management's perception of customers' expectations.
3. The third gap is between service quality specifications and service delivery.
4. The fourth is between service delivery and external communication to customers about service delivery.
5. The final gap is between customers' expectations and perceived service.

The gap between customers' expectation and management understanding is common and serious, because it is often the result of lack of commitment to the creation of a quality service from top-level management, who should be providing motivation, resources and a good example. Unless resources of personnel and finance are made available, it is frequently impossible to match organisation performance to customer expectation. The lack of commitment might equally rest with middle management. An underlying lack of understanding of quality management techniques is often the root cause of failure. It might, of course, be due to lack of capital, or market conditions, ill-designed premises, anything, in fact, that affects the potential and will for change.

The service performance gap occurs at any point where the employee is unable or unwilling to perform service tasks to the level required. Organisations that are highly interactive, labour-intensive and perform in multiple locations are especially vulnerable to this gap. Opportunities for mistakes and misunderstandings exist when service providers and customers interact.

The next gap occurs when promises do not match delivery. This happens when overpromising. It is a significant cause of customer dissatisfaction. Often, the cause is not in the tangible sense of late delivery, but of there being some extra expectation on the part of the customer that is not satisfied by the product or service. Advertising regulations prohibit overpromising in respect of technical matters, but in unquantifiable matters such as friendliness, quality and so on, any claim is arguable. Underselling, or underpromising can also cause a problem. Organisations often have many controls and checks to ensure that the product is delivered, but because the customers are unaware of these, they have an inadequate sense of the service provided. Customers, as a rule, only really want organisations to be efficient.

Internal communication breakdown is another potential cause of trouble in this area. It may occur when advertising and marketing people start to promote a new product or service before the frontline people have been trained in how to deliver it. The same problem arises in multi-chain organisations like hotel groups. A customer who experiences superb service in one of those in the chain, will expect the same in another. The group as a whole has to set and maintain consistently high standards in all its outlets if this gap is to be avoided.

The fourth gap is between service delivery and external communication to customers about service delivery. Advertising and marketing claims can lead to misapprehension and false expectations on the part of customers. This makes it difficult for frontline employees to work efficiently.

The gap when perceived service fails to match customer expectations summarises the effects of the other four, from the customer's standpoint. All other gaps that are in the hands of management to close affect this one. Management's objective must be to bring what is actually delivered as close as possible to customers' expected and desired service. Understanding what is wanted, having the management will to achieve that, ensuring that the service specification is carried out and controlling what is promised are the keys to closing the final gap.

Quality initiatives and examination of key processes, properly controlled, should close all five gaps. All problem areas should be defined, solutions chosen and improvement plans set in action.

Process review

A first step in dealing with key processes is to describe exactly the process that possibly requires improvement. Next, determine start and finish points and flowchart the process from beginning to end. At every stage in the process or phase, list all the customers and determine their key expectations. This is best done by asking each customer to identify his/her own key expectations.

Monitor the process and establish how delivery of each stage compares to key expectations. The data you gather by this method indicates where expectations are not being met. It is necessary to determine quantifiable indicators for each area of key expectation, determine the method of data collection, collect the data and make the comparison against key expectations.

Having analysed the work process, list the opportunities for improvement, and the unmet expectations. Note the redundant stages, the unnecessary complexities, inconsistencies and potential problem areas in the process (see Figure 4.2).

It is vital to be clear at the outset just what work process you wish to tackle. In most companies, work processes intermingle at various

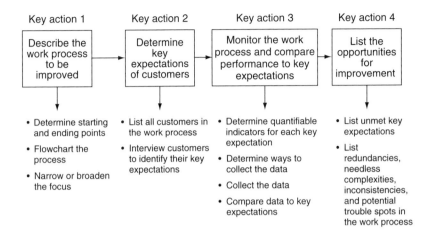

Figure 4.2 Analysing a work process
Source: *Analyzing a Work Process*, Zenger Miller (1996)

stages, and can be difficult to isolate. The flowchart should enable uncertainties in the process to be clarified. The flowchart will indicate whether you have properly encompassed the process, or whether its scope needs to be narrowed or broadened in order to be useful.

Keep it simple, if you can. To start the task, only one person should decide on the process to be explored and define the outline. It is better to work by degrees and do a good job on one part of the process than to do an unsatisfactory job on the whole.

Processes can easily be redesigned one at a time, without challenging the total functional structure of the company. Those who perform the process will know best what, if any, problems are faced.

Work processes necessarily involve a number of people and several departments within the company. Their knowledge and cooperation are essential tools. It should be made clear that it is only the actual process that is under scrutiny, and not the people who perform the process. They should understand that their specialist knowledge of their own piece of the process is valuable and welcome. If one process, or department, has a history of problems, that might be the most productive starting point, since the workers will probably welcome the chance to set things right.

It is tempting to start solving problems as they emerge, but the object is to get an overall picture before attempting to alter anything. It is only when the exercise has thrown up a picture of the process as a whole that remedies for problems can be considered. In organisational terms, the objective is to add value for customers by improving and sustaining quality. To be side-tracked is unproductive. When the process overhaul and documentation are complete, many of the minor problems will have disappeared anyway.

Once the process has been identified and described, with its start and finish points clarified, a team should be formed with the responsibility of searching the process for anomalies. If the team comprises someone, or several people, from every stage of the work process under examination, there will be a broad input of information. It will also furnish data about key expectations at each transition point in the process. The team should contain enough people with the authority to implement any changes in the process that the team as a whole deems worthwhile.

A process review can be time-consuming and requires input from many people. It is important, therefore, to gather as much relevant data as possible from as many sources as can usefully supply it. Interviews are helpful to find out how customers rate staff members, and to discover what problems staff members have with their work processes. They take longer to conduct than questionnaires, but they provide deeper insights. A questionnaire is useful to obtain input from several people involved in the work process and to acquire customer responses to a product or service.

While gathering your data, it would be valuable to try to discover whether your competitors are following your lead, or making you follow theirs. Identify the tactics used by rival companies. Your frontline staff and your customers probably have a good idea about which of you is ahead.

The precise methods used to collect data need to be determined. Some data can be measured from existing records, such as length of time required to despatch orders, faulty goods booked in for repair/replacement, credit notes issued and so on. Modern IT has removed any excuse for not retaining, updating and analysing data.

The data will also highlight what types of errors occur and where. Repetitive processes can be quantified on run sheets, which show progress at timed stages of output. Run sheets pinpoint where there is a bottleneck in the process, so that remedial action can be taken.

Where physical location and relationships are important, the workflow can be shown in diagram format. Movements can be charted and, if necessary, reduced.

Having collected all the customers' key expectations and summarised them for the customer group, it might transpire that it is not possible to meet all expectations at once. They should be prioritised, and a decision taken about what can be done now and what should be aimed for later. Quality improvement is a continuous process. There are always more steps on the ladder. The key expectations of customers, legislation, competitors' offerings, the economic situation of the country and other external factors and circumstances change continuously. The time for surveys and process reviews is always NOW.

Every organisation is, to some extent, dependent upon outside suppliers, for raw materials, components, deliveries, advertising and janitorial services, for example. These are always potential sources of problems. If possible, there should be a strategy in place to meet problems, should they arise. If supplier organisations also have effective quality control systems in place, there should be few occasions to give rise to concern. The consumer organisation should make plain to suppliers its own quality requirements and insist that they are met.

All the foregoing steps must be repeated regularly, at predetermined intervals, to absorb changes in customer expectation and economic circumstances, and to control new processes as they are introduced. Many organisations, which were exemplary by their success a few years ago, have fallen victim to complacency and lost their market leadership. There can be no last stage in quality management. Failure is due to either lack of a system, or lack of passion for quality management.

A quality management system must be more than rhetoric. It is the vision which should permeate an organisation and be self-perpetuating, or it will not endure. Vision is the essence of leadership. Vision provides strategies that operate in terms of customers and how to deliver value to them.

It has been said that, 'Satisfaction is, as it should be, mute. Its prior presence is affirmed only by its subsequent absence'. The point being made is that customers are not aware of satisfaction, while they have it, but are aware of failure and dissatisfaction. This makes them susceptible to the blandishments of competitors.

Problems

Commonly, problems of processing arise because the systems are, usually, inflexible. They cannot cope well with unusual situations. They are often used as an excuse for not trying to meet customers' needs. They are often blamed for inadequacies in the service. They tend to be unresponsive to changes in the needs of customers or the organisation. They might have become so familiar that people are unable to think of other and better ways of doing things. There might be a redundant set of customers somewhere in the process, or even a segment of external customers who are unprofitable and who impede the process because of their special requirements. It is often the case that a simple task might be redesigned to obviate minor mistakes that lead to faulty products being produced.

To be valuable, procedures and systems have to help the customer, and be as relevant to the customer's present-day needs as when they were set up. If they are unhelpful or irrelevant, ways should be found to alter them to improve customer service. Above all, they must have in-built flexibility and be responsive to changes in customer requirements.

Areas that might repay investigation on behalf of the external customer are: sales and ordering systems; accounts and invoice systems; delivery systems; after-sales service systems; and customer feedback systems.

The last stage of process control is to check how the improvements you have just made to the process, or the new process you have introduced, now meet customers' key expectations. The answers you obtain are the measure of the success of the process review.

Business process re-engineering

The idea behind process management is to try and organise the way in which a business operates, and that will make sense from a work point of view. The term applied to this approach is *business process re-engineering* (BPR). It is capable of wholesale application throughout a large organisation, or can work equally effectively at individual, or unit level. At the end of successful BPR, organisations should have been rebuilt on the strength of collective and collaborative intelligence. In fact, organisations have always seen a number of the strategies described below as integral to some at least of their own processes. It is the philosophy behind process management and BPR that we need to examine, and then consider the practical steps to be taken to bring BPR into a structured format that can be applied to any part, or the whole of, any organisation.

The principle guiding all BPR activity is to identify the value added and cut out the rest. It has to be a team effort for every work process, for it to be successful. It can only be defined by what the customer regards as value-added. Non-value tasks should be eliminated where possible, or reduced to a minimum. Non-value tasks are time-wasters or work-wasters. It should be recognised that interruption is one of the greatest sources of errors and, ideally, a process should be one in which work is uninterrupted from start to finish.

Quality in the service industries

Processes in manufacturing allow for the investigation of readily identified processes. Such processes form a concept that might well be unfamiliar to service provision organisations. In fact, there are probably far more service providers than manufacturers, but the customers for each type of offering want the same standards of service quality and need to be treated as though they are important.

From the dog-grooming parlour to the insurance company, there is scope for the sort of process review mentioned already. Are appointments kept? Are premises and staff clean and friendly? Is information readily available? Does the company offer something more than its competitors? Is the invoicing satisfactory? Can goods be delivered to suit the customer's convenience? How are complaints handled? Is new legislation understood and are its implications appreciated? These are the same questions that large organisations ask when making a process/systems review. Every business, large or small, can improve the way it works for the benefit of its customers.

So far, we have dealt with general service qualities. It is time, perhaps, to look in detail at the sort of service standards that might be set.

Formal quality systems describe service quality criteria applicable to all customer 'moments of truth', but service standards are quantifiable and should also be set for every customer interface. Employees should have a key role in setting service standards. They, more than anyone, understand what is realistic and they, after all, will have to meet the standards when set.

In today's world, good manners are something of a rarity, yet the use of good manners is the way in which frontline employees render superb quality service to customers. Awkward customers, impatient customers, angry customers and dishonest customers have, most of the time, no objection to impeccable manners and a friendly smile. The way in which even the most recalcitrant customer should be dealt with can be taught. Like all other processes, deficiencies in the existing way of doing things should be identified. Staff should be empowered and provided with the means to deal with all types of people, and this includes other employees as well as outsiders. There should be written rules, to codify and clarify service standards, so that there can be no mistakes.

Some of the causes for customer dissatisfaction are simple to correct, but management is not always aware of the need for improvement. The advantage of investigating and identifying critical processes and systems is the way in which certain previously unconsidered processes and systems are revealed as critical. Trouble arises when organisations think they know better than their customers. The type of review that looks closely at exactly what happens, step by step, in an organisation throws up some interesting facts. Some of the more obvious examples where attention to detail repays the effort are the contact points of telephone, correspondence and face-to-face meeting. *Service standards and performance levels* should be set to make these contacts satisfying to customers and staff.

The number of times a telephone rings before it is answered, how many people can be allowed to queue at a checkout, how long door-to-door deliveries take, by what date should reports be completed; all these are examples of *service quality occasions* where fixed *service standard targets* can be set.

Whatever process is under review, there have to be specific measurements set all the way through the process, and they need to be concise, based on customer requirements, and written into job descriptions and performance reviews. They should be jointly created with staff and fairly enforced by managers. These measurements are useful to set *service standards*.

To answer the telephone promptly is service quality. To answer the telephone within three rings should be service standard.

Return customer calls in a timely fashion becomes 'return all calls within 24 hours', when that is the service standard. Be empathetic with an upset customer is part of service quality. The service standard should be, 'always apologise if a customer is upset'.

If you are to take personal responsibility for helping the customer, give your name, telephone number and extension. The customer knows that you are personally responsible and he/she is able to contact you again. That is service standard. To dress appropriately for work means wear your full uniform at all times. That, too, is service standard.

The service standard is the rulebook for frontline employees. The most commonly used method of communication between customers and suppliers is the telephone. Unlike written communications, there is no second chance to make a first impression. Tone of voice, clarity of expression, willingness to help are all part of the message that comes via the telephone. Thus, it should have a complete set of service standards. These should be studied and applied by every employee with telephone access to customers.

Telephone service standards

The telephone, in particular, is often misused, yet it is a commonly utilised channel for dialogue with customers, and it is of critical importance. The way in which it is answered can have a profound impact on the image of the organisation. Customers use it to ask for information, to expedite deliveries, to make complaints and to offer suggestions. It offers the caller a reflection of the organisation; this is often a first impression. It can also be a method for obtaining customer feedback. It is a resource rather than simply a tool.

Many companies receive far more telephone calls than letters. Unlike letters, which can be amended before posting, the telephone provokes an instant response. It has to be the right response.

- Answer the telephone within three rings.
- Use a friendly tone of voice, identify yourself and give the impression that you are helpful and knowledgeable.
- Always speak slowly and clearly.
- If you have a bad line, suggest at once that the caller rings you back.
- If you are on the switchboard, find out to which department the call should be transferred. (Switchboard staff should have a good working knowledge of which department does what within the organisation. An alphabetical list of all employees and their departments should be available to switchboard staff.)
- The instructions to callers to press *, numbers and # to pass quickly to the department they want are not always appropriate. There should be a facility to bypass this and find someone who will listen to customers whose problems are not routine.
- Never leave a caller waiting because the line to the department they want is busy. Keep talking to them, say what you are doing and apologise for the delay in making the connection.
- If you cannot connect the call, offer to take a message and have the department return the call. Ensure that the message is dealt with. To do this, you need the caller's name, telephone number, the company they represent and the person they wish to contact. Take down the message and read everything back.
- Answer with, 'Good morning/afternoon,' and name the department and give your name.
- Take a contact name and use it in conversation.
- Always say, 'Thank you'.
- Return telephone messages within 24 hours.
- Always take calls when you are in the office.
- Callers using your Freephone number are still not happy to be left hanging on for several minutes. Their time is valuable.
- Conclude the call politely and wait to hear the caller replace the receiver before you replace your own.

- If there is a telephone answering machine on your line, check it regularly, and if you are away for any length of time, delegate someone else to do this for you.
- If you have a fax machine, always ensure that it is switched on and has adequate stationery. Check for fax messages and emails regularly. Treat them with the same urgency as ordinary correspondence.

Correspondence

- A reply should be sent to all correspondence within 24 hours.
- When a reply is not imminent, forward a letter or card of acknowledgement.
- Mail should be opened centrally, unless marked 'Personal/ Confidential', and circulated daily. (It is useful to have a senior member of staff present when mail is opened.)
- All replies should be neat and free of errors.

Meetings

- Be on time for ALL meetings and phone ahead if there is any delay.
- Hold a team meeting each week.

Retail outlets

Customers will feel that they have received polite, efficient and friendly service, if service standards state that:

- They are never left waiting at a till.
- They are given no cause to feel that they have been delayed unnecessarily.
- The transaction is handled at a speed appropriate to the individual customer.

- Offers, campaigns and other useful information, where appropriate, are pointed out.
- A member of staff helping a customer is interrupted by another member of staff only to offer help.
- Products and payments are handled with care, and goods handed to the customer.

When customers and staff meet, service standards demand that:

- Customers should feel that they are being given priority over other tasks.
- Staff should make eye contact and greet each customer.
- Attention should be focused on the customer.
- Staff should be polite, friendly and interested throughout.
- Individual customer tastes and preferences should be respected.
- If there is any delay in giving service, apologise and advise what steps are being taken to help.
- Each customer should be thanked, and the contact ended in an appropriate way.

Management's understanding of customers' expectations

One way in which management can identify more closely with customers is from the complaints received. If all complaints are logged regularly and a summary made in such a way that it indicates the solution, and the logs or summaries are distributed to key staff, action can be taken at the stage where it is needed. There should be a personal response to every complaint, as well as responsive action taken to remedy the cause. Customers should be advised on exactly what action has been taken.

In the same way as there should be written policy and procedures for other processes, complaints handling should also be committed to writing and communicated to all employees. It need be no longer than:

> This company and its employees welcome complaints, and are committed to ensuring that every complaint will be received courteously, investigated as thoroughly as necessary, and acted on swiftly and appropriately.

Back up, in the form of complaints handling and assessment training, should be provided for those employees most likely to be recipients of complaints. These employees should also know how to disseminate the information concerning serious complaints to interested parties, for the further improvement of the process that gave rise to the problem in the first place.

Complaints

Complaints and the way in which they are handled play an important role in customer retention, or in customer defection. There was a time when complaints were regarded as a nuisance. Top management avoided dealing with them. The consequences of mishandled complaints had not then been comprehended.

Recently, it has been appreciated that a complainant is a valuable source of information for a company. It is essentially free market research. Also, for every one person who makes a complaint about some aspect of quality or service, there will be many others who simply cease dealing with the company and take their complaints to competitors, who will quickly find ways to exploit them, to the disadvantage of the original company. The person who complains, therefore, is doing the company a service by bringing a problem to its attention.

A caveat should, perhaps be offered. Sometimes one customer in a thousand has a complaint that is purely subjective. Before an organisation rushes to remedy the situation, it is advisable to check with others. If there is support for the complainant from other customers, action is imperative. If not, the customer should be told why no action will be taken, and an apology given.

The cost of losing one dissatisfied customer is far more than was once imagined. It is no longer one single source of lifetime income that is lost, but there is a domino effect among existing and potential customers, some of whom might also defect. The original fault, unless tackled, will cause more defections and dissatisfaction.

Today, systems are in place in companies whereby customers are positively encouraged to complain, and their complaints are analysed in depth. The faster a problem is solved, the less damage is inflicted and the fewer customers are lost. If a complaint is received and the customer dealt with politely, quickly and efficiently, that customer probably retains loyalty to the company. There might be a stronger bond with the company after the event.

There are several options when we consider ways in which customers might be prompted to complain, should cause be given. These will vary from business to business. It is the same process as provision of ways to listen to customers, and the same ground rules apply. Once the complaint is made, how it is dealt with is crucial.

Someone from the company must *listen* to the customer. The customer must know that he is receiving *full attention*. In order to avoid any misunderstanding, the person dealing with the complaint should *probe deeper* into the difficulty experienced, to get a fuller picture of the problem.

A customer should be asked what the company can do to win back their business. What the customer says at this point must be the key to the way in which the company deals with them in future.

Let the customer show anger. Empathy must be the response, and an immediate start on problem solving. The customer should be asked to suggest how the problem can best be solved.

One company within the financial services sector has a structured procedure for handling written complaints, and this applies to all teams across the company. It stated:

1. Read letter thoroughly and ensure that you have a complete understanding of the complaint.
2. Identify individual responsible for the complaint. If in doubt, check first.
3. Contact that individual and confirm that they accept responsibility for the complaint.

4. Hand over the complaint directly to that individual (*one pass only*). The complainant should be told who is to deal.
5. Record the complaint in a customer feedback log.
6. Check for any information on customer. (The telephone number might be on database, even if ex-directory.)
7. Telephone customer on same day. Talk through the complaint. Rebuild customer's confidence.
8. Reassure customer; ask for more information; discover expectations of the customer; try to resolve complaint OR confirm actions being taken and by whom, if known. Confirm in writing what you have agreed to do (if appropriate).
9. If unable to contact by telephone, acknowledge correspondence on same day; reassure customer and confirm actions being taken and by whom, if known.
10. Facilitate resolution of complaint with appropriate person or team/s.
11. Confirm resolution in writing.
12. Update customer feedback log. Share what has been learnt with team at next opportunity.
13. After seven days, ring customer and confirm their satisfaction. Ask 'How can we help you in future?'
14. Complete customer feedback log, return log to customer feedback team, for the matter to be fed into the relevant processes.

Most customers are willing to come to an agreement with the company, and if the suggested agreement comes from the customer, it should be accepted by the company. Often, it is far less onerous than a suggestion the company might itself have offered. Having come to an agreement, it must be implemented as swiftly as possible. Complaints should always be followed up. It is advisable to contact the customer and enquire whether everything is now satisfactory and if they are happy with the outcome. There will be situations where finding a solution to the problem belongs up the management scale, and there should be a channel through which such complaints are directed.

Customers who complain are angry people. They might well have defected already, had the complaints procedure not been in place. If they do defect, they can damage the company's reputation by telling their friends and acquaintances about their grievances. It is important to catch the problem early.

The way in which the complaint is handled, rather than the status of the person handling it, is the key. Staff cannot be expected to do the right thing, unless they have been taught how and given the authority to take what steps they feel appropriate. Complaints are not always put in writing, and unhappy customers sometimes have no patience with forms and free-phone help lines. They often approach the nearest employee of the company and pour forth their anger. If the right service culture is in place and staff have been trained in the way in which complaints and defects in service are handled, it will not be difficult for them to cope when faced by an angry customer.

Those customers who were angry but who were treated properly and had their problems resolved will often become an organisation's most loyal customers in the future.

Translate customer complaints into specifications for new products and services

A complaint should also be a tool of strategic planning. If it is made easy for customers to complain and the organisation responds empathetically, a great deal of valuable information can be gathered from those customers whose expectations are not being met. The information can be passed to management and used when planning product or marketing changes.

Customer service and complaints handling should be a key results area, and complaints should receive a rapid response.

In the *National Complaints Culture Survey (NCCS) of 2003*, under the headline 'The Director's View', we read that nearly 75% of the senior directors surveyed believed that customer loyalty levels were decreasing in their industry. Nearly 80% of these directors indicated that customer satisfaction (and loyalty) was of vital strategic importance to their industry in the next 12 months.

From the same publication, under the headline 'The Customer's View', lack of time is given as the main obstacle to customers' complaints; the deterrent given by one-third of respondents is that they believe 'the organisation wouldn't do anything about it, anyway'; 37% of respondents believe that organisations never encourage complaints; and nearly a quarter believe that organisations never welcome them, when they actually receive them.

Expectations for resolution

Customers are, indeed, becoming more demanding. Expectations for resolution have increased for all forms of complaints. NCCS claims that:

- 65% of all customers now expect complaints in person to be dealt with immediately, or on the same day, an increase of 9%.
- Virtually all customers want their written complaints to be acknowledged, and nearly one-third of them expect this acknowledgement within two days.
- 43% of customers also expect written complaints to be resolved within one week (an increase of 10% from the previous survey).
- Over half of all customers expect their telephone complaints to be resolved immediately, or on the same day.

The employees' view

Employees believe their organisations are becoming better at encouraging customers to complain but are still poor at recognising and thanking these customers for their trouble (NCCS, 2003).

Empowerment levels have improved but this is a critical area, given customers' ever-increasing expectations for complaint resolution.

The bottom line

NCCS 2003 concludes that nearly 90% of respondents will repurchase from an organisation if their complaint has been handled well. Even more encouraging was that nearly 60% of customers will pay at least 5% more for better levels of service.

The basic process for dealing with complaints follows a short sequence:

- *Listen* (to find out the cause of the complaint)
- Apologise
- Take speedy action to remedy cause of complaint
- Refund costs incurred
- Assure customer that it will not happen again

When the complainant is kept informed of the action being taken, even if the problem is intractable, he/she will find some satisfaction in knowing that everything that can be done is being done. Employees will also realise that being seen to try is vital, rather than just saying 'No'. The person who takes original ownership of the problem should ensure that all frontline employees are advised of its origins and its resolution. They should then check within their own areas of responsibility, to satisfy themselves that the root cause is eliminated.

Compliments

Compliments, though received less often than complaints, provide fast feedback on company behaviour. It is not enough to thank the customer and forget it. To deliver a compliment requires more of a customer than does a complaint, which is often delivered in the heat of the moment, when something fails to meet expectations. Behind the compliment is a window on customer expectations and customer satisfaction. It marks the current level of service and customer satisfaction. More importantly, it shows that there is still room for improvement in meeting customer expectations. A sincere compliment signifies that there is already an appreciable improvement in supply of goods or services above what was expected by the customer who praises the company. Complacency and self-congratulation are the wrong responses to a customer compliment.

Investigate compliments

In the same way as complaints are investigated and managed and the findings fed into the processes of the company, compliments need to be investigated and similarly managed. Customers, who are so delighted that they take the trouble to say so, would not object to being thanked for taking that trouble to give positive feedback, nor to being asked what, specifically, caused their delight. To listen carefully to what the customer says is both polite and expedient. From the answers given, the company can learn much about itself and should be able to identify where it has room to improve its processes and systems so that the cause of the unexpected compliment becomes part of routine customer expectations.

The factors that engendered the compliment should be integrated into the company's service quality standard. As with complaints, compliments, the factors that gave rise to them, and their significance with regard to customer retention and profitability should be communicated to all staff. The aim should be to raise the levels of service at which compliments are given, and in the same way as all other improvements in service quality are measured, compliments should also be logged and measured, to ensure that customers' expectations are continually rising. Compliments form one of the most valuable indicators of continuous improvement. Each compliment can be regarded as a step in the right direction on the profitability ladder.

Compliments from internal customers

Employees' compliments are less easily absorbed into company culture, since they are often inaudible to management. Given a chance to express themselves *formally*, on changes to the working environment, working practices, opportunities and training, internal customers' compliments should also form part of the overall customer service quality initiatives. Employers and managers who encourage feedback from external and internal customers, and integrate the compliments as well as the complaints into any future improvement processes, will reap dividends.

National Blood Service (NBS) compliments and complaints procedures are based on their *core purpose*: to save and improve patients' lives; and their *mission*: to deliver world-class services, build ever stronger partnerships with donors and the healthcare community. Loss of customers for the NBS is not so much a matter of profitability; it is a matter of life and death.

The NBS customer feedback leaflet gives opportunities to donors for feedback. It explains briefly the NBS policy of continuous improvement, and contains a small questionnaire with a tick-box for:

- Compliment
- Other feedback
- Complaint

There is a set of further options following the question: Do you require a response to your feedback or complaint? These options are:

- No
- Letter
- Email
- Telephone.

Below these is space for the respondent to give personal details and to say when it would be convenient for NBS to contact him/her. It is pre-addressed and postage paid. It makes customer feedback simple, fast and cost-free. The leaflet explains how and to whom complaints may be addressed and offers an opportunity to donors to tell the NBS face to face, by telephone, fax, e-mail, or by visiting the website, how it is doing. It contains a thank you.

Donors quit for personal reasons, they move house, develop health problems, become too old to donate blood, are unable any longer to attend donor sessions. There are some who find cause for dissatisfaction with the service and stop donating blood. There are others who become advocates and recruit new donors. In this respect, the NBS is like any other service provider. It gains and loses donors for a variety of reasons, it strives to discover why, and is continuously monitoring its processes to improve its service quality. It rewards and encourages loyalty by issuing tangible gifts to donors after a certain number of donations. It trains its staff to be competent, friendly and show empathy with those of a nervous disposition. It endeavours to make its venues as comfortable and inviting as possible, it reminds donors personally about forthcoming sessions, and it advertises locally when sessions are to take place, to encourage new donors to come forward.

Only one matter remains to be settled, when all else is in place. How often and in what way is the quality initiative to be reviewed and improved? Each organisation will have its own answer to this. Management, having made the commitment to the review and approved its findings, and established an overall strategy and quality improvement charter, has to keep the momentum going and be prepared to move ahead at a steady pace, reviewing and updating as necessary.

Summary

Customers are the main drivers to identifying those processes that are critical to the success of a business. For high-level objectives, top management is responsible for identifying the appropriate processes. Ideas also filter up from teams, such as the quality steering team, or its equivalent.

Unless excellent and ever improving product or service can be consistently provided, all other efforts to retain customers are wasted.

Products and services go through a series of processes from start to final delivery. At each stage, there will be a customer, internal or external, waiting to take the goods and services forward. It is the expectations of each customer, at each stage, that need to be met. To do this requires that key stages of the process system, having been identified, require careful attention, with these expectations in mind.

There are three basic areas to be covered, according to the National Blood Service, in obtaining feedback from customers: compliment, complaint and other feedback. While much has been written about complaints handling, compliments are equally useful to an organisation, because they identify what is going well and, as a consequence, is becoming part of customers' overall expectations. Other feedback might concern itself with present or future product or service quality and development. This type of feedback directly influences processes and systems just as much as do complaints and compliments.

Manufacturing processes can be more easily monitored than service provision. The use of run sheets, flowcharts and other documentation allows for day-to-day control of either. Allied to customer feedback, processes can always be subjected to continuous improvement. The objective behind improvement to processes is to generate increasing value for customers and other stakeholders. This, in turn, creates greater satisfaction for customers and employees. It also raises levels of expectation. What gave rise to yesterday's compliment has become today's expectation and, possibly, will be tomorrow's cause for complaint. Nothing stands still in modern business. What is applicable to outside customers is true also of internal customers: the employees who run the systems and processes in the company. Like the external customer, they can contribute complaints, compliments and other valuable feedback, to influence process and systems for the improvement of quality service provision.

Managers, when dealing with process re-engineering to improve service to internal customers as well as external, should allow all customers, internal and external, to have input. One sometimes overlooked but valuable question to ask in this connection is whether the attendant paperwork helps or hinders processes. In taking action on systems and processes, therefore, the bureaucracy also requires inspection and adjustment.

Processes and systems are similar to the circulatory system of the human body. They can suffer from blockages, infections and stagnation, which might cause the body to become sick, or to die. They need to be subjected to a regular keep fit regime, and all parts of the organisational body require to be monitored at all times. Every body consists of interactive parts, the health of one part affects the rest. In a business, all components within the framework consist of several processes and systems. They are all equally vital to the good health of the whole organisation.

5

Employee Involvement

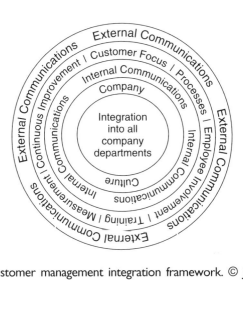

Figure 5.0 Customer management integration framework. © John A. Murphy 2005

We saw in the previous chapter that employees form part of the customer satisfaction continuum, in that they each have a part in the service provision process, and themselves become customers as work is passed to them from the previous stage of the process. To involve employees in the customer management integration framework is unavoidable. How this is done is worthy of consideration by top management. Unlike the tin of beans, a clone of every other tin, people are different from one another, with a variety of skills, aptitudes, personalities and prejudices, which they bring to the workplace. The previous chapters concern aspects of organisations that are easily approachable by management with intent to change for improvement. Employees, unlike amorphous segments of customers, systems and processes, can present intractable problems. At the time of cultural change within an organisation, employees are already in place, under contract. They are people with personalities and attitudes. They have their spheres of influence, and they have legal rights, as well as obligations to their employer. They cannot be disposed of in one fell swoop and replaced by others who better fill the new roles allotted to them. Employees are the engine that makes an organisation run, and engines do not run for long without constant care and attention.

The customer management integration framework puts *employee involvement well within* the boundaries. The responsibility for employee involvement begins with the recruitment or personnel director, who decides whom to employ. This hiring process is supercritical. The wrong person in the job can spoil every effort by his or her team. The right person in the right job is cheerful and enthusiastic. Enthusiasm is infectious. Responsibility for employee involvement is shared, further down the line, by those responsible for management of human resources, training and assessment.

In *Back to Basics: How Well Are Your Customers Treated by Frontline Staff?* (June 2003, IOMA's Report on Customer Relationship Management), the following advice is given on how to improve employees' contentment/customers' experience:

- **Step 1: Hiring/training right**. Getting the right people to do the right thing is the first step, based on: Standardised processes (*screening*)+Automated tools (*software*)+Equitable practices (*equal opportunities*)=High-quality hires.
- **Step 2: Rewarding right**. Although pay motivates people at one level, it seldom acts as a motivator when people move up in the organisation, or when their need gratification moves to a higher plane. Base pay+incentive pay+work experience+training+benefits=Total compensation.

- **Step 3: Recognising right.** As individuals grow in the organisation, more emphasis shifts towards recognition of what they do for the organisation.
- **Step 4: The culture and work experience.** In addition to rewards and recognition, organisations need to offer an enviable work environment that would enhance employee satisfaction, resulting in productive employees.

Before anyone makes a major, rather than an impulsive, purchase, there will be a recognised need, a knowledge of what meets that need, a budget to pay for the product or service, and a plan for its future use. Hiring an employee can be compared to this type of transaction. It consists of selection of the right person for the organisation and for the specific job, a plan for how best to utilise him or her, and provision of any training that would enhance performance. This forms Step 1 above.

Step 2, as applicable to a new employee, concerns itself in the main with monetary rewards allied to training. The work experience, however, is the critical element that engenders enthusiasm for the job and commitment to the company.

Step 3, as applicable to an employee of some standing in the organisation, recognises that monetary rewards are of less significance; and status, responsibility and recognition of their role in the company become predominant considerations leading to continued satisfaction.

Step 4 refers to such things as a larger office, better company car, less supervision, more responsibility for decision making, steps on the ladder that lead to the top of the organisation and are worth striving to achieve.

The same report, quoting Hansemark and Albinsson (2004), also says, 'Employee satisfaction of intrinsic and spiritual character is the source of excellent quality and customer satisfaction'.

Intrinsic here means ingrained, and spiritual refers to a non-materialistic attitude to work. Some people continually think beyond their immediate task or duty and seek for ways to improve what they do, or to solve problems for team members by devising better systems and processes. This can become a habit that makes the work more challenging, interesting and satisfying. Such people might be described as self-motivated, and, with adequate recognition and thanks, they are happy to continue in this productive and satisfying mode of working. If such an employee interacts with customers they are likely to increase customer satisfaction. An employee who is bored with the job, unhappy about the working environment or the management's policies, or has an axe to grind, can put customer satisfaction at risk.

Retention of customers

Retention of customers is an expression we bandy about without always understanding what we mean by it. One definition of retention puts it as '…a commitment to continue to do business or exchange with a particular company on an ongoing basis.' A more elaborate definition defines retention as '…the customer's liking, identification, commitment, trust, willingness to recommend and re-purchase intentions, with the first four being emotional-cognitive retention contructs, and the last two being behavioural intentions'. It has been argued, however, that customer satisfaction on its own cannot produce lifetime customers, even though satisfaction can result in retention.

Open dialogue and frequent contact with the customer are regarded as the key to customer satisfaction. There is more to it than that, as we shall see. One major concern for managers with respect to employee/customer interface is how uniformly all members of the organisation understand key concepts. To keep people on track it is vital continuously to communicate to staff and customers the key concepts of the organisation, report on how they are functioning and watch how employees, especially frontline people, implement the strategies designed to make them work. Horizontal and vertical, two-way, ongoing communication and measurement are critical tools for the top management of any company to measure the efficacy of its key concepts and the uniformity of comprehension among employees and line managers.

In thinking about customer/employee retention and satisfaction, we have overlooked the third party that has an interest in outcomes of the organisation, and that is the shareholder, with whom relationships must be cultivated as assiduously as with customers and employees. Irreparable harm can be done to businesses that fail to build strategies to enhance and cultivate relationships with all three groups of stakeholders.

Figure 5.1 shows the way in which a set of latent variables, such as customer expectations and customer perceptions of quality and value, link to a customer satisfaction index. There is not one gap in the chain that marks the steps from perceived employee satisfaction to customer loyalty. Nothing is perceived until it is believed. Nothing is believed until it is proved. The company's image attracts customer interest. Customer interest arouses expectations about the product. Satisfied, committed, loyal employees enhance customer satisfaction by creating perceived quality service. There is a direct correlation between perceived value, customer satisfaction and customer loyalty. Interestingly, this model shows how important it is for a company, in all its dealings with customers, to live up to its image, if those customers are to be captured permanently. Thus, the company's image has to be reflected at every link in the chain that ends in customer loyalty. This emphasises the importance of everyone knowing what the company image means to the customer, and how essential it is for every employee to sing from the same hymn sheet.

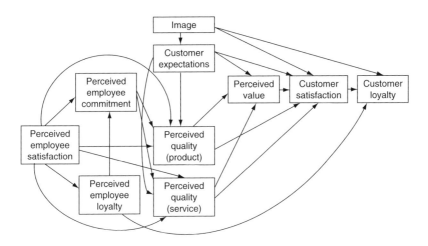

Figure 5.1 European customer satisfaction index

Source: Vilares, M.J. and Simões Coelho, P. (2003) The employee–customer satisfaction chain in the ECSI model. *European Journal of Marketing*, **37**(11/12): 1703–22. Republished with permission, Emerald Publishing Group Limited: http://www.emeraldinsight.com/ejm.htm

How customers view employee satisfaction is *perceived employee satisfaction*. In the same way, *perceived employee commitment* is the way customers view employee commitment. Those employees who are perceived as committed, act as advocates for the organisation, and represent employee dedication to help the organisation achieve its goals. They are also perceived as loyal employees.

It can, therefore, be concluded that customer expectations have no direct impact on customer satisfaction. The impact is indirect and comes through perceived quality and perceived value.

Perceived employee satisfaction has important, direct impact on perceived service quality.

Some studies of the links between employee satisfaction, loyalty, productivity and profit in one of the UK's four largest superstore retailers were carried out by the Operations Management Group of Warwick Business School. The researchers claim that there are reasons why the relationship between employee satisfaction as perceived by customers and customers' own satisfaction is not necessarily direct. Thus, employee dissatisfaction does not always impact adversely on profitability. Equally employee satisfaction does not always impact positively. However, in time, employee dissatisfaction will eventually be translated into customer dissatisfaction.

The key message here is for practising managers not to take it as gospel from management consultants and academics that employee satisfaction drives profit, but to take the initiative and do the analysis in their own organisations.

Understanding key concepts

In an organisation bent on cultural change, management of human resources requires skill and patience. Employees, who are generally inclined to fear and resist change, can seriously hinder what they do not comprehend and are not trained to perform. There might also be people who hold positions in an organisation as a result of nepotism. They regard themselves as invincible. If anything illustrates the need for total management commitment to cultural change in an organisation, nepotism is it. Such people can always be re-educated, or persuaded to depart quietly.

Organisations invest heavily in recruitment and training, in setting up workstations, in provision of pensions and peripheral benefits for employees. Training new people involves the time and effort of established employees. It costs as much, or more, to replace a valued employee as a top customer. A disgruntled employee is potentially more destructive than a dissatisfied customer. Satisfaction among employees is shown to be mirrored in customer satisfaction. Reciprocally, customer satisfaction is the cause of employee satisfaction.

The question often arises as to whether happy employees make happy customers. Extensive research carried out by Dr Rosa Chun, at Manchester Business School, would indicate that the answer is 'maybe'. There is certainly a link connecting employees and customers, an intervening variable that, in most instances, is a process, thus ensuring repeatability of performance. The format is (Chun, 2003):

Employee/Customer Satisfaction Continuum
Employee satisfaction – Intervening variable – Customer satisfaction

---

Controlling the continuum

The employee/customer satisfaction continuum, for many companies, contains a series of interchanges between production and sale. The success or otherwise of these is only marginally in the hands of the primary manufacturer/provider, unless the company assumes control of the product or service from the source of raw materials or bought-in components. It is also necessary to exercise control from the moment goods leave the works until they arrive in the hands of the end user. Undisputed is the fact that punctual delivery of quality product, excellent back up and supportive advertising are factors that are critical to the creation of an image and define what end-user customers expect. The manufacturer or supplier understands this and recruits, trains and motivates employees with these objectives in mind. What happens when goods leave the manufacturer, however, has a major influence, or none, on customer satisfaction.

One has only to think of a petrol producer, where the end user is biased towards the product by the company's image but his purchasing decision depends on availability, quality and price. On the other hand, a large supermarket chain sells goods and services manufactured or provided by hundreds of organisations. The motivation behind end-user purchase from retail outlets, again, relies on brand image, availability, quality and price. Only a handful of employees who work in a large retail store are frontline people. None represents the original suppliers, or any of the intervening handlers of the merchandise. At each interchange between originator of the goods and their final sale to an end user, there is a new set of frontline employees to promote customer satisfaction.

It is difficult to think of any sizeable organisation entirely responsible for product or service and, at the same time, having face-to-face contact with and feedback from the end user. Significantly, the length of the employee–customer satisfaction link is equal to the length of the customer–producer feedback link, and the latter is potentially littered with obstacles and misunderstandings. It is evident, then, that every organisation in the delivery chain should take the same steps towards achieving customer satisfaction as the original supplier.

For any large organisation with many links in the chain between production and sale, it is vital to ensure that all hands through which goods and services pass are 'clean and competent' to represent the parent organisation and its products or services. Top management and boards of directors must be aware of potential weak links in their own distribution chain, and take steps to strengthen them. This means looking beyond the organisation, at competitors and intermediaries, and at the way in which products and services are brought to the end users.

The satisfaction quotients of employees in companies where consumers of their goods and services are remote, indubitably impinge on company image, in terms of quality of product, and of price. In this sense, then, it is reasonable to claim that employee satisfaction connects directly and indirectly to customer satisfaction. Study of the intervening links between individual companies will indicate how many more processes and measurements must be undertaken by top management to maintain the company image, quality and availability of product, and price competitiveness.

In a Manchester Business School paper entitled *The Links between Employee Satisfaction and Customer Satisfaction*, prepared for the CMLG project, Dr Rosa Chun came up with certain intriguing conclusions. Recent literature seems to have found a *negative* or no link in the service profit chain between internal and external satisfaction. It is, however, still considered by some managers to be good policy to offer rewards to encourage employees to stay with the firm and provide good customer service. Internal and external satisfaction are usually linked and affected by other factors than employee satisfaction/customer satisfaction. Research at Manchester Business School suggests that the assumption of a direct link cannot be made without investigating the organisational context. Links between the two satisfaction types are neither clear nor valid for all businesses.

There is, for example, no evidence that increasing staff pay will influence the customer, although it will improve staff satisfaction. Quoting Reichheld (1996, p. 46), the MBS paper says, 'Motivated employees stay longer with the company and get to know customers better, and this builds greater customer satisfaction, and further improves the relationship and the company results'.

Dr Chun says, too, that, '...the empirical evidence has recently been challenged. The chain has not been tested rigorously across large numbers and different types of service organisation'.

She concludes that probably the best way to see both the service profit chain and business excellence is as frameworks, idealised models that do not always reflect reality. Her team, researching internal and external perspectives of 17 organisations over five years, have compiled a database comprising nearly 10,000 interviews, half with customers and half with customer-facing employees. Having explained her methodology, Dr Chun concludes that the reality of the satisfaction link is better explained at the level of business unit and firm. If there is a link between employee and customer satisfaction, there has to be some *intervening variable* that affects both. However, that link has not been firmly established.

With those warnings in mind, this chapter suggests what might, *ideally*, be done with a workforce, to improve customer service and to achieve harmony of purpose in the workplace. The starting point is recruitment and this is followed by the building of trust between individuals. This might lead to some measure of employee empowerment. We look at the importance of a team approach, and examine how to involve employees in setting performance and service standards. We consider the setting up of performance agreements, and how to incorporate service quality issues into performance agreements; the ways in which management can listen to employees; conducting performance reviews; reward and recognition – linked to customer retention; employee retention; and the value of performing exit interviews.

Recruitment

Before a chef assembles ingredients for a dish, he decides on the recipe to be used and the method of preparation and cooking. In the same way, before selecting people for employment, the job they are to do and the talents required to do it must be considered. People are a resource in an organisation. Like the materials used in production, the choice of appropriate people for the jobs they are to perform is critical in achieving organisational goals.

Best practice: employee involvement

- Recruit people with the right attitude (Schindlerhof).
- Ritual for new employees – flowers, photo (Schindlerhof).
- Clearly defined culture is sent to job applicants (Schindlerhof).
- Employee surveys – using web – key question: 'How effective is your manager at following up survey results?'
- Link between customer satisfaction and staff rewards (Centrica 33%; Oracle 33%; Celestica 25%).
- Link between employee satisfaction and customer satisfaction.
- Employees participate in user group meetings (Oracle).

(Source: BQF Benchmarking Project, 2001.)

There are formal qualifications for most types of employment today. These give one measure of a candidate's suitability. Other useful measures include appearance, personality, confidence and previous experience. The qualifications and personal qualities needed for a prison officer will differ from those demanded of a funeral director, a ballerina or an airline steward (source: Quest Report).

ISO 9001:2000 – Section 6 – deals with resource management, under which category it lists human resources. It deals with assignment of personnel:

. . . to ensure that those who have responsibilities defined in the quality management system are competent on the basis of applicable education, training, skills and experience.

Under the heading Competence, training, qualification and awareness, the ISO says that,

The organisation shall establish and maintain system level procedures to:

a) *determine competency and training needs;*
b) *provide training to address identified needs;*
c) *evaluate the effectiveness of training at defined intervals;*
d) *maintain appropriate records of education, training, skills, and experience.*

This takes into account the fact that structural change within an organisation, following re-engineering of processes and new quality initiatives, highlights the need to re-educate, re-deploy and retrain existing people to fit them for their new roles within the organisation. Particularly in the service sector, the human dimensions of the job are as important as the technical qualification.

It is essential to know what prospective recruits expect from the job, as well as what they can offer to the employer organisation. Where a new employee is to form part of an existing team, the characteristics of the other team members also have a critical bearing on the selection process. The laws against discrimination are specific, but they cannot deal with personal prejudices, except as defined by the laws. The average age of a team, or its shared outside interests, or any number of other binding factors, might militate against a newcomer who does not share some or all of them.

Formulation of a precise job description, prior to advertising for someone to fill the vacancy, is of prime importance. The description should be detailed and accurate, within the confines of the law, to attract the right people and eliminate unsuitable contenders. The job description should be drafted *initially* by someone who knows the requirements from personal experience, rather than by a personnel officer (source: Schindlerhof).

Unless the person who drafts the description takes part in the interviewing process, additional information about the job is needed, to guide those who make the selection. A written questionnaire would be useful. It should define the purpose of the job, the ultimate service required and the desired end result of the service.

Job Title.
Why is this person necessary to the organisation?

- What is the purpose for which they are to be employed?
- What will the primary duties be?
- What secondary duties will there be?
- How often are the duties performed?
- What is the scope for and nature of decision making?

How is the job to be performed?

- What methods, practical skills and/or technologies apply to the job?
- What interpersonal skills are required?
- What are the general working conditions (place, hours, hazards, advantages, colleagues etc.?)

Standards

- What procedural standards apply to this job?
- What personal service standards apply to this job?
- How is the quality of the job measured?

Relations

- What internal and external contacts are involved?
- What are the reporting relationships?
- What are the rewards (salary, pension, advancement prospects, recreational facilities, holiday entitlement, crèche facilities, etc.)?

No job is perfect and no employee is ideal. Fitting job to worker is a compromise, with best-fit as its optimum outcome. Unless major changes in working practice or training are envisaged, it should be easy to decide what to look for in a replacement for an existing member of staff. The task is most difficult when the position is newly formed as a result of internal changes within the organisation.

To facilitate matters, a list of required performance factors should be compiled, to define more closely what would be expected of the new employee. These might include:

- Task and target achievement/reliability.
- Flexibility/responsiveness to challenge.
- Assurance – would internal and external customers trust this person?
- Market knowledge/empathy with customers.
- Professional expertise.
- Industry/product knowledge.
- Communication/selling/customer relation skills.
- Planning.
- Staff management.
- Administrative and financial skills.
- Technical skill and knowledge.
- Controlling and developing work quality.
- Problem solving/continuous improvement.

When asking a previous employer for a reference for the prospective new employee, it is advisable to run through the foregoing list and check how well the interviewee performed in a previous position. Written references cannot be regarded as accurate sources of information. A telephone call is useful as a means of determining employee quality.

No matter how many excellent qualities the applicant brings to the job, a career path should be available. If a higher position might not be available, other inducements should be produced, to offer something positive for which to aim. The quality policy of the organisation should be explained to prospective recruits at the outset. The better the qualifications for the job, the better the starting salary should be. Employees are cynical, nowadays, about long-term prospects in any field of employment, and this leads to feelings of detachment towards the employer of the moment.

Reassurance should, where possible, be given early that the job is long term and will be rewarding.

Many organisations like to offer a position subject to a period of mutual assessment before final confirmation. Often, the starting salary is lower than the in-house rate for similar work, and should rise when the probationary period is over. It is vital that this type of arrangement is formalised, so that it cannot be overlooked when the probation period expires. Promises need to be kept on both sides of an agreement, if people are to learn to trust one another. It is advisable to have no verbal agreements when it comes to employment matters.

Choosing frontline staff

Change of some sort is inevitable in most organisations, brought about by new technology, by staff working more from home, by splitting certain functions and relocating them. The more dispersal happens, the more important the frontline staff are in keeping customers happy. For the right people, with the right training and support, regular customer contact is satisfying of itself. For those who are prone to self-doubt and lack of confidence, it can be demoralising. These people are also useful, but in the back room, not the showroom. Happy staff make for happy customers. People who know they give good service to customers have job satisfaction. Their smiles are genuine and evoke genuine smiles in return. Customers who deal with satisfied employees perceive quality service and derive satisfaction. The converse is also true. Selecting the right people for the job is what one expects from good management.

Employee audits

When culture change is being implemented an opportunity arises for an audit of current staff, to see where there are, or might be, problems. It is common today for employees in responsible positions to work long hours, yet this can lead to tiredness and inefficiency. Equally demoralising is underemployment. People with too little to occupy them, or who feel that what they are asked to do has little point to it, find it difficult to motivate themselves to do anything. They are unsatisfied, as distinct from dissatisfied. Inadequate skills also act as a damper on productivity. Demoralised staff leave, and must be replaced. New organisational culture provides an occasion to look to the future, so that training schemes can be put in place to cope with forthcoming changes in staffing requirements.

Short-term, part-time contracts, particularly in non-profit-making organisations, such as universities, copyright libraries and hospital administration departments, for example, are usually dictated by funding shortfall, but the people who are thus employed always have their eye on the clock and the calendar. There is no sense of participation in the organisation, no loyalty to it, and no meaningful association with established staff. Another motive for short-term hiring is the present income tax, pension and national insurance structure. If it can be avoided, this type of contract should not be considered. The best employees are those who feel secure in their posts and who have time and confidence to develop a good relationship with their employer, their colleagues and the employer's products, service and customers. The best employers are those with the time and inclination to canvass the opinions and absorb the ideas of employees at all levels within the company.

As a long-term customer becomes familiar with the way in which an organisation operates and what it offers, so a long-term employee, accustomed to the organisation and its customers, learns how best to give satisfaction to employer and customer. Privatisation of public utilities saw massive job losses, but for those who survived the earthquake, new opportunities came into being and led to increased satisfaction all round. It is common sense for employers to retrain people as necessary, rather than recruit new people and start from scratch to integrate them.

The days when rows of ill-educated, poorly paid, job-secure, factory workers spent the day screwing tops on bottles and dreaming dreams have passed. Drudgery vanished with industrial smog. Automated processes emptied factory floors of people and led to improved production and higher quality goods. Now, the human touch is required in serving the customer directly, with information, with products and services and with delivery. Interpersonal skills, aligned to technical qualifications make for a very different type of employee.

Humans cannot be replicated as machines can. They can be qualified and trained, but each one remains an individual and needs to be treated as such. The major scourge of modern business is the high level of absenteeism due to work-related stress. Managers should be aware of the reasons for absenteeism, and sufficient staff should be employed for any process to ensure that those who perform the task are not subjected to more pressure than they can handle. A recent BBC Radio 4 programme on employment, discussed some changes made to an office, with the intention of delighting the workers there. When the interviewer questioned employees about whether the new working environment was what gave them job satisfaction, the consensus was that it had little effect on how they feel. What matters to the majority is the knowledge that management is interested in them as individuals, shows them respect, has time to talk over work-related matters with them, and is sympathetic in helping them to deal with personal problems. The frills make no difference to employee satisfaction. Many, indeed, would rather the money spent on them was used in other ways.

Increased leisure time, rising affluence, self-sufficiency and educational opportunities spell success for the right person in the right job. Higher salaries and a shorter working life *in a supportive environment* make for happier, more dependable and longer serving employees. It is clear that anything invested in recruitment, management and training, for the right people, will pay handsomely and yield profits for further investment. New employees need to be able to integrate smoothly and to enjoy the company of colleagues. The trick, then, having found the best-fit recruit, is to define precisely the job and tell the new employee what he/she needs to know and needs to be, in order to perform satisfactorily. Having engaged the employee, it is necessary to nurture and support him/her.

Tools for the job

Employees who are given the tools for the job will perform well. The term *tools* encompasses clear systems, procedures and processes, and requires a clear definition of what is expected of employees. Support and respect from managers build confidence in frontline staff and enable good performance.

Building trust between individuals

Trust is something that people share. In the sense of 'trust within an organisation', it depends upon consistency and fairness of treatment. Where there is lack of trust, that an employer might not believe the true reason for an absence, for example, an employee will find a convincing lie. If there is a mistake made, it will be hidden, or the blame will be put onto someone else, unless the employer or manager is known to be understanding and reasonable. Equally, managers and employers who do not take responsibility for what happens within their departments or companies will rapidly lose the trust of their subordinates. In the same manner, employers need to trust employees to give of their best consistently and be reliable.

Trust requires that matters of confidence are treated as such. Gossip is harmful, and what employees say to managers about personal matters should always be kept confidential. Employees should always be encouraged to talk frankly to managers if they find that some aspect of the way in which a company conducts itself presents a problem. Managers can use the information without revealing the source, if there is a problem within the department or organisation that requires attention.

Whistle-blowers are people who do not trust their employers to act to right perceived wrongs, and who fear for their jobs if they question company decisions. Many matters that concern employees can be cleared up by an explanation of the necessity for what is being done. People must know that their concerns merit a hearing and that action will be taken when and where needed. Whistle-blowers can do irrevocable harm to a company when they take their grievances into the public forum.

Information is the tool to tune a corporate engine efficiently. Employers might feel justified in what they do. They might convince employees to agree with their arguments, but critical feedback from employees might reflect an attitude prevalent among the wider public.

Then, a major rethink is called for, right or wrong. In this scenario, managers need to trust the instincts of the employees. Genetically modified 'suicide' seeds are a case in point. The producers have publicly changed their practices in line with public unease.

Trust between individuals

In the workplace, trust is needed in day-to-day relationships with colleagues. Fair play is maybe a good way to express what is meant here. A generous act on the part of a manager or employer towards a reliable employee yields dividends in an improved relationship. Honesty between people begets trust. Customers who deal regularly with certain employees learn to trust them for service, for advice, for information and for that friendliness that makes everybody relax. However, in the work situation, as with the staff–customer relationship, one mistake, and years of good work can be undone.

In terms of people management, it is important for managers to be aware of the moods of their staff. Someone who is sick should not be sent to handle an irate customer. Someone who, for personal reasons, cannot work alongside someone else should be moved elsewhere. Trust is a fragile plant. In the wrong growing conditions it will wither. The fact that people can sometimes be unpredictable, moody and unreasonable makes managing them interesting and challenging, but nobody ever said it would be easy. Establishing and nurturing trust between individuals is also a rare talent.

Empowerment

The unqualified proposition that empowerment benefits employees does not bear close scrutiny. Empowerment can be seen as something akin to water flowing from a management-controlled tap. It can be turned on to allow a trickle, or it can give a surge, and all the stages in between the two extremes. There is no norm about it. Circumstances dictate policy. The flow can be adjusted at any time.

If it is part of a company philosophy to empower frontline employees in their dealings with customers, this does not necessarily imply simply giving them complete freedom to act at their own discretion. Employees are individuals and require individual training and treatment, to encourage them to give of their best. It is the job of managers to manage. Empowerment, even a limited amount, removes the 'parrot complex' that can be irritating to staff and customers. Strict guidelines for verbal interchange, for example, soon become an automatic reaction on the part of staff. Customers recognise the total lack of interest and sincerity in the body language and are antagonised.

Whom to empower? First, there are some people for whom empowerment is anathema. They are often loyal, conscientious and productive people, but they resist assuming extra responsibility. They work best within a tight framework of understood rules. Rather than risk failure, they will do nothing. Empowerment requires training in what is expected of the right types of people, so that they know how far to go when acting on their own initiative. It also means not interfering with those for whom this type of responsibility is unwelcome. They are best deployed where they are useful and satisfied.

An example of the latter type is Margaret, secretary to a departmental sales manager, and an intelligent, conscientious and valued employee. Her boss proposed that she retrain as his personal assistant, with commensurate rates of pay and other benefits. She declined. She was paying off a mortgage with her partner. She lacked the self-confidence to take up the challenge, and threatened to resign if the offer was not immediately withdrawn. She feared failure and subsequent job loss. The failure here was on the part of the boss, who knew too little about Margaret's circumstances and made an error of judgement in offering promotion.

Secondly, there will always be untrustworthy managers and supervisors who are happy to pass the buck when something is mishandled, but who take credit for other people's successes. These people use empowerment as a way of shedding their responsibilities onto others. Too many of this type will discourage initiative from lower levels of employee. They will no longer trust managers to support them and they will fail to respond well to empowerment. This, in turn, leads to job dissatisfaction, to mistakes being made and to resignations.

Before organisations utilise empowerment, the concept should be examined like a work process, to see what benefits derive from it, where problems might occur and under what circumstances and in what measure it should be implemented or changed. Employees should have the opportunity to be consulted and offer their own suggestions, just as they should in production process changes. Once levels have been agreed, they should be mutually respected. If the levels are not correctly set, the process can always be changed again, with staff involvement.

To some extent, the service or product will suggest the optimum level of empowerment and upon whom it might best be bestowed. In certain occupations, where almost all employees are frontline staff, such as hotel workers, chamber maids might know that they can provide extra linen, at their discretion, or, in an emergency, call out a doctor to attend to a sick guest. A receptionist might have yet more powers to serve customers *ad hoc*. However, fiscal limits might be set in respect of dissatisfied customers who demand compensation or service beyond what might reasonably be provided. Managers are, after all, paid to manage and to take final responsibility for what happens in the organisation for which they work.

Employees who suspect that they are doing a management job for a worker's wage cannot be expected to work well. This will be seen as a breach of trust. It will encourage some of them to behave in ways that are detrimental to good customer relationships, or to good financial management. Friendly customers might be favoured, while customers who complain are neglected. It can also lead to traps being set for unwary managers by disgruntled employees. A person who is unhappy at work, especially because of unwelcome responsibilities, is probably about to leave the job and has nothing to lose by sabotage. Rather than allow this type of person to work out the period of notice, it is better to dispense with them immediately they tender their resignation. It is worth talking with them, however, before they depart, to see what can be learnt from the mutual experience. This subject will be dealt with later in the chapter.

Team empowerment is equally fraught with potential disaster. Teams are formed to manage work processes. Accountants manage money, sales teams spend it. There is a rational conflict of interests between them that team empowerment can exacerbate. All teams have their own territory, which has to be defended against that of other teams. The larger the organisation, the more dangerous unrestricted empowerment can be. If a whole team takes action that management regards as totally inappropriate, either the team leader carries the can for the rest of the team, or blame is shared equally. For management to seek retribution among a work team is a limited option. Blame, in any case, lies with management, who has the last word on empowerment and how it is applied.

Every type of organisation will have its own views on empowerment, and its own ways of giving power with one hand and curbing it with the other. As a business strategy, it cannot stand alone. It is part of employee selection, training, involvement and management, and it works as well or as badly as the rest of the process. The best chance of success with empowerment is when the organisation offers customised service to customers with whom it has a long-term relationship. It is appropriate, too, where non-routine, complex technologies are employed, where managers have already experienced empowerment working well for the organisation and its customers, and where employees have the necessary skills and desires to extend themselves in this way.

Use of the term empowerment is perhaps misleading. It implies something that cannot properly exist outside management circles. Encouragement can be given for employees to *show initiative*. This expression implies knowing what management would expect to see from the outcome of the initiative, which in turn guides the employee or the team in the action to be taken. Management must trust the employee to know and to do what is appropriate. The employee must trust managers to understand what was done and why, and to support the decisions taken.

The team approach

The EFQM excellence model, criterion 3, looks at people in the following ways:

- People resources, to be planned, managed and improved.
- People's knowledge and competencies are identified, developed and sustained.

- People are involved and empowered.
- People and the organisation have a dialogue.
- People are rewarded and cared for.

The involvement and empowerment of people (sub-head 3) proposes the encouragement and support of individuals and teams participating in improvement activities. Empowerment, as we have seen, is something of a two-edged sword, to be wielded with extreme caution. However, a well-founded and well-led team can be a powerhouse within an organisation, provided that the team is well chosen, well motivated, shares goals, and has someone special to lead and inspire.

It is worth reminding ourselves that much of this chapter applies in an ideal world of perfect jobs and perfect, or would-be-perfect, people. In real work situations, there are those who cannot relate to team practices and the ethos of teamwork. The main concern of such people is what effect the team as a whole will have on their personal career path. This brings us back to the old question of trust. Can other members of a team be as career-orientated as oneself? Can management be trusted to advance all members equally, and if not, whom will they promote and why? Can the employee trust that the job is safe for the foreseeable future?

The EFQM criterion for people specifically advocates encouraging people to work together in teams, and this is clearly not quite the simple task it might appear at first glance.

Teams, then, might simply be people, engaged in performing together a particular work process, who act as individuals within the constraints of the actual process itself. In this case, it is every person for him/herself. Alternatively, there is the ideal team, a coordinated group of people who share common aims, and exchange information and ideas for improvement. This type of team can cut across departments and processes and function as a powerhouse of innovation and inspiration, but there has to be one person to stoke the fires and stimulate the minds and imaginations of the rest. There has, essentially, to be managerial support for what emerges from such a team. The product is often unexpected, controversial, eccentric even.

The ideal team can be trusted to overcome any difficulties and find solutions to its own problems. They are most fruitful where they receive most support and understanding. If generous empowerment is going to be successful, it will be within this type of team framework. One of the constraints that strangle good team effort, apart from worries about advancement within the organisation, is often budgetary. If a team can measure itself against similar teams, or against past performance of itself, and show improvement, it should be allowed to make a claim for some relaxation of the purse-strings for a given project.

To move from a group of individuals participating in a task to forming a cohesive unit (ideal team), to take the task forward, requires seven recognised elements to be put in place. There has to be a strong platform of understanding, a shared vision, a creative climate, ownership of ideas, resilience to setbacks, network activators and learning from experience. All these have to be present for excellent results. Where none are present, there is no team. Where some are present, or all are intermittently present, there is average performance and a less than fully functioning team.

With the creation of teams, there are various things to consider.

A strong platform of understanding

Team members understand and respect each other's viewpoint. This has a powerful cohesive effect and strengthens performance in the other six areas. It includes shared values, beliefs and goals.

A shared vision

Every team has a responsibility for achieving something. When this is converted into a shared vision, it motivates and sustains a team's progress. When this shared vision is missing, it might be difficult to notice. When it is present, results speak for themselves. It permits the team to assume control of what it does. It is another essential link in the chain of ideal team composition.

A creative team climate

This is the psychological climate for creative change within teams. Its presence allows for new ideas and innovation towards ongoing improvements in output.

Ownership of ideas

Where ideas are supported by all team members, they receive the greatest attention and show the best results. The idea belongs to the team; the individual members of the team look for ways to adopt parts of the idea for themselves.

Resilience to setbacks

Things occasionally go awry, even in the best teams. Where all the other required elements for success are in place, an ideal team will work together to overcome setbacks. The easy option is always to find someone or something to blame, but the ideal team does not consider this to be an option. If the idea was shared, the vision shared and the implementation shared, there will be a mutual problem-solving mentality at work.

Network activators

Teams require one or two members to be good at working with key individuals inside and outside the team. These have outside contacts and fresh sources for ideas. They give impetus as well as support, by demonstrating how their team's efforts impact on those of other teams, in other departments. This gives rise to a ferment of ideas and innovations stimulated by the broader base of lateral interaction. The perfect situation is when a whole organisation works for improvement as one ideal team. The word used to describe this unified approach to service quality is *voluntarism*. People do what they do, and do it well, from choice, not coercion.

Learning from experience

Unless a team learns from experience, it can make no progress towards developing the other essential ingredients of success. In this context, experience is not totally limited to quality effort; it is experience of the way in which the effort is judged by management. Encouragement and support is the key to helping teams forward.

Involve employees in setting performance and service standards

Motivated people are capable and willing to set their own performance and service standards. If, however, anyone is set an apparently impossible task, they are discouraged from attempting to perform it. If they know the object of the exercise, and are asked what they think it is fair and reasonable to be expected to do, there is every chance that they will complete the task satisfactorily. Once employees understand the aims and goals of the organisation, it is possible for them to cooperate in setting performance and service standards. Probably, they will set these at a higher level than would be acceptable to them if standards were imposed without prior consultation.

In the matter of involvement of teams in work processes there are certain characteristics to be discovered when teams succeed:

- Good teams find ways for improving performance and service beyond what management would ask of them.
- Cooperation is good; confrontation is bad.
- The more people understand of the outcomes desired from what they do, the more inclined they are to work together to attain those outcomes.
- Teams that are given responsibility for assessing customers' needs and desires find it easier to adapt and accommodate to meet those needs. The management skill is in providing direction.
- Information that teams gather for themselves is of more value than information gathered by others.

Performance agreements

Newly engaged staff, when they are given contracts of employment, expect to have their role clearly defined, in writing, in the contract. That, however, is not the last word on the matter. If an organisation really puts customers first, implements all the process re-engineering steps necessary to streamline production, surveys customers, segments customers and provides everything for customers' delight and satisfaction, employees still have the major part to play. Unless they agree with the overall aims of the organisation and accept the fact that attention to service quality issues is necessary for customer retention, the rest is a waste of time and resources.

To get agreement to anything, both sides of a discussion must see things from the same perspective. Management has a duty to share information, if there is to be any hope of a shared vision. Management, too, must be seen to be working towards the same goal as employees. If every person in the company understands the company's mission, they tend to agree among themselves and work towards the common goal. If there is lack of knowledge, there will be lack of understanding, and resistance to cooperation.

The success of performance agreements, as an abstract concept, depends on management, who must also be seen to be working in parallel with the workforce as a whole. Like everything else about a customer-orientated organisation's changes, such agreements should be committed to writing and employees should have a copy where they can see it, to remind them of what they agreed to do.

Incorporation of service quality issues into performance agreements

Every person in the organisation needs to know exactly what is expected of them. Service quality is the template for what is done but, on a specific level, people need to know their tasks. To ask a man to produce 100 printed circuit boards in a four-hour period is not the same as expecting him to produce them without defects in that time span. If he is sufficiently motivated, he will try to make every product perfectly. If he is not motivated by service quality ideals, he will know that his work is checked for defects, and will leave it to the checker to right the wrongs. The gain to the organisation whose employees want to do things right the first time is obvious, even from this simple example. The savings made can be ploughed back into new customer initiatives and in rewards for those employees who earn them.

Listen to employees

Why should employers listen to employees? There are plenty of jobs out there. If people have a complaint, let them take it elsewhere. Too many companies, especially in times of high unemployment, took a tough line on employees with something to say. But, employees sometimes have very useful comments to make, have innovative, cost-saving suggestions to offer, carry feedback from customers, warn of problems looming.

Employee opinion surveys (EOSs) are as valuable as customer surveys, and are as effective, providing the results are acted upon. If they are ignored, as with customer surveys that are not used, they are worse than useless, because employees feel insulted and disillusioned. To stop customers from defecting to the competition, the composition of surveys and the results they generate are carefully considered. Customer surveys are routinely carried out, and new measures are taken to meet shortfall in service quality. Is it as useful to look at employees in the same way?

Where does a dissatisfied employee go?

Dissatisfied customers take their business to the competition. Dissatisfied employees take their skills, *and their knowledge of your business*, to the competition. Dissatisfied customers might be lured back to your company. Dissatisfied employees will never return. In financial terms, the loss of a valued customer might be considerably less, in the long term, than the loss of a valuable, knowledgeable member of staff.

What to ask in an EOS

There is one difference between surveys of customers and surveys of staff. Customers have nothing to lose and everything to gain by honesty. This is not always true of staff, or is often seen by them as not always true. This means that questionnaires must be carefully formulated, or else staff will give the answers they think management wants to receive, rather than answer honestly. Respondents must know that what they say will be held in confidence. Many work-related problems are to do with personality clashes, aggravated by long working hours, the stresses of combining work with domestic responsibilities and difficulties with personal relationships outside work.

Compare the EOS with what customers are asked. Job satisfaction might be measured on the same type of five-point scale as customer satisfaction. Additional questions such as:

- How we can improve the service we give?
- What are we doing wrong?
- What would make you go to the competition?
- How do you see your future with this company?
- If you were the manager of your department, what would you do differently and why?
- Do you feel that you are valued enough?
- Is your work station comfortable?
- Do you feel safe when at work?
- Are you at ease with your colleagues?
- How free do you feel to use your initiative?
- Is what you do appreciated by management?
- What worries you most about your present employment?
- Do you always know why you do what you do?
- Do you understand the company's mission?
- Do you feel as if you belong to your team?
- If not, why is this?
- If you were offered training in a new skill, what would you suggest?
- In terms of promotion hopes, what is your ambition?
- Does your future lie with the company?

Employee motivation

No tool has been developed to quantify the value or contribution that an employee could bring to an organisation, but that does not signify that there is an insoluble problem here. The equation to be solved is the ELV (employee lifetime value). A possible avenue for research into this subject would make an in-depth study of the factors that influence learning and sharing knowledge from an organisational and individual perspective.

The EFQM criterion 7a lists some of the perceptions by which employees' motivation might be measured. It includes:

- Career development.
- Communication.
- Empowerment.
- Equal opportunities.
- Involvement.
- Leadership.
- Opportunity to learn and achieve.
- Recognition.
- Target setting and appraisal.
- The organisation's values, mission, vision, policy and strategy.
- Training and development.

In the same way, the EFQM looks at measures of satisfaction with:

- Organisation's administration.
- Employment conditions.
- Facilities and services.
- Health and safety conditions.
- Job security.
- Pay and benefits.
- Peer relationships.
- The management of change.
- The organisation's environmental policy and impact.
- The organisation's role in the community and society.
- Working environment.

The ideal EOS, or a focus group of employees, should address all these matters of motivation and satisfaction and act on any shortcomings revealed. Employees, like customers, deserve to be informed what measures have been and will be taken. As with customer surveys, there will be some matters that are quickly remedied, others that require preparation and planning. Such surveys, like pedigree dogs, are expensive, require regular exercise and daily grooming. The cost of not paying attention to these so-called *perception measures* might be devastating in terms of profitability, both in terms of employee and customer churn.

While on the subject of surveys for customers and employees, it might also be worth asking the employees of companies who supply the organisation with goods and services what they think might improve the working relationship. It is not unknown for seemingly intractable problems to vanish with such an exercise.

Motivators

Things that satisfy employees bear no relationship to what makes people dissatisfied, and many factors contribute to the psychology of motivation. If any single factor has been identified in the search for the most effective employee motivator, it has to be to do with empowerment. The employee who is given an interesting job and the tools and authority to perform it, and who is given recognition for what has been achieved, will be motivated to perform well. Demotivators, things that make employees lethargic about their own performance, are linked most strongly with two aspects of company behaviour, namely, company policy and administration, and supervision. Other influences play a part in providing, or depriving employees of, satisfaction, and they vary from company to company. Herzberg (2003) offers the following terse advice: forget praise, forget punishment, and forget cash. Make their jobs more interesting.

In the same edition of the *Harvard Business Review*, Nigel Nicholson offers advice about how to motivate the recalcitrant employee, the person who, in spite of being offered challenging and rewarding employment, never seems to want to do what his employer expects him to do. The root of the problems that he gives as examples lies more with the employer, or manager, than with the employee. Specific examples are given and the methodology of change is explained. Each recalcitrant employee has unique difficulties and these have to be explored if there is to be improvement. Failure results in resignation of the employee and reflects badly on the manager.

Performance indicators

The EFQM criterion 7 deals with performance indicators, which it describes as, 'These measures are the internal ones used by the organisation to monitor, understand, predict and improve the performance of the organisation's people and to predict their perceptions'.

If it is expected that organisations will survey staff and customers to see where improvements might be made, it is also justified in asking employees whether they are doing all that they might do for the benefit of the company, and for the company's customers, and in what areas the organisation can help them to improve performance. Appraisal interviews, properly designed and conducted, are one form of employee survey that is common, useful and should be mutually beneficial to employer and employee.

Appraisal and appraisal interviewing

Staff appraisal is one way in which the changes taking place today in businesses of all types can be absorbed and expanded to the benefit of company and employees. Its primary objective is to help improve individual performance, realise potential and achieve better results for the organisation. It should deal with three essential areas:

1. A review of past performance, and the lessons to be learned.
2. Identification of the future needs of the individual, the department and the organisation.
3. Formulation of an action plan specifying what has to be done, by whom and by when.

For success, top management must be committed and involved in the appraisal scheme. The immediate boss should perform the appraisal interview. All line managers should be trained and the drill should be monitored through the line. In a large company, a senior person should be accountable for monitoring the mechanics, consistency and results of the scheme. The method of looking at performance should be objective and regular. The job-holder's views need to be taken into account. This is the opportune time to uncover, discuss and obviate problems tending to employee dissatisfaction. The appraisal looks to the future as well as reviewing the past. The objectives and workings of the scheme are explained to the person who is being appraised.

If employees' remuneration is linked to *how* they live the values, they will certainly know them. Colgate-Palmolive has a list of behaviours that reflect the *living* of their values, and, at their annual appraisals, employees are assessed on their performance relative to those behaviours. Colgate-Palmolive's values are:

- Caring.
- Global teamwork.
- Continuous improvement.

Benefits of an appraisal system

For the job-holder, the system provides an opportunity to discuss all aspects of the job, with the boss, in depth, in private and free from the pressures of the daily workload. It clarifies for the job-holders how best they can contribute to the objectives of the department and the aims of the organisation. It identifies strengths, which can be built on, and weaknesses to be addressed. It clarifies what is expected in the job and involves people in planning their work and their future. The written record of the interview and action plan signifies that there is a bilateral commitment to make things happen. It also saves the individual from having to repeat the performance, should a new boss be appointed. Defects in systems and processes, or in the hygiene of the work environment, can be addressed.

For the managers, the appraisal system creates the opportunity for them to think seriously about what they expect from their people and what plans they have for the period ahead. It allows for recognition of new ideas and for problem areas to be identified and tackled.

For the organisation, appraisal is a visible commitment to recognition of the importance of its people. This can be reflected in the morale of staff and can be transmitted to potential employees. The organisation should aim for greater individual effectiveness and commitment in areas such as: corporate aims; succession planning; identification of training needs; feedback from employees; recurring problems; obtaining objective information on performance for use in business planning, and promotion and salary decisions.

Target setting

To avoid problems associated with personal qualities and subjective judgements, target setting is now regarded as the best means of measuring the performance of individuals. This system relies upon identification of the key result areas for the job and setting standards of performance which are measurable, recognisable and achievable. It also means setting targets which are priorities over and above the routine work. These are about change and development and relate to the individual job-holder. The view is forwards to the future, not back to the past.

The system relies on regular meetings and consultation and should not be an imposition. Then, it provides the best method of meeting the need for an objective appraisal scheme based on dialogue. At one time, such appraisals were almost exclusively backward looking and associated with salaries and promotion. Today, in many organisations, there would be two separate meetings, one to do with the past and rewards for what has been achieved; the other is the dialogue session, where new targets are set.

Again, as with other processes, management takes the first steps in preparing an appraisal system, by deciding why it is needed, its objectives and how it might be expected to help the organisation. Management next decides on the structure of the scheme, the paperwork, frequency and timing, who is involved, what support information is to be produced, how information is to be used and how the scheme will be monitored.

Before implementation, all those concerned in any way must be informed of the objectives and methodology of the scheme, and appraisers must be trained in how to conduct the appraisals. If salary is linked to performance, the way in which this operates must be explained to staff and managers. Salary decisions should only relate to those parts of performance that can be substantiated.

Paperwork should be simple, and should include guidance notes for appraisers and those being appraised. It should be completed immediately after an appraisal has been conducted. Targets should be set against the important parts of ongoing work, they should be specific, one-off priorities, and build on strengths, address weaknesses or explore new ideas. The report should be duplicated, one copy to be accepted and retained by the employee until the next appraisal meeting. At this time, the successes and failures can be reviewed and investigated, and any problems thrown up can be resolved.

Employees are often uneasy about appraisal, fearing that it implies criticism of their performance. They should know that its aim is to achieve results, encourage them to give their best performance, and help to develop their skills, abilities and knowledge, provide them with a challenge and a sense of achievement and improve communication between them and their boss. Appraisals should always be approached in a positive way and employees should feel encouraged and inspired afterwards.

Before an interview, employees should be given notice, the objectives stressed, areas for discussion outlined and any relevant paperwork exchanged. The interviewer has time to speak with other people who are affected by the work done by the interviewee, and the interviewee has time to review what has been done, or not done, and suggest their own ideas for the coming period.

Managers need to think about the needs of department and individual, establish a purpose for the interview, set deadlines for completion of the process, know when the process is to be repeated, and conclude the interview on a positive note.

As with all work processes and systems, appraisal benefits from regular review, to stop it losing direction and purpose and becoming a valueless routine. The recommended frequency for review is about once in three years, but will vary with the type of organisation and the rate of staff turnover. New managers should be trained at once in how to conduct the interviews and should be given time, before the next run of interviews, to read and evaluate the summaries left by their predecessors. Employees who continue to meet targets, will appreciate receiving praise in terms of salary increase and in promotion. Promotion implies greater responsibility, and for some, this is almost reward enough in itself.

The emphasis on appraisal has shifted from chastisement to improvement. It has become a generally welcome, 360° investigation and discussion, with staff and management working together to find new and better ways of company performance enhancement. Employee feedback and management input further the creation of a deeper understanding of the company's values and targets, and provide a guide to improved systems and processes. Appraisals are now seen as an opportunity to obtain helpful feedback on what employees, or managers, are doing well or badly, and for comparisons to be made between teams, to discover what can usefully be carried over from a successful team to the rest of the organisation. The element of fear that once accompanied appraisals has disappeared from the best organisations.

The *Financial Times* (2 September 2004) carried an interview with Michelle Peluso, head of Travelocity, the US online travel company. Ms Peluso attributes her speedy rise to the top in the company to her appetite for new thinking. Her top tips for handling staff are: regular, informal lunches with employees to encourage feedback and discussion, regular emails to staff, weekly prizes to employees at all levels who are nominated by colleagues for outstanding and innovative work, and mentoring 'exceptional' people. She says, 'You have to make employees passionate about their work.'

Reward and recognition – linked to customer retention

As its title states, this book is about maximising customer retention and profitability, and all the chapters have as their backbone the notion that the customer is the life-blood of a company. Reward and recognition for employees should, therefore, relate to how far they contribute to the retention of customers. As we have seen, customers can be retained by a quality of service over and above anything that the competition can offer.

Employees can only perform well in the sphere of customer retention when they know what strategy management has decided to adopt and how it is to be implemented. If employees are not told what is expected of them, they cannot meet expectations. There are some people who, no matter how difficult the task, will do their very best to complete it. Others will do the least amount of work compatible with retaining the job, until it suits them to move elsewhere. The most ardent employee, who is unsure of the goals for which to aim, is the one whose defection can be most costly. They will bear the greatest disappointment.

Employees who know the aims and objectives of the organisation, but who receive no encouragement and support from the managers, will grow discontented, too, and leave. Many organisations do not consider this to be a problem, but a closer inspection will prove otherwise.

To advertise, interview, employ and train someone to fill the shoes of an experienced person will cost in time and money. That newcomer is not initially as productive or as useful as the one who resigned. It will take time before he/she has learnt all there is to learn about the position. Existing staff, especially where a team is concerned, have to learn to adjust to a new person and help to settle him or her into the job. They might resent having to do this. One discontented person in a team or department, like a bad apple in a barrel, can spread discontent. Trust flies out of the window.

There might be a domino effect. If the others become disaffected, but choose not to resign, the situation is hazardous for the organisation. Suddenly, targets will no longer be met. Excuses and evasion will be the new order of the day, and managers who are less than alert might find it impossible to explain what has gone awry.

Meanwhile, the ex-employee has taken everything he/she knows about the organisation, and all their experience of the way things are done, and offered it to a rival. If that ex-employee was one of the frontline staff, someone with a long-standing relationship with one or more of the organisation's best customers, what will the customers do?

How long will it take to rebuild the broken relationship with them? Will some of the customers relate more to that ex-employee than to the organisation, and take their business to the person whom they know and trust?

People are sensitive; they want praise and flattery from time to time, as well as a rise in salary at predictable intervals. To have a senior manager or director come down and say, 'Well done, thank you very much,' costs nothing, but is worth a lot. To make it personal is to make it count for something. To a team that has just achieved a difficult target, a lunchtime drink or an evening meal is always a nice way to register the organisation's appreciation. Some organisations use visible rewards, certificates or photographs of 'Employee of the Month', but the less obvious ways of saying thank you are often less embarrassing to the recipient and cause less friction among not quite so successful work-mates. A day off with pay, for a special occasion, is another much valued gesture towards a person who does well.

Recognition

A study by Beverly Kaye and Sharon Jordan-Evans, in their book *Love 'Em or Lose 'Em*, offers guidance in how to show recognition of good performance.

- *Spontaneously.* Catch people doing something right and thank them then and there.
- *Specifically.* Praise people for *specific* (rather than generic) accomplishments or efforts.
- *Purposefully.* Take an employee to lunch or dinner in a great restaurant to show your appreciation of work well done.
- *Privately.* Go to your employee's office to give a personal thank you and praise.
- *Publicly.* Praise an employee in the presence of others (peers, family members, your boss).
- *In writing.* Send a letter, memo or email. Possibly, send a copy to team members or higher level management.

Recognition is reward, reward is recognition

If employees were asked for just one reason why they go to work, it has to be for the income it brings. A salary rise is very welcome, but it is not special. If the boss throws a spontaneous party in his office and invites a team that has performed very well to come inside, have a drink, and allow him to make a speech of thanks, it will be remembered long afterwards. Some organisations are much more generous in recognising excellence. They give trips abroad to top performers. One farm-supplies company sent its top salesman to Texas for a month, to see how things operate there. Some companies will allow champion employees to take a sabbatical for a year, or they organise holidays for ideal teams and their families. Accurately targeted rewards are specific to the recipient. A free holiday abroad, for example, is of little use to someone with a partner who is unable to share it, for whatever reason. Sometimes, alternatives have to be offered to individuals.

How to reward your staff

In 2004, *The Sunday Times* published a list of the 100 best companies to work for and how they reward their employees. The following is a random selection:

- 85% of staff say managers regularly express appreciation. (Beaverbrooks)
- Parents able to take time off for school plays/sports days. (Pannone & Partners)
- Access to Timpson Senior's Harley Street doctor, holiday homes for use of staff with more than five years' service. (Timpson)
- Matching charity donations of up to £7500 per employee. (Microsoft)
- Helicopter ride, Orient Express for best suggestion each quarter. (Richer Sounds)
- Time off for employees to take part in community activities. (Boehringer)
- Recent team bonus was trip to Disneyland, Paris. (Electronic Arts)

- Free breakfast at work, organic produce for staff restaurant. (Computer Associates)
- Perfect attendance rewarded with gifts such as hi-fi systems, theatre tickets, meal vouchers and hampers. (Loop Customer Management)
- Annual entertainment budget of £500 per head. (Honda)
- Staff get two days' extra paid holiday before marriage. (Wragge & Co.)

What makes a great employer?

Microsoft says, 'For Microsoft to become an employer of choice means creating a flexible working environment, allowing our employees to play to their strengths and give them the opportunity to do what they do best every day.' This approach covers physical, emotional and intellectual aspects of employment. The physical aspect is approached by the provision of a range of services on the premises, from having one's shopping delivered to the company car park, to photo processing, car valeting, dry cleaning and other facilities. The emotional side deals with health, leisure, personal finance services, and aims for a balance between employees' home and work lives. Intellectual provision comes in the form of mentoring with a view to promotion. Interestingly, the providers of these services are local companies for whom a block of 1000 Microsoft employees forms a viable customer base. The employees' verdict on what it is like to work for Microsoft is overwhelmingly favourable.

In their book, *Now, Discover your Strengths*, Buckingham and Clifton (2001) developed a Strengths Finder, and looked for the top 34 innate talents to be found in a workforce.

Not every employee appreciates every form of reward mentioned above, and care must be taken to discover what will generate appreciation and satisfaction. However, from a smile and a few words of appreciation to the magnificent gesture, as they say of Aunt Maude's birthday present, 'It's the thought that counts'. The point about recognition and rewards is that they promote repetition of the behaviour that earns them. Rewarded behaviour should reflect the organisation's service quality goals and be customer-retentive. If managers are themselves paid on service quality improvement results, they perceive this as important down the line. If an organisation as a whole does well in this, it is due to employees who are motivated to succeed. The philosophy of rewards for improvement in customer service casts a glow over the whole organisation and leads to interdepartmental and multilateral team efforts. These take the organisation ever forward. Recognition is an essential, yet under-used, quality improvement tool.

What about when things go wrong? Even the best efforts sometimes founder on an unexpected rock. There is no sense in recrimination. The sooner the damage is rectified the sooner things are back on an even keel. It is worth considering how a good recovery might also merit recognition, especially if a lesson can be learnt from the incident. Strong teams find faster ways to put the company back on course.

Recognition and reward should never be arbitrary. There should be a yardstick of quantifiable indicators, based on feedback from the external or internal customers served by individuals and teams. Keep everything highly visible and transparent, so that the whole company knows who is making the greatest contribution to continuous service/quality improvement. Immediacy is essential, to keep the excitement alive.

As with other processes, those to be rewarded should have input into who receives the rewards and what the rewards should be. Senior executives should be highly visible in the recognition process. If possible, rather than reward by promotion a valuable person to a second-rate manager, investigate what other reward might be effective in giving him/her satisfaction and motivation. It is important for any reward and promotion scheme to be seen to be fair. As with unwanted rewards, unwanted promotion offers can have the opposite effect to what was expected, and the employee concerned will resign. If in doubt as to how rewards and promotion offers will be received by employees, enquire. Reward the small steps as well as the giant strides. The more employees who feel good about themselves, because of a gesture of appreciation from management, the more cooperative and motivated the workforce becomes.

There is always a danger in any reward scheme that some people will regard it as unfair. To avoid this, use peer review, customer feedback and solid service/quality measures. Train managers to feel competent and confident to build a sincere 'thank you' culture. Remember that customers are internal as well as external. Internal customer feedback is as important as that from external customers. Many small rewards yield many motivated staff. A few expensive rewards for a few top people are not as cost-effective or as motivational. They yield a few happy, motivated staff.

Employee retention

Staff resign for a number of personal reasons that have nothing to do with work *per se*, and there is little to be done about them. When customers leave an organisation for personal reasons, replacements have to be found. When staff leave because, for one reason or another, they no longer derive satisfaction from their work, it is valuable to discover why it happened. Those who have been a short time with the company might well have decided that they do not fit. Those who have been for any length of time with an organisation, and who have benefited from training and experience, are a serious loss.

Steps should be taken, before the door closes on them for the last time, to try to discover what went wrong and how it might be rectified. It takes one sheep to lead a flock, and where there is cause for dissatisfaction, the first resignation might be followed by others. Why bother to deal with complaints from customers, if you have no interest in complaints from employees?

In a fully integrated organisation, where the customer, internal and external, dictates policy, the internal customer, the employee, is as important as the external customer, and his/her complaints deserve the same level of attention as the external customer's complaints. The cost of losing one valued employee, due to dissatisfaction with some aspect of the job, is as high, or even higher, than the loss of a valued and dissatisfied customer. The loss of either is an indicator of some aspect of the organisation in need of adjustment. To ignore the one and attend to the other is nonsense.

In *Back to Basics: How Well Are Your Customers Treated by Front-line Staff?* (IOMA, 2003), quoting John McKean's research in *Customers are People: The Human Touch* (2002), it says 'that 70% of what determines which company customers will purchase goods or services from is based on how humanely they are treated.' McKean also said, '...that there is a direct link – an 80% correlation – between how businesses treat their employees and how they treat their customers.'

A 1% loss of top customers could result in a 25% reduction in profits. A CIPD study indicates that the more satisfied employees are with their jobs, the better the company is likely to perform in terms of productivity and profitability. Sears Roebuck found that a 5% improvement in employee attitudes will drive a 1.3% improvement in customer satisfaction, which in turn will drive a 0.5% improvement in revenue growth. To maximise profits is the name of the game, and the end product or service is what the customer purchases. Most people make a few major purchases in a lifetime: house and furniture, car, student tuition fees, annuity/life assurance policy, and pension, for example. Some of these are subject to further purchases, but only long after the initial decision to buy was made, and the next purchase will be based again on company image, quality of goods or services and price. It is the small, regular, repeat purchases that add up to company profitability. Fail to satisfy at this level and profits will soon start to decline. Take care of the pennies, and the pounds will take care of themselves, as the old proverb had it.

The value of performing exit interviews

As with the customer who is dissatisfied, the departing employee can be asked about what gave rise to their resignation. This is best done while they are still working out their notice. If it is done in a friendly way, in private, and with the genuine desire to amend matters made fully apparent, the employee will respond. Once a person has tendered their resignation, there are no inhibitions left to plain speaking. There is nothing to lose by exposing the flaws in the system, or the thorn in the flesh. It is easier to plug a small leak than to stem a torrent.

Aggrieved people leave a company with no feeling of obligation or regret, and they can take valuable information about the company and its products, services and business methods to a competitor. This is something upon which no price can be placed. If warning signs are heeded, the loss might be contained. The leaver, suitably mollified, might even be prepared to keep the old employer's secrets safe.

Once the problem has been exposed, it must be visibly rectified and the remaining employees affected by it should be informed that the problem has been identified. They should also be told what steps are being taken to put it right. If the remaining employees concerned are consulted about what to do in order to remedy the situation, they will have no reason to complain about it themselves. If it is a major problem, it requires top management to intervene and to do so in a high-profile manner.

It is seen that human resources management is similar in many respects to all process and systems management. It is more difficult, due to the fact that human beings are all different, and they have lives outside the organisation. Their day-to-day involvement in making decisions that affect them and what they do within the company can bring about massive increases in output of service/quality improvements and ideas. Humans appreciate rewards, respond to motivation, have the ability to solve their own problems, run the organisation, and satisfy external and internal customers. They gain strength and effectiveness by teamwork. This gives them satisfaction in return. If the chain breaks down, and something interrupts the satisfaction exchange, employees leave the organisation and take valuable knowledge and experience with them, possibly to a competitor.

A wise manager looks behind the letter of resignation for the true reason why a valued and trusted employee is about to depart. Having found the problem, the manager tells the rest of the workforce that he knows about it and, unless it is very straightforward, asks them what should be done to set things right. The more involved and important that employees feel, the more willing they are to shoulder responsibility for forwarding the organisation's aims and goals.

People, like processes, need constant attention. All the steps in the processes of human resources management merit regular examination and should be utilised for the main goal of customer retention and ongoing quality/service improvements. Appraisals provide the basis for rewards for past performance as well as for setting future goals. As with other processes, these should be properly documented and monitored.

Summary

Every organisation requires people to work for it. The recruitment selection process is a critical step in fitting people to employment. People should be chosen, not simply for their qualifications and experience, but for their ability to become part of a team, to share knowledge and skills with others openly and frankly, and to work to achieve the company goals. Before anyone is interviewed for a position, the exact requirements of the job must be set down and explained to those who make the selection.

Employment is a two-way engagement, between employee and employer. Employees respond to being treated with respect and to being valued. They expect to be treated fairly and to be able to trust management, both at the top and at team level. They look for a career structure that will bring them job satisfaction and enhance their self-esteem. As they understand the company's culture, enjoy its training opportunities, experience its success and share in its rewards, they move into a new phase. They gain in standing in the organisation and become integrated into its culture and aspirations. They become self-motivating and feel competent. Their satisfaction flows over to the customer and is reflected in the company's profitability.

Employees who feel competent to perform and are happy with their colleagues and working environment are usually well disposed to be creative and enthusiastic. The ideal organisation forms one cohesive team, whose goal is service excellence. Employees who are happy at work are those who feel that their opinions matter and that their contribution is appreciated, not just by colleagues and managers, but also by customers.

A highly successful company, Hewlett Packard, surveys its entire workforce every two years and performs sample surveys every quarter. Like others who understand the importance of employee involvement, this company is sure that high levels of employee satisfaction will generate customer satisfaction, leading to customer retention and profitability. Hewlett Packard recognises that efficient processes are essential to its service delivery excellence, and the best way to assure good customer satisfaction and retention is to have people who are motivated to do a good job for the customer. Recruits are screened for that attitude. The organisation acknowledges all the key areas of the customer management integration framework, and considers that, at the end of the day, it is the people who count.

Staff who contribute to the setting of service goals, who are trained to achieve, who are expected to assess themselves on a regular basis, who feel that they are part of a happy, progressive, team, are satisfied. They pass on their joy and enthusiasm to customers and to one another. People form the backbone of company culture. If they are involved and happy, they are assets. If they are uninvolved and unhappy, the company suffers as much as they do.

For many companies, there is no overt link between employee and end user, due to the supply chain length. However, there is a link, and employees along the supply chain play their part in creating customer satisfaction. Everyone should be able to take a part in helping to further the company's aspirations, even when the goods and services are passed along the line.

Initially, remuneration is the carrot that catches the employee of the future. Working environment and perquisites act like glue, to hold them in place until they mature. Different companies employ various strategies to retain staff. The longer people stay with a company, the more valuable they become. It is a parallel that can be made with customers who purchase the product or service. Whether there is always a direct and measurable relationship between employee satisfaction and customer satisfaction, or between employee loyalty and customer loyalty, has yet to be proved.

It is indubitably the employees who make the difference between a company and its competitors. The more the employees understand about how the company integrates its framework for service excellence, the better they can cooperate with one another to achieve it; therefore, people yield the most benefit to a company from its overall investment in improvement.

Recruitment and training are expensive. If employee churn is high, there are serious problems within the company, which inevitably incur unnecessary costs in finding replacement staff, and training and integrating them. There is the knock-on effect of disgruntled employees, who are about to resign, infecting others with their negativity and persuading others to leave. For these reasons alone, any organisation that aims for maximum profitability will give close attention to staff recruitment, training and motivation. Some companies have a set of procedures, which are used to integrate newcomers, so that they start 'on message' as far as the organisation's core values and culture are concerned.

Employees are the seed corn of the business's future, and unless they are given every encouragement to grow, there will be no harvest. In this sense, the HR manager is the farmer, whose task is to select and tend the seeds, and encourage their growth. The responsibility that attends the role of HR manager is not always properly understood, but it is critical to the success of any organisation. It is his/her task to ensure that all parts of the company are under his/her supervision, as far as development, retention and satisfaction of its employees is concerned. It is the task of all managers to take the time to listen sympathetically to employees and take on board what they have to say about the job, the company and the products and services it supplies. Most employees consider this to be the key to their satisfaction and enjoyment of the job.

6

Training and Development

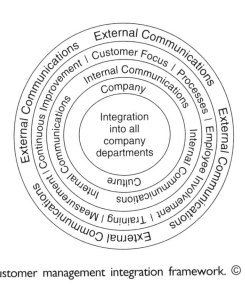

Figure 6.0 Customer management integration framework. © John A. Murphy 2005

The value and usefulness of the employees of a company lie in the skills and knowledge these people bring to the task they are required to perform. In most cases, skills and knowledge can be nurtured and grown, with the measurable benefit to the company from the employees' enhanced contribution to customer service, and benefit to the employee in increased job satisfaction arising from deeper involvement with the aspirations of the company towards its customers.

The customer management integration framework *puts training between employee involvement and measurement*. The following chapter describes the relationship between them.

In the previous chapter we spoke in general terms about the importance of training and development as part of staff deployment, and how teams and teamwork stimulate new ideas and more integrated work practices. In this chapter we take a closer look at training and development for individuals and teams. As with all the aspects of employment so far examined, training and development in this context form another process that has customer satisfaction and service as the primary goal. The responsibility for the training and development of people rests primarily with the director of human resources, or the equivalent. It is delegated through supervisory staff and on-the-job trainers, often with the assistance of outside consultants.

Many organisations have adopted the principles of *Investors in People* (*IIP*), the national quality standard for effective training and development of people to achieve business goals. Simply expressed, this standard is a process based on four key principles:

- Commitment to develop all employees to achieve business goals and targets.
- Reviewing regularly training and development needs in the context of the business.
- Action: taking relevant action to meet training and development needs throughout people's employment.
- Evaluating outcomes of training and development for individuals and the organisation as a basis for continuous improvement.

This IIP standard identifies the many and varied business gains to be made by its adoption. While some organisations have yet to be convinced about its claims, their competitors, who have adopted the standard, are leaving them far behind.

This chapter covers identification of training needs; competence-based training; service quality training; teamwork training; coaching; just-in-time training; and formal recognition.

There are Scrooges to be found in business, and these miserly people postulate that employees are an expense, which is to be kept to a bare minimum. Of course, employees are necessary to run an organisation, but cutting costs is not the way to maximise their profitability. Of course, training is expensive, it takes time and it is sometimes assumed that it is unnecessary by organisations whose attitude is, 'Our people are doing fine already, without any training.' This chapter takes a different view. No matter what other priorities seem more important, money spent on proper training for staff at all levels is the surest guarantee of reward. It should be taken seriously by those in authority within an organisation. The question is what training should be given and to whom?

In the introduction to his book, *The Learning Organisation*, Bob Garratt argues that it requires conscious and continuous learning between three groups to make an organisation simultaneously effective and efficient: the leaders who direct the enterprise, the staff who deliver the product or service, and the customers or consumers. Without this triangular, conscious learning on a regular and rigorous basis, the enterprise will die.

The IoD recognised its role in the learning process when they launched a tough, new, professional qualification – *The Chartered Director* in 1999 – as a measure of a director's understanding of the integrative nature of their work, which is truly to give direction and leadership to their organisation. Within the syllabus are embedded key principles such as *The Learning Organization* and *The Learning Board*. It is expected that, in the next decades, there will be evidence of a welcome and significant change in the mindset of directors, and in the importance of organisational learning, due to the numbers who have applied for training since the launch.

Employees are assets

In the same way as money invested properly will grow, investment in employees enables them to grow in value to an organisation. The investment in people and in providing them with the right type of training is expensive, but it yields astonishingly high interest. Anyone wishing to invest takes time to look for a good yield before putting money into anything. The larger the investment, the better the return one anticipates.

We understand already that loyal customers provide the best route to higher profits for an organisation, and that knowledge governs the choices to be made when we talk of investment in people. We have also seen that the relationship between employees and customers influences levels of satisfaction for both parties. Employees provide the service; customers who appreciate what they receive become loyal. This customer reaction, as we know, delights employees. Profits rise accordingly, and this should enable employers to pay higher salaries and to further improve service quality. The cycle is self-perpetuating, if it is properly constructed, monitored and guarded. It is, therefore, good business to enable all employees to enhance this relationship with customers, by all possible means. To this end, they must be substantially informed about all aspects of the product or service they are providing to internal and external customers. They should be provided with the skills and knowledge to give them the capability of effectively and consistently satisfying customers' varying expectations.

Previous chapters have demonstrated the reasons for, and methods to employ, in seeking to give the sort of quality service that attracts and retains customers. To skimp on training the very people who are expected to deliver that service quality, from the most junior to the most senior, renders all other initiatives worthless. To use a pelagic metaphor: if one sees the organisation as a net and the customer as the fish, the net must be strong at every part and regularly maintained, to keep the catch intact. Employee competence is one part of a company's strength. Service quality provision is the other.

There is always a payback

As companies started to invest financially in their people, people began to invest psychologically in their companies. Forward-looking and successful companies have taken one step further. They have coupled their training and development initiatives with a restructured hierarchy of power. The new ideas incorporate horizontal rather than vertical empowerment. These changes entail people working in teams and groups within a network of trust-based relationships. It takes time to redesign radically a corporate structure and yet maintain cohesion. The capable people that are necessary to run a modern corporation have to be wooed and won, and they expect a firm commitment from employers if they are to respond with whole-hearted participation in achieving the corporate ambitions. They expect to be decision-makers and are willing to take responsibility for what they do.

Delegation of more power to frontline staff, who are often some of the lowest paid employees, to ensure their development of service quality, and to get rapid feedback of customers' changing needs, represents a major shift in the traditional hierarchy of power.

The coming decade will see further and more rapid changes. Responses have to be immediate. Teams of motivated employees, who share common aims and who have made that vital psychological investment in their company, will be able to cope. Managers will give way more and more to leaders. Leaders work with, across and through teams and departments, liaise with outsiders, give guidance in problem solving, facilitate work processes and grease the bearings of the employee engine that runs the company. Technological change also will not stop now. People have to be trained to meet that type of change as and when it happens. There must be anticipation of and preparation for change.

We are still in the process of refining organisational learning at the day-to-day, operational level. When we include the new thinking on leadership skills of formulating purpose, vision and values, developing strategic thinking skills, more effective risk assessment, and greater clarity about responsibility, a powerful vision of the twenty-first century organisation begins to emerge. The organisation will, in future, be driven by regular and rigorous learning, particularly through continuous, open, critical review and debate, at all levels, as part of its normal work.

Before exploring the other aspects of training, it is worth looking more closely at the roles of teams and leaders, since they are the future. Teams of tomorrow are not simply those people engaged on a process or stage of a process, whose only consideration is his, or her, own small function. The teams that matter and that are worth developing are an entirely new style of group. They do not appear by chance. They grow, like a tree, from the basic seed. Management selects certain people for a specific area of responsibility. Note that there is no longer any mention of 'task' in the old sense of the word. Like anything that is worth having, the acquisition of teams and team leaders is far from simple, but there are basic rules for its success.

Team establishment

The process of team establishment is not something to happen overnight. It takes time and is not without teething problems. Teams are made up of individuals; those same awkward human beings to be found everywhere. It takes considerable expertise to mould them into tight-knit units. Before thinking in detail about training for teams and leaders, therefore, it is worth examining the process by which they are established and organised.

Stage 1 – Forming

Management, first having carefully selected what is hoped to be a good mix of people, and appointed a leader, leaves them to become acquainted with one another and with the work they are expected to accomplish. Team members, while assessing one another, will also try to find how far they can provoke the team leader, in a subconscious attempt to set limits to his/her authority. During this exploration period, they will seek to define or redefine the task in their own terms, and decide how it will be accomplished.

The team will also be trying to decide what acceptable group behaviour is, and how to cope with group problems. Next, the team has to decide what information it must gather in order to perform the task. The pendulum swings the other way, once the initial stage is passed, and some people might begin to discuss abstract issues and concepts, while others in the team might become impatient with these discussions. Splits develop. Matters irrelevant to the task are likely to take up discussion time, and this can lead to complaints about the organisation and perceived barriers to performance of the task.

Team leaders, who ought to be aware of the likely distractions at the formation stage of a team, should provide structure and focus. This is done by holding regular meetings and assisting in task and role clarification. Each member should be encouraged to participate, but no one should be allowed to become dominant. The leader should help people to learn about the work areas, expertise and preferred working methods of other team members.

Information relevant to the task and the team should be shared, and members should be encouraged to ask questions of the leader and of one another. Basic ground rules should be agreed. The leader should use team-building exercises. Things sometimes become worse before they improve.

Stage 2 – Storming

Having overcome the first hurdle and started to examine the task, teams move into what has become known as the storming stage. The leader will know when this happens because members begin to argue among themselves, even when they agree on the central issue. Defensiveness and competition is the mood of the individuals. Team members start to question the wisdom of those who selected the project and, worse still, the team that has to implement it. Next, unrealistic goals might be set and this would lead to concern about excessive work. Then, there will be incidents of disunity, tension, even jealousy. At this stage, the team can make itself, or break itself.

The helpful leader encourages joint problem solving and makes members give their reasons why an idea is useful, or suggest how to improve it. The expression of different viewpoints should be encouraged. The group decision-making process should be examined, and the decision-making responsibility shared appropriately. Members ought to be encouraged to say how they feel, as well as what they think, if they obviously have feelings about an issue. Adequate resources to do the job must be provided where possible. If there is a problem with provision of resources, it should be explained.

Stage 3 – Norming

Although this word 'norming' is not found in the dictionary, it perfectly describes the stage when teams realise that they can complete the task and achieve. They become friendlier to one another, engage in discussion of the team's approaches, they confide in one another. A common spirit and sense of purpose emerges. They begin to maintain the ground rules and any defined boundaries (the norms). They start to devote their time and energy to completion of, rather than discussion of, the task.

The leader can now talk openly about his/her own issues and concerns, allow group members to manage agenda items, give and request feedback, negative and positive, with the group, and assign challenging issues such as budget allocation for consensus decisions. This is the stage at which the leader can delegate as much as the team can handle, with help where required.

Stage 4 – Performing

When the team settles down to the task, there will be noticeable differences in the individual members. They will be familiar with the strengths and weaknesses of the team, they will feel a greater attachment to the team and this will enable them to work openly through team problems. They will have become interdependent and happy to share skills and experiences. They have rehearsed, now they are ready to perform.

Leaders whose teams are ready to perform, look for challenging goals, and see that they are jointly set. They find new ways to increase the team's scope. They question assumptions and traditional ways of behaving. The leader develops mechanisms for ongoing review by the group, and openly recognises each member's contribution to the common aims. The leader's task is to develop members to their fullest potential through task assignments and feedback.

This is a type of training that will be new to many managers. It requires careful consideration of the tasks and the people ideally best suited to accomplish them, if teams are to be strong enough to weather the storm and grow to perform. Selection of team leaders is also highly critical. They are both the accelerator and the brake on the team. Teams need to be urged forward, but there will be times when there is need for a brake to be applied. Training for leadership, then, is a prime requirement, if teams are to become the powerhouses of an organisation. Managers for whom this is a new and radical concept are advised to seek professional advice and help before they embark on recruitment and training for teamwork. This brings us back to the basic matter of training for the future.

Rapid changes in technology, in marketing, in advertising opportunities, in combinations with other producers or service providers to give superb service quality, all impose new rules. These indicate that training and development are not investments to be made once and then relegated to the filing room. It must be a dynamic, ongoing, anticipatory preparation for the future, and the people who have to face that future must at all times be equipped to fulfil the roles the organisation has for them. An investor takes a long-term view of the money invested. As with the saver, so it is with the corporation. People are the assets; their training and development create the yield.

Identification of training needs

With horizontal sectioning of organisations, managers are not about to be made redundant. Where this restructuring has already taken place, they have become facilitators and example setters. They, more than any other employees, should receive retraining for their new role. In terms of training programmes, they provide the impetus, the wherewithal and the opportunities. They select the employees who will move the organisation ahead.

Until people are technically qualified to do their jobs, there is no possibility of them being able to concentrate on service quality. Therefore, the first aspect of any training must be focused on competence. Within a large organisation, no two people have the same levels of competence. Even if they have equal 'paper' qualifications, their experience might be unequal. For this reason, training needs will vary from person to person.

As new technology is introduced into teams and departments, skill levels must be improved to take advantage of it and to maximise employee output. Technology is the means whereby organisations take the lead over competitors, but this only happens when employees are capable of using it fully. Identification of training needs has an extra dimension. It highlights existing skills and where they are not being fully exploited.

Individuals should be assessed individually for training, and personal schedules designed to meet their needs. A sequence of revision and review should be established, documented and followed. At an employee's appraisal session the opportunity arises for an assessment of the success or otherwise of the training schedule, and for its amendment, if this is demonstrated to be necessary. To be effective, measurable standards must be set against which performance can be accurately measured.

Competence-based training

Competence-based training, especially for graduate-entry employees, might seem superfluous, but new technology and new methods of doing business require ongoing training at every level. The learning curve is continuous and should not be broken. No one can know, without proper training, all there is to know, when change is so rapid and so revolutionary. Alongside their culinary skills, canteen staff should understand about health and hygiene and balanced diet, about special requirements for employees with health problems or religious dietary needs, and about budgeting. An outbreak of food poisoning and its consequences for the organisation would be extremely grave. The packer must be able to handle the latest tools and materials of the trade, understand how to pack goods safely and avoid unnecessary weight and wastage. Every team, at every level, has something new to learn and practise, and has a customer, internal or external, to satisfy and delight.

Many employees are capable of much better performances than they have been giving, or have been expected to give. Training enhances performance alongside provision of greater job satisfaction.

If promotion or increased remuneration follows, employees quickly see the advantage to themselves in following training schedules and utilising what they have learnt. Job satisfaction and pride in what they do will follow.

Until training needs have been properly assessed, no scheme is of value. Management at top level must understand that targeted training, for individuals and teams, with quantifiable results and employee involvement in design and implementation, is the surest way for their organisation to surge ahead.

Measurement of results

Once the process has been started, how does one know if it is being done properly and producing the required results? Is it possible to measure the outcomes, and is it worth doing so? Why measure anything, and if you measure, what do you measure? The answer is, it all depends on what you decide you need to measure and why.

A man undertaking a very long walk will first study a map. He will work out how many miles he has to travel, then pace out his journey and check progress against milestones, in order to conserve energy and organise appropriate meal breaks and overnight stops. He has his goal and he knows the route to it. He plans ahead, so that he arrives at a hotel before midnight and travels along clearly defined paths. He knows his walking pace and he will recognise the destination when he gets there. He takes sufficient money to pay for his needs along the way. These are the important aspects of his journey. To count how many photographs he takes of the scenery and how many times he has to use his umbrella is an irrelevance. Similarly, measurement of anything should follow the same rules as apply to the walker. If they are relevant to the ultimate goal, let them be measured. If not, they are to be ignored.

An organisation might ask itself what it currently measures.

- Are there clear 'top-down' requirements?
- Are there measurable improvement goals?
- Are there specific process outputs?

- Are there numerical targets and milestones?
- What customer-related measures are in place to clarify requirements and to receive ongoing feedback?
- Are there process performance measures which are focused on key points?
- And are these clear, simple and relevant?

From the 'bottom-up' aspect, employees are concerned with:

- What measures of achievements focused on work teams, compared to targets, and visible to team members are there?
- Does everyone in the organisation know what is being measured and why?

Finally, in general terms, does your current approach provide you with the answers you need? Unless an organisation knows how far along the road it has travelled and where it is going, it can only make uninformed guesses. There is a need for a map, a goal and milestones along the way. Rather than allowing itself to be swamped by unnecessary data, sensible management chooses critical criteria by which to assess progress and uses only those criteria for its measurements.

The logical sequence of measurement follows established guidelines. First, the objectives should be defined. Link measures to what you have to achieve. Develop non-financial measures and convert to money where it makes sense. Ask yourself, what are your customers telling you? What are customers' requirements and what is their response to your measures? How can you anticipate changing needs quickly? Can your process meet customers' requirements? Is it delivering? After delivery, did it fulfil the customers' requirements? What do your employees (internal customers) have to say?

Measurement of what is wrong is as useful as measurement of what is right. Focus on what is important for customers, define your priorities for developing or maintaining a competitive edge and identify the milestones that will tell you if you are on track for your destination. Encourage teams and individuals to create their own measures and track their own performance. Make the data visible and timely. Be consistent in what you do.

Competence training, then, concerns itself with how people do their work. As far as this type of training is concerned, an organisation should be confident that everyone within it knows and understands what they need to do. People should have the right tools/equipment and information they need to do their job, and they should all have been trained sufficiently to work effectively and utilise all their potential. Finally, management should be sure that its teams are organised to tackle problems and react swiftly to unforeseen events.

Service quality training

Having assessed competence training needs, implemented a schedule of training and set up the control mechanisms to monitor results, and ensured that every employee is qualified to perform his/her task, the next consideration should be service quality training. With the present move towards team-based work units, with teams rather than managers responsible for every stage of all a team's processes and for setting and meeting targets, service quality training is essentially a team-training requirement, but one to which individuals also need to be totally committed. People, team leaders and teams must be allowed the leeway necessary for manoeuvre and innovation. After initial training, this becomes a continuous improvement process. It should follow the discipline applied to problem solving in such a way that improvement follows. The four steps are PLAN–DO–CHECK–ACT. This provides a structured framework for improvement. It goes hand in hand with empowerment.

When we looked at empowerment as a general concept, there was an obvious downside, for instance, in cases where incompetent or lazy managers expected managerial work to be done by employees, and when things went wrong, the managers passed the blame down the line, or, conversely, took credit where it was not due to them. Empowerment, in a horizontally structured organisation, leaves no room for buck-passing down the line. In fact, the use of the word 'down', in the sense of power cascading downwards, will soon fade from business jargon. There will be new management structures where power flows outwards rather than down. The fully trained and empowered team members are the constraints under which such lateral empowerment operates best. To them belong both blame and credit, and they bear the responsibility for righting wrongs and correcting mistakes.

When we looked at team composition and development and the role of team leaders, the types of training each would require has far more to do with service quality issues than with the specific task they are to perform, but there is some blurring at the edges. In the case of an established and functioning team, competence and service quality become one issue. Ongoing training, therefore, has to address both aspects of the issue.

Like competence training, service quality training should be applied to every employee. The van driver must be tidy, polite and helpful to customers; he must be punctual, handle goods carefully and respectfully and project the company's image of itself, in exactly the same way as frontline staff and top management. Every employee should, cheerfully and without the need for instructions, keep the workplace clean and tidy, behave decorously and offer help to others when there is pressure. Every little step towards excellence is part of the service chain and should be encouraged and applauded.

Irrespective of the industrial sector, all employees should receive specific training in service quality, in addition to the product-specific training they receive. This will, of necessity, include:

- Training on interpersonal skills.
- Listening techniques.
- Communication.
- Appreciation of service standards (e.g. returning phone calls within a specified time).
- Responsiveness.
- Empathy.

Within teams, the greatest thrust forward is usually to be found where there are the proper foundations in place and the organisation gives whole-hearted support. Training of leaders and teams for service quality often requires specialist help to get started. Leaders should be taught to understand the mechanism of the team but also learn how to control and direct it and how to get the most from every member.

Teamwork training

Outside consultants who train newly appointed leaders and teams for service quality have their own methods, but most engage trainees in some form of participation in theoretical models. The use of role-play, or of focus groups, to reveal members' characteristics and to discover and solve theoretical problems in work processes is a useful method. With skilled leadership, teams can pass through the four development stages more rapidly than would otherwise be true, and after training, they should be almost ready to perform without further urging.

Teams usually include a selection of personality types. The training identifies these recognisable categories. Some are natural leaders; others have innate loyalty to colleagues and enjoy the closeness of the team. Others have problem-solving skills and some are natural communicators. A few are by nature loners but they can work with other teams and people towards organisational goals, and some need a chance to express their creativity. Service quality training helps to identify the structure of teams, so that members learn what each person has to contribute, over and above basic competence skills, and reveals possible weaknesses. This knowledge breeds mutual respect and trust. Training also builds a strong bond between the team members that outlasts setbacks, difficulties and internal differences.

If an organisation manages complete horizontal layering, teams see themselves as part of a whole, an element within a larger team that encompasses the whole organisation. There is no envy where all are equal and all know exactly what is expected of them. In a tug-of-war against the competition, everybody on the rope has a critical part to play in winning the game. There will emerge from integration of an exchange of information and ideas, innovation and problem solving across layers and throughout the organisation.

It is important for trainers to ensure that teams interrelate with one another in clearly defined ways and for specific purposes. This means writing reports. Reports are intended to be read. Before a report is written, the readership should be identified and the purpose and scope of the report determined. Reports should be brief, clear, accurate and simple. Reports should always be signed and dated.

Snakes in the grass, or master spies

Whatever name they work under, the technical competence and service quality training of this team's members should be of the very best and their rewards should be proportional to their input of useful material. The team leader will be someone with extra special qualities. Many companies leave this aspect of modern business out of their calculations, to their ultimate cost, or rely on trade magazines to supply the latest news to anyone with the inclination to browse their pages. If the work of these observers is seen as yet another process and governed by the general rules that apply to all processes, including the documentation and report rules, the benefits are immediately obvious, both in terms of production improvement and for service quality. These are the people who should attend trade exhibitions and study the latest offerings in their own field, and compare prices and quality. They also have an opportunity to talk *anonymously* with competitors and customers and obtain useful, frank, free feedback and information. They can provide answers to those questions that management always wanted to ask, but never discovered how or whom to ask.

Play fair with employees

Management, to benefit most from all training initiatives, but especially so in the case of service quality, should recognise that effort deserves reward. To train someone to do their work well and to strive for maximum service quality is good. Employees who respond positively need to know how they benefit, as well as how the organisation benefits. The organisation has to treat them justly and offer them advancement. It has to shelter them from the brutal impact of economic storms and technological change, and it has to show them that they are valued and important. It has to be willing to maintain regular training programmes for everyone, and it should document and assess the outcomes of these on a regular and mutually understood basis.

There are certain major organisations who offer new skills training to anyone who wants it. This has the advantage of enriching the overall skills level of the workforce and facilitates job transfer, to meet demand at peak times and places. One other advantage is that employees, whom the present job no longer satisfies, are encouraged to stay within the organisation, where their service quality training is not wasted and where their competence in another field, thanks to training, is already assured. It is always better, cheaper and more satis-factory to swap employees around and broaden their experience within the organisation than to let them go and employ newcomers.

Thus, we can see that training is certainly another work process, with two objectives. The first is to give all employees competence to perform their tasks, and the second is to provide them with motivation to focus on service quality. It requires total management commitment, it should have written procedures, and it should involve every employee in the standards set and the methods used in training. It requires measurement against known criteria and it should be capable of cost analysis against long-term profit gain. Having set up the training modules and linked them to job categories, newcomers to the organisation can be processed routinely and their competence assessed according to the work they are to undertake.

There will, of course, be times and situations where constructive help is needed in a particular work situation, but where training in the broad sense of the word is not appropriate. This happens when an employee requires to be extended, to develop his/her potential further. This is where a more experienced employee, or a team leader, might act as a coach.

Time and effort can be saved with the LATCH method of training (Figure 6.1). This means starting at the top, with managers, and training them. They, in their turn pass on what they have learnt to the next layer of the company, who take it on in the same way.

Coaching

There is a difference between learning how to do something and regular coaching in the practice of that something. One can, for instance, study the theory of soccer or cricket until one knows all there is to know about the game, but one cannot play unless one trains and

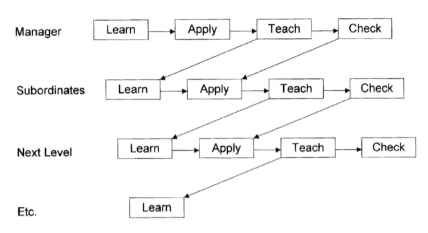

Figure 6.1 LATCH cascade training concept
Source: S.T. Microelectronics

practises, not just once a year, but every week, and the motivation behind coaching comes from the coach. The coach, team leader, or fellow member of the team, notices that there is a chance for improvement, and helps the person who needs coaching to increase their scope or improve their performance. This is done by means of direct discussion, questioning and by guided activities.

The coaching process

Coaches should be taught how to approach the person to be coached, in order to inculcate the right attitude to what will follow. In outline, coaching starts with identification of the topic for the coaching process. It must be agreed with the person to be coached, and the objective for the coaching identified. Means should then be employed to promote discovery and set parameters.

The coach should prepare a schedule of what is to be done and how. Only when everything necessary for the coaching session is prepared and to hand should the coach begin.

The person being coached will probably feel apprehensive, so that a good coach will immediately involve the person in the coaching.

If this is handled tactfully, the trainee will be responsive. The coach can confirm with the trainee the objective for the coaching and set the standards to be reached. The more the trainee is able to participate in the initial part of the coaching and understand its importance, the more likely it is that he/she will be interested and cooperative.

If the coaching is to extend the employee's role, the coach might ask the coached person to think through what can be done to achieve the objectives mutually agreed. The person should be encouraged to formulate answers to questions like the following:

- What options have you thought of concerning how to do this task?
- What would be the first step?
- What are the consequences for staffing, budget, other departments etc.?
- How have others tackled this in the past?
- What is the pay-off/cost of each of these options?
- Which option do you think is most viable?

The trainee should continue to think about and practise the task, until it can be performed correctly and safely. Suggest that trainees talk their way through the process. This helps to consolidate in the mind what has just been taught.

The coach should not offer advice or help to the coached. The idea is to encourage them to think for themselves, so parameters should be set. Establish exactly what needs to be done and by when. Ensure that the coached person knows how far he/she can go without reference back to the coach, and never assume that he/she understands this otherwise.

Human beings are unpredictable, can be awkward and stubborn, or just obstructive. If you are the coach and you authorise someone to do agreed work or research, tell others, so that the person being coached has a smooth passage and does not meet barriers to cooperation. Give the coached person the resources and administrative support they require to carry out the task. Record what a trainee has achieved and how safely and speedily they can now perform the task.

Benefits from coaching

Coaching helps to improve performance and employee development, it is important in achieving empowerment, it improves morale and self-confidence, and it releases management time.

Training costs are sometimes wasted

Yes, managers *sometimes* have a point when they see training as a waste of time and money. This is only true under certain circumstances. The blame for those circumstances arising can often be laid at management's door. There will always be times when the old is overtaken by the new before training in use of the old is complete. This might be due to the adoption of new technology, or new products or services coming on line. It could happen when companies are taken over by others, or when they combine with others to make a value-added product or service. None of these things happens overnight, but they can arrive at short notice. There is a way to cope. It is known as just-in-time training.

Just-in-time training

This is reaction to events for which precise prediction and preparation were impossible. The idea follows from the Kanban system of material and production control. Kanban's basic premise is 'Buy one – Order one – Make one', and it is used to ensure that the customer draws product through the system. Kanban maximises use of labour, materials and production. Your fax roll, petrol gauge or box of envelopes, for instance, might have a marker to indicate that supply is getting low and it is time to replace or re-order. The marker is there so that you need not carry stocks of the items, but have a warning of when it is time to obtain replacements. Just-in-time training is similar, in that it is demand led.

Every training programme should have just enough spare capacity to react swiftly to surprise demands for competence skills. It is unlikely that the whole workforce will need extra training when the unexpected happens. At first, anyway, only those who need hands-on experience require retraining. If the need is shown to be more extensive at a later date, the essential training can be incorporated by coaching during routine work processes, or slotted into the established training schedules.

There might be times when a company decides to re-equip from top to bottom with new machinery, as happens in printing companies, for example, where bottlenecks in work flow would arise from partial re-equipment. In this case, with foresight, staff training can begin at the manufacturer's premises, before the machines are installed. Most major machine producers have some form of in-house training for future operators. There are obvious benefits when manufacturers train customers/operators on new equipment. Any problems can be tackled at source, and the trainer, on the supplier's payroll, will be enthusiastic and knowledgeable.

Just-in-time training applies, too, when an unforeseen training need is identified within the existing work processes of an organisation. If coaching is too narrow to handle it, the general training programme has to be enlarged and the necessary training incorporated into future training schedules. Every training need that is identified after a programme has been designed and implemented must be integrated swiftly, documented and absorbed, and be subject to the same conditions of employee involvement as the other training schedules. There has, also, to be something in it for employees, if they are to cooperate in training schemes.

Formal recognition

If staff work hard to learn from their training and show willingness to undertake the additional responsibilities that come afterwards, there should be a formal recognition of their efforts. A good approach to this is for them to take a short examination at the end of a course. This can be constructed to show what has been learnt and how it will be utilised. This latter aspect is particularly effective in proving to employees that what they have learnt is valuable to the organisation as well as to them. Some organisations use modules for training and the results obtained after completion of each module are accumulated and might eventually lead to an NVQ, diploma or a Master's degree. Salaries should also reflect educational achievements. All achievement should be highly visible and publicly acclaimed, at the annual dinner, perhaps, or at an award ceremony. This will encourage others to strive for improvement, and it gives trainers satisfaction because they had a major role in the successes of their trainees.

In the days of master craftspeople, there was a seven-year apprenticeship and the apprentice, having qualified, would be entitled to regard himself/herself as a master craftsperson. The pace of change today is so fast that the long apprenticeship is a thing of the past. The demands made on a modern workforce, however, far surpass anything that would have been anticipated 50 years ago. People come to a job, today, with certain formal qualifications, or having attained certain educational standards, but what they actually do when they start work cannot be learnt in advance. For this reason, companies that value their employees and managers offer them ongoing 'apprenticeships' and ensure that they are always fit for the job.

How is the person at the top affected?

Managers currently face innumerable major challenges. They have need of an astonishing range of skills, from personnel selection, to statistical analysis, operational research and company law, cost analysis and accounting, market research, new product design, failure mode and critical analysis, not to mention computer skills and database management and so on. If they begrudge training for their staff, how necessary do they regard it for themselves? Too many managers came into business from university, with a degree that had nothing to do with business at all, or might just have touched on company law, perhaps. Training, like other work processes, requires total commitment from senior managers. They, too, need ongoing, structured, tested and appraised training schedules, and their time spent in training will, of necessity, be longer than that spent by someone lower down the line, due to the complexity of their tasks.

Managers as trainers

When outside consultants have done the initial training, the appropriate next step is to utilise line managers to deliver skill-management sessions. The manager should be a role model as far as learning goes, and demonstrate by example that learning is just as important as doing. Managers must encourage and support learning by acting as facilitators and allocating time and resources to the process. There is no better way to keep training relevant. Managers engaged in training others, are training themselves and learning to practise what they preach. They know their people and can deal with more of them faster than outside consultants could. It sends a clear message to all employees that skill development is important. Managers are best placed to provide follow through and on-the-job coaching. The use of line managers to develop skills among staff in their own areas hastens the overall skills development of the organisation as a whole.

Managers, then, have a vital role in training, skill development and in impressing the organisation's vision into the hearts and minds of employees. Line managers need to be taught how to do it before they can demonstrate to others.

Training customers

So far, we have mentioned consumers as part of the learning triangle proposed by Bob Garratt, but we have not discussed here specifically how and by whom customers are to be trained. Customers are not expected to demonstrate the skills of management and employees in the organisation that they patronise, but the effect of that in-house training builds certain expectations in the consumer and teaches the organisation's people to *satisfy those expectations*. This is the main plank of *consumer* training. Previous experience of, or information about, an organisation's image, reputation and products or services are the textbooks from which the customer learns what to expect. The discussion of how to create service excellence, which forms the background to this book, indicates how customers are to be trained in what to expect, and to be satisfied. Failure of one side of the *training for satisfaction* triangle causes the collapse of the whole structure.

New products, new technologies, new demands and new thinking, underline the need for training for improvement to be continuous and rigorous. Customers' demands and organisations' methods of meeting those demands prohibit any slackening of the learning process. To visualise the three elements of production and consumption as a triangle clarifies the integrated nature of training and underlines the need to keep the three parts moving forward as one.

Summary

Having discovered that training is similar to other processes and requires the same circumstances to prevail and the same single-minded attitude to customers if it is to be satisfactory, we can summarise this chapter briefly. Once again, the message is clear: everybody, from top to bottom, left to right, needs to be involved. There is a universal need for ongoing training and development, and those with most experience should be encouraged to pass on their knowledge and the benefits of their experience to others down the line. Training is used to improve competence at the task and to continue to improve service quality. Whatever it costs, it is a good and necessary investment and will bring in handsome dividends. The old proverb, 'Look after the pennies and the pounds will take care of themselves,' has become, 'Look after the employees and the employees will take care of the customers.'

In this connection, the rapidity of change in the modern business environment, the immediate availability of information via the Intranet, and expansion of air travel, all make it necessary to consider how best to make an immediate and appropriate response to any perceived training need. Increased mobility across international borders brings with it a need for training in how to behave properly in other countries, how to communicate effectively in languages other than one's own, and how to handle unfamiliar currencies and trading habits. Training affects management as much as it does the run of employees, and especially frontline people.

Well-trained, service-quality focused staff allow organisations the flexibility and opportunities for improved productivity and service that yield customer satisfaction. This, in turn, yields employee satisfaction. Employees will expect to be able to continue giving and receiving satisfaction, in exactly the same way as customers expect to continue to receive and give it. As standards rise, employees and customers grow accustomed to them. To keep the one aspect healthy, the other aspect needs constant nourishment. Ongoing training of employees, in improved competence and in service quality, meets the aspirations and expectations of both employees and customers. This situation brings in the greatest profits to the organisation and does most harm to its competitors. This, in its turn, enables the organisation to increase the rewards it offers to its best performers.

Action on training and development for the improvement of employees will include performance reviews and appraisals, evaluation of results before and after training courses, employee opinion surveys of training need and provision, surveys on the effectiveness of training, qualifications and certifications obtained and the anecdotes and testimonials that accrue from training and development. Management action should be geared to cover these factors.

There is another aspect of training that is coming increasingly to the fore: training customers. The organisation that has regular discussion with its customers, and involves its employees, at all levels, in the exchange, is also aware of what competitors in the field are offering, or are about to offer. This enables the company to inform those customers who matter most about what to expect from the organisation in the future, and suggest how its offering might be better than the competitors' goods or services. This form of training is as important as employee training. Customer development, based on a frank and open exchange of information between customer and company, is what informs future product and service enhancement, and improvement in design. It is also the way in which problems can be explored and rectified quickly. The more that the employees, who have been taught this lesson, participate in communication with the customer, the greater the payback in customer satisfaction and profitability.

To expend time, money and labour on any development, without knowing that the outcome is desired by the customer, is to pour money down the drain and give competitors a huge advantage. Customer training, therefore, includes training them to pass back vital information about current product and service, as well as the desired product and service of the future. When employees understand this, they are able to facilitate the information exchange, and they understand what changes the company makes, in order to implement customer service quality expectations. Training and skills enhancement of employees, therefore, is always a worthwhile investment of time and money.

7

Measurement

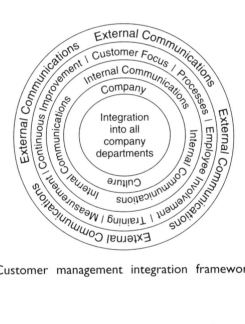

Figure 7.0 Customer management integration framework. © John A. Murphy 2005

Measurement is the process whereby we ensure that supply matches demand, that endeavour reaches targets, and that there is a mutually acceptable standard that can be applied to our exchanges with one another. We measure the physical and mental growth of our children by means of continuous measurement against many standards. We measure things every day of our lives, consciously or unconsciously.

Measurement undertaken for a purpose leads to action. This applies in business as much as in anything else. Before we purchase wallpaper, we measure the walls we wish to paper, and we accept that there is a standard length and width for a roll of wallpaper, so that we know how many rolls to purchase, and, from the instructions on the packet, we know how much adhesive we need and how to prepare it. We measure, then, to ensure a level playing field, to avoid argument, as a tool for making comparisons, to ensure economical use of time and materials, and to provide industry standards for the benefit of users.

This chapter concerns itself with organisations that measure, what they measure, why they measure and how they measure, and it discusses setting benchmarks against which to measure. Top management sets the targets for measurement, and managers and supervisors provide the raw data for the reports.

At this stage, it is time to look again at the customer management integration framework diagram that encapsulates the whole of this book. From the outside circle comes the basic outline of the framework, and it consists entirely of *external communications*, from and to the customer, from and to the company. Within this we have the second circle, containing the main ingredients of the chapters of the book. These form a closed circle. For convenience, but arbitrarily, for our starting point we can take *customer focus*, followed by *processes*, then *employee environment*, *training* and *measurement*, followed by *continuous improvement*.

External communications govern the shape of all these ingredients for customer service, and they are all directly linked to one another and to the external communication process. Within this second circle lies one further catch-all element: a third circle of *internal communications*. This, again, impinges upon and is governed by all parts of the second circle. Finally, at the very heart of the framework lies the *company culture*, upon which all the other circles are centred. The framework is complete when all facets of its construction are fully integrated. How is this harmony recognisable?

The answer lies with one subject on our second circle yet to be explored in detail, and this is *measurement*. A company that strives for improvement can only establish whether it is making progress in the right direction when it couples improvement with measurement. The processes it undertakes during production, administration and delivery form part of service quality issues, and these, therefore, should be subjected to regular measurement, from which action must follow for there to be logic behind the measuring processes. The success or otherwise of the action is itself a matter for measurement. First, we might consider the flow pattern from the first steps we mentioned and what might be measured.

We thought, early on, about definition and acquisition of a customer base – *segmentation*. The next step was to define the key quality indicators, from the customers' standpoint, and link them to the business objectives. This led us to study processes. Next, we saw that it was necessary to train quality review teams. Employees are taught to conduct quality reviews of their own work areas and to react to immediate customer needs. The results of quality reviews are analysed, and reports presented to management. Steps are taken to respond to customer needs. Finally, customer needs and the action plans to meet them are communicated throughout the organisation and to customers. This is all evident from the framework, which also shows clearly how every part is dependent upon and directly related to every other part.

Thus, we recognise that measurement must take into account every part of the framework. External communication is the source from which a company obtains the views, feelings and needs of its selected customer base. Only when accurate measurement of these is taken can a company take the necessary steps to meet the needs, understand the feelings and appreciate the views of its customers, and make known to them in return what the company has to offer. The company desires to give total satisfaction to its customers, from which follows employee involvement, empowerment and satisfaction. This is an ascending spiral and it works when there is continuing improvement in customer service quality, in processes, in training, in customer focus and in employee involvement. As customer satisfaction grows, it carries employee satisfaction with it. Employee satisfaction generates customer satisfaction, and so on *ad infinitum*. The rates at which these things happen and the consistency with which they happen can and should be measured.

Benchmarking

In the field of service quality, in contrast to product quality and employee performance, finding ways to make accurate measurements of quantifiable areas sometimes presents difficulties for managers. There is one tool that often helps them to perform this task, and it is benchmarking. The idea of benchmarking, in the business forum, is for non-competing companies to compare notes on the ways in which they successfully measure and perform, and see if there are any ideas that can be copied or adapted. This interchange of ideas between companies can be beneficial to both parties and stimulate yet more ideas and suggestions. Imitation is, as they say, the sincerest form of flattery.

Always measure customer reaction

We have already looked at some of the ways by which customer needs and basic requirements can be explored, and experience shows that the closer the interaction and communication between the organisation and its customers, the more profitable and enduring the relationship between them. Everything an organisation does, no matter how trivial, should relate directly to external communication. For this reason, customer reaction and expectation in every sphere should be monitored closely in ongoing surveys, focus groups, face-to-face discussion, post-purchase questionnaires, follow-up of complaint handling, and by any other means that have been found effective. The objective of all businesses is the generation of profit, and the purpose of all measurement is to see how well the organisation behaves, in all parts of the framework, towards this one end.

In a CMLG (2002) report, *Building Customer Capital*, there is an 11-point ladder illustrating what the authors describe as a best practice creation process. It is shown in Figure 7.1.

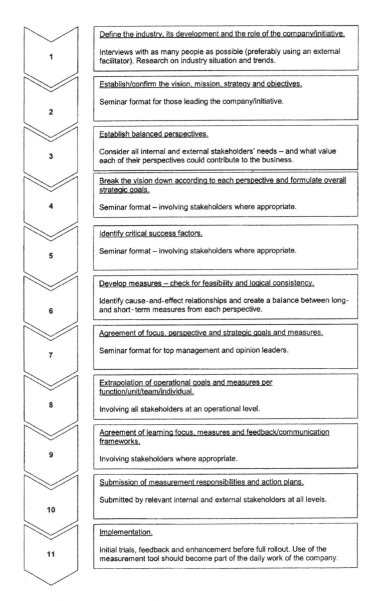

Figure 7.1 Best practice creation process
Source: CMLG Manchester Business School. © 2002

Measurement tool creation

Before a company chooses what, when and why to measure, certain questions pertaining to relevance need to be asked, in order to create a measurement tool. Measurements either waste time and money, or they lead to greater profitability. The management of measurement tools, as with all aspects of management, is to keep the organisation on track towards increasing profitability. The questions to answer at the outset are:

- How does each measurement relate back to the corporate mission?
  How do the measures taken relate back to added value for the company?

- What is expected by way of a result from this measurement?
  Can the rewards of taking these measures be quantified?

- Is there an interrelationship between each performance driver and an outcome measure?

- What are the performance drivers?
  Performance drivers are those aspects of management already dealt with in previous chapters: customer focus, processes and systems, and employee involvement.

- Has each measurement been clearly defined?
  The outcomes should be measured in rising levels of satisfaction for employees and customers, in company growth and increased profitability, in better products or services, and in contented shareholders.

- Is there a balance between short-term and long-term measures?
  Long-term measures will cover such things as expansion of premises, re-tooling, recruitment of an increased workforce, take-over of other companies, major expenditure of all types, and this has to be set against the thousands of small, day-to-day steps that can be taken for immediate and short-term results.

- Is there a balance of perspective between employee, management team, customer, partner, supplier and shareholder?
  Satisfaction for all parties will derive in part from different sources; everyone has to be included in the measurement process.

- How were employees and customers involved?
  Having measured, management has to think about how to communicate and integrate its findings and measure the effect of them on all parties involved in the measuring process.

Landhotel Schindlerhof, a prestigious hotel and conference facility in Nuremberg, has its own system of satisfaction measurement. This hotel considers that a customer has made a complaint if he/she has not put a check mark against the highest evaluation, on the hotel's feedback cards. For every customer who takes the time and trouble to make a specific comment, even if it just a 'thank you', the hotel will send a personal answer. There is a budget of approximately €5,000 set aside just to pay for the replies to feedback cards.

All measurements must be followed by actions for improvements

The results of such actions should be continuously re-examined and checked for their success or otherwise. They should be fed back into the organisation, to extend employees and develop their potential; and to keep the company culture on track. Measurement results should set new targets, stimulate further improvements, enhance employee and customer satisfaction, and maintain cohesion between them. It should prove to management and shareholders that the organisation is running as efficiently as possible, with further quality objectives always within sight.

EFQM excellence model, criterion 6 – customer results defines what an organisation is achieving in relation to external customers under two categories. The first are the customers' perceptions of the organisation, obtained from customer surveys, focus groups, vendor ratings, compliments and complaints, for example. These measures, depending on the purpose of the organisation, may have to do with the following:

- Overall image:
  - accessibility;
  - communication;
  - flexibility;
  - proactive behaviour;
  - responsiveness.
- Products and services:
  - quality;
  - value;
  - reliability;
  - design innovation;
  - delivery;
  - environmental profile.
- Sales and after-sales support:
  - capabilities and behaviour of employees;
  - advice and support;
  - customer literature and technical documentation;
  - handling complaints;
  - product training;
  - response time;
  - technical support;
  - warranty and guarantee provisions.
- Loyalty:
  - intention to repurchase;
  - willingness to purchase other products and services from the organisation;
  - willingness to recommend the organisation;
  - duration of relationship;
  - effective recommendations;
  - frequency/value of orders;
  - life-time value;
  - numbers of complaints and compliments;
  - new and/or lost business;
  - customer retention.

The other category concerns performance indicators, which are the internal measures used by the organisation in order to monitor, understand, predict and improve performance of the organisation and to predict perceptions of its external customers. These performance indicators for customers may relate to matters that include the following:

- Overall image:
  - number of customer accolades and nominations for awards;
  - press coverage.
- Products and services:
  - competitiveness;
  - defect, error and rejection rates;
  - guarantee provisions and warranty provisions;
  - complaints;
  - logistic indicators;
  - product life-cycle;
  - innovation in design;
  - time to market.

This book is not a DIY handbook for organisations that want lessons in management of the everyday aspects of business. It is an overview, to stimulate the mental processes and to help managers to get properly organised to maximise the potential of their own organisation and people.

Priorities for success

Siemens AG, a world leader in many fields, is proud to advertise its corporate culture, which is based on the EFQM guidelines. From the top, its list of corporate principles, which are the basis for its commitment to business excellence, are these:

1. Customers govern our actions.
2. Business success means we win from profits.
3. Learning is the key to continuous improvement.
4. Excellent leadership fosters top results.

5. Our innovations shape the future.
6. Our cooperation has no limit.
7. Corporate citizenship is our global commitment.

How is total measurement relevant to business success?

Measurement is based on exploration. Like the navigators of old, it starts with a voyage of discovery around customers and creation of maps of what they expect from an organisation, and of the rocks on which the company ship might founder. The success of the voyage is measured in terms of increased profits. It took many voyages, many ships, many explorers and many years, and it cost many lives, to map the globe. It has been a similar experience for businesses to learn the route to profitability, but there are always shifting sand-banks, changing currents, storms and hurricanes to be avoided, which is why ongoing measurement is necessary.

The One Number You Need to Grow by Frederick F. Reichheld (2003) deals with key performance indicators in a novel way, when the author points out that, by substituting a single question for the complex black box of the typical customer satisfaction survey, companies can actually put customer satisfaction survey results to use and focus employees on the task of stimulating growth.

The author states that, in most industries, the percentage of customers who were enthusiastic enough to refer a friend or colleague (the latter being, perhaps, the stronger sign of customer loyalty) corre-lated directly with differences in growth rates among competitors. This contradicts earlier assumptions about the correlation between loyal customers and organisational growth.

Existing approaches to measuring loyalty and its impact on growth have not been very effective. The best companies have tended to focus on customer retention rates but the measurement is merely the best of the mediocre lot. Retention rates provide in many industries a valuable link to profitability, but their relationship to growth is tenuous. That is mainly because these companies track customer defections – the degree to which a bucket is emptying rather than filling up. The author argues further that retention rates are a poor indication of customer loyalty in situations where customers are held hostage by high switching costs or other barriers, or where customers naturally outgrow a product because of ageing, increased income or other factors.

Customer satisfaction surveys are an even less reliable means of gauging loyalty. In general, it is difficult, according to the author, to indicate that satisfaction lacks a consistently demonstrable connection to actual customer behaviour and growth. Based on the information by the American Consumer Satisfaction Index (ACSI), which reflects the customer satisfaction ratings of 200 US companies, the author cites examples of cases where there are inverse relationships between customer satisfaction ratings and outstanding sales growth. One such case is Kmart, where a significant increase in the company's ASCI rating was accompanied by a sharp decrease in sales as it slid towards bankruptcy. Another classic example of the unreliability of customer satisfaction ratings came from an interview with one of the dealers of big three car manufacturers. In most cases the dealers revealed that customer satisfaction ratings were a charade, which they played along with to remain in the good graces of the manufacturer. They put pressure on their sales people to boost up the score, which often meant pleading with the customers to provide top ratings, if that meant giving them something like free mats or oil change.

Which, then, are the right metrics for gauging customer loyalty? To determine this, the author matched survey responses from individual customers to their actual behaviour – repeat purchase and referrals over time. The resultant data allowed the author to determine which survey questions had the strongest statistical correlation with repeat purchases or referrals. The aim of the research was to find at least one question for each industry that would predict the above behaviours. The result revealed the question that was the best for most industries. The top ranking question that was the most effective across industries was:

- How likely is it that you would recommend (company X) to a friend or colleague?

Reichheld found two questions that were effective predictors in certain industries, and they were:

- How strongly do you agree that (company X) deserves your loyalty?
- How likely is it that you will continue to purchase products/services from (company X)?

The research concluded that in most industries there is a strong relationship between a company's growth rate and the percentage of its customers who are 'promoters', that is those who say that they are most likely to recommend the company to a friend or colleague. This conclusion highlights the need to track down net promoters.

Tracking net promoters

The percentage of customers who are promoters of a brand or company, minus the percentage who are detractors, offers organisations a powerful way to measure and manage customer loyalty. Firms with the highest net promoter scores consistently garner the lion's share of industry growth. So how can companies get started?

Survey a statistically valid sample of your customers with the question, 'How likely is it that you would recommend (brand or company X) to a friend or colleague?'

It is critical to provide a consistent scale for responses that range from zero to 10, where zero means not at all likely, five means neutral, and 10 means extremely likely. Resist the urge to let survey questions multiply; more questions diminish response rates along with the reliability of your sample. You need only one question to determine the status – promoter, passively satisfied, or detractor – of a customer. (Follow-up questions can help unearth the reasons for customers' feelings and point to profitable remedies but such questions should be tailored to the three categories of customers.) Learning how to turn a passively satisfied customer into a promoter requires a very different line of questioning from learning how to resolve the problems of a detractor.

Calculate the percentage of customers who respond with nine or 10 (promoters) and the percentage who respond with zero through six (detractors). Subtract the percentage of detractors from the percentage of promoters to arrive at your net-promoter score. Don't be surprised if your score is lower than you expect. The median net-promoter score of more than 400 companies in 28 industries (based on some 130,000 customer survey responses gathered over the past two-plus years by Satmetrix, a maker of software for managing real-time customer feedback) was just 16.

Compare net-promoter scores from specific regions, branches, service or sales reps, and customer segments. This often reveals root causes of differences as well as best practices that can be shared. What really counts, of course, is how your company compares with direct competitors. Have your market researchers surveyed your competitors' customers using the same method? If they have done so, you can then determine how your company stacks up within your industry and whether your current net-promoter number is a competitive asset, or a liability.

Improve your score. The companies with the most enthusiastic customer referrals, including eBay, Amazon and USAA, receive net-promoter scores from 75 to more than 80. For companies aiming to garner world-class loyalty – and the growth that comes with it – this should be the target.

Measurement of people

The EFQM excellence model, criterion 7 – people results, puts the same headings to its sub-criteria here as is used for criterion 6, namely, perception measures and performance indicators.

If one considers what Siemens has to say about its service culture and the key principles by which it strives to operate, we can see that there is more to it than is immediately obvious. The EFQM criterion 6 elaborates on what is to be measured with regard to customers. EFQM criterion 7 deals with what the organisation is achieving in relation to its people, and again uses perception measures and performance indicators as the basis for its sub-criteria.

People perception measures, obtained by way of surveys, focus groups, interviews, structured appraisals etc., may include those relating to:

- Motivation:
  - career development;
  - communication;
  - empowerment;
  - equal opportunities;
  - involvement;
  - leadership;
  - opportunity to learn and achieve;
  - recognition;
  - target setting and appraisal;
  - the organisation's values, mission, vision, policy and strategy;
  - training and development.
- Satisfaction:
  - organisation's administration;
  - employment conditions;
  - facilities and services;
  - health and safety conditions;
  - job security;
  - pay and benefits;
  - peer relationships;
  - the management of change;
  - the organisation's environmental policy and impact;
  - the organisation's role in the community and society;
  - working environment.

People performance indicators are internal measures used by the organisation in order to monitor, understand, predict and improve the performance of the organisation's people and to predict their perceptions. Performance indicators for people may include those relating to:

- Achievements:
  - competency requirements versus competencies available;
  - productivity;
  - success rates of training and development to meet objectives.

- Motivation and involvement:
  - involvement in improvement teams;
  - involvement in suggestion schemes;
  - levels of training and development;
  - measurable benefits of team work;
  - recognition of individuals and teams;
  - response rates to people surveys.
- Satisfaction:
  - absenteeism and sickness levels;
  - accident levels;
  - grievances;
  - recruitment trends;
  - staff turnover;
  - strikes;
  - use of benefits;
  - use of organisation provided facilities (e.g. recreational, crèche).
- Services provided to the organisation's people:
  - accuracy of personnel administration;
  - communication effectiveness;
  - speed of response to enquiries;
  - training evaluation.

In the context of Siemens and of the EFQM guidelines, learning, the key to continuous improvement, is not just about employees improving competence and caring for customers, it is the acquisition by management of comprehensive data about all aspects of the business, followed by intelligent analysis of that data, and action as necessary being taken. Learning, therefore, is applicable to all and always applicable to all.

Leadership

Excellent leadership refers to more than supervisors, team leaders and line managers. It includes total management commitment to corporate principles and provision of the means to develop them until they become the backbone of the company. True leadership always starts at the very top. Its signals to the troops are clear and its understanding of the ongoing situation, on all sides, is comprehensive.

Corporate citizenship means that nothing the company does, anywhere in the world, causes alarm or distress to others, or has an adverse effect on the environment. International businesses tended to assume that they could override local susceptibilities, and there have been many reported cases of immense damage done to the health and well-being of poor, ignorant peoples, of environmental damage on a monumental scale, of companies who rode roughshod over laws and human rights, all in the name of profits. With the present availability to gather and disseminate news at high speed, such activities earn nothing but contempt and notoriety for the perpetrators. Corporate citizenship requires measurement of the impact company activities have on people and the environment, and an awareness of the way in which its behaviour impacts upon customers' perception of service quality.

Measurement, therefore, is not a simple and clearly defined set of statistics for the amusement of accountants. It is the management who should be responsible for deciding what is to be measured and how, for setting benchmarks, creating the environment for measurement, analysing the results, and communicating them throughout the organisation. Measurement is the chief tool of management, as the saw is the tool of the sawyer. It is also the mirror of success.

What to measure?

SECOR produced a customer metrics member survey, in the form of a detailed questionnaire for CMLG member organisations, the purpose and scope of which was to collect the specific customer measures currently used within the members' organisations.

It is a lengthy document and, in order to complete it accurately, the organisation has to have a truly comprehensive knowledge of itself and its behaviours. The guidelines recommend the approach to be used. The manager responsible for completion of the survey should review the areas of management identified with the individual measurement areas, and confirm who has ownership. Owners should be asked what existing customer measures are being reported within their sphere of responsibility, and they will need to provide proof and explain what rules they apply. For each identified measure, the definition of the measure, the rules for calculating the measure and an example value of the measure, and its target value within the organisation are required. Details of each measure are to be recorded in the appropriate sections of the questionnaire.

The fields cover four strategies for creation of a customer lifecycle: *attracting, transacting, service and support,* and *enhancing.* Attracting begins when a customer becomes aware of the company, develops an interest and tries to understand the company, product or service. Under this heading come brand building, customer value management, customer behaviour modelling, product development and market operations.

Transacting comes when the customer decides to purchase, and concerns product customisation and sales force operations. Service and support are concerned if the customer needs assistance from the company in installing, using or servicing what was purchased. It encompasses service centre operations, field service operations, supply chain/ logistics and website operations.

Enhancing is when the customer may think of purchasing additional products or services. It is to do with customer value management, customer knowledge and balanced scorecards.

The actual survey begins with the attracting phase, and asks about brand loyalty, brand awareness, perceived quality, brand associations, percentage of market share, company's market ranking and number of customer enquiries. As with all the sections of the survey, there is space in which to record what measures are used, in this case, to measure brand equity, to describe the measurement approach and the rules applied to achieve each measure noted therein.

Similarly, there is a section on customer value management, much of which would be impossible to complete without a very thorough knowledge of the company's customer base and the value of the customers to the company. This part is followed by a short but probing section on customer behaviour modelling and measurement.

It moves on to product development and asks about the level of customer input that goes into product development, and the satisfaction derived therefrom. Logically, this is followed by marketing operations measurements.

The transacting phase mentioned above is next, and deals with product customisation and how customisation is appreciated by customers. Having a new product to sell, the sales force operations are put under the microscope, and the survey asks how these operations are measured.

Servicing and support, where applicable, is examined from two standpoints: service centre and contact centre operations, and this section embraces matters such as telephone response times, complaints procedures and the effectiveness of complaints resolution procedures. Field service operations come next, and this covers, among other things, response times, time taken to resolve problems and the percentages of failed service visits and of customers who have never asked for a service visit.

Many goods and services pass through a supply chain before reaching their destination, and there is a part of the survey that deals with this. Like the other sections, this also has a place for customer feedback measurements.

Website operations and email services offer several opportunities to take measurements, and these form part of the survey, following from the supply chain and logistics section.

Enhancing: customer value management deals with customers who are of greatest value to the company; their loyalty, advocacy and retention rates. It deals with the way in which the company measures the health and value of its existing customers.

Where many companies begin their research and measurement by taking steps to acquire knowledge of their customers, this matter is left until near the end of the survey, and deals with measurements to do with segmentation of customers, their expectations, and how well the company understands their behaviour.

Each section has room for an evaluation of existing procedures, and to record the rules employed for measurement. It is probable that many companies will have only a moderate idea of how well and how comprehensively they measure their efforts, and, in some areas, they might feel that the information is impossible to obtain, for accurate measurement purposes, or that it will be too costly and time-consuming to gather. However, the survey offers a valuable template by which to gauge measurement. It suggests ways in which a good insight into the company might be obtained.

One thread runs in parallel with the rest, throughout the survey: the interaction of employees with customers and the effect of such interaction on customer satisfaction levels. Thus, without specifically enquiring into the matter, recruitment, training, motivation, empowerment and employee satisfaction are measured alongside the other factors addressed by this type of survey.

There is nothing that cannot be measured by some standard or other, and business provides ample scope for analysis and measurement. There is no hard and fast way of tackling the richness of the fields to be measured, and many organisations have offered useful suggestions to those who have not yet picked up a measuring stick. No two businesses are exactly alike, and each must choose what it recognises as the critical areas for scrutiny, within its own activities. Measurement can become addictive, and, in time, it might be possible to measure every aspect of what a company does. It is better to measure some things, to get the feel of it and see what it reveals, than not to measure anything, and hand all your potential advantages to your competitors.

Measurement of performance

The EFQM excellence model, criterion 9 – key performance results, completes the measurement sectors by looking at how and what organisations can measure, in order to gauge how well they are achieving in relation to planned performance. As this is another practical exposition of what to measure, it is worthwhile detailing the headings for this criterion, too. The sub-criteria for this are key performance outcomes and key performance indicators.

The *key performance outcomes* are a measure of the key results planned by the organisation and which may include those relating to:

- Financial outcomes, including:
  - share price;
  - dividends;

- gross margins;
- net profit;
- sales;
- meeting of budgets.
- Non-financial outcomes, including:
  - market share;
  - time to market;
  - volumes;
  - success rates.

Key performance indicators are the operational measures used in order to monitor, understand, predict and improve the organisation's likely key performance outcomes. These may include those relating to:

- Processes:
  - performance;
  - deployment;
  - assessments;
  - innovations;
  - improvements;
  - cycle times;
  - defect rate;
  - maturity
  - productivity;
  - time to market.
- External resources including partnerships:
  - supplier performance;
  - supplier price;
  - number and value added of partnerships;
  - number and value added of innovative products and services solutions generated by partners;
  - recognition of partners' contribution.
- Financial:
  - cash-flow items;
  - balance-sheet items;
  - depreciation;
  - maintenance costs;

- return on equity;
- return on net assets;
- credit ratings.
- Buildings, equipment and materials:
  - defect rates;
  - inventory turnover;
  - utility consumption;
  - utilisation.
- Technology:
  - innovation rate;
  - value of intellectual property;
  - patents;
  - royalties.
- Information and knowledge:
  - accessibility;
  - integrity;
  - relevance;
  - timeliness;
  - sharing and using knowledge;
  - value of intellectual capital.

Now we know what to measure, there is room here for a few practical suggestions about how to do it. We could start with customers, which are the alpha and omega of every business measurement. An informative survey of how well customers' current expectations and needs are being met might be obtained by asking managers to suggest seven or eight key areas of service which they think are critical to customer satisfaction, and to prioritise them. Next, ask customers which key areas are most important to them, and ask them to state their priorities. There might well be discrepancies. Study of these, where the exercise has been undertaken and differences revealed, usually points up one common cause. Many companies still tend to think of customers in terms of groups, or segments, not as individuals. Customers are individuals and behave accordingly. Each organisation has to become familiar with its own customers' needs. These will vary from company to company as well as from customer to customer.

The man who, on one occasion, buys a luxury apartment in the south of France also buys milk and bread daily. He wants the latter to be fresh and wholesome and available when he needs it. We know this because we all buy milk and bread daily. What he wants of his apartment has to be discovered by probing questions. We do not all have the means to make such a purchase, so, until we ask the purchaser what he requires, we have no experience of the needs of such a person.

Individual customers have their own priorities and know what level of service or product features is important to them, when they approach a company. They want, as we have emphasised continuously in this book, a predictable service of a certain standard and quality. This means that they want the goods they order to be available, at a known price, delivered promptly and in good condition, when they order them. They also want to know how they operate, if they have not had previous experience of the particular goods before.

Matters such as constant communication, reliable sales personnel and good public relations are often of no direct interest to the customer. In fact, the average customer neither knows nor cares about the wheels within wheels that turn to provide what is wanted. Thus, a reliable price list and plentiful and reliable stock, properly packaged and promptly delivered are what the customer actually values most. Of course, the other items are necessary, but only to make sure that what the customers actually care about can be supplied to order.

There are 10 factors that contribute to the overall perception of service quality from the customer's standpoint. These are:

- Credibility
  Trustworthiness, believability, honesty of the service provider.

- Security
  Freedom from danger, risk or doubt.

- Access
  Approachability and ease of contact.

- Communication
  Listening to customers and keeping them informed in language they can understand.

- Understanding the customer
  Making the effort to know customers and their needs.

- Tangibles
  Appearance of physical facilities, equipment, personnel and communication materials.

- Reliability
  Ability to perform the promised service dependably and accurately.

- Responsiveness
  Willingness to help customers and provide service.

- Competence
  Possession of the skills and knowledge required to perform the service.

- Courtesy
  Politeness, respect, consideration and friendliness of contact personnel.

These have been amalgamated and reproduced as five broad dimensions, derived from customer-orientated focus group research into service quality. These key dimensions are reliability, responsiveness, assurance, empathy and tangibles.

If you can measure your own performance in these areas, the obvious next step might be to check on how well your nearest competitor judges these customer requirements and how successfully these are met. The crux of the matter is that customers know what they value, what they expect and what standards are acceptable to them, and they have their priorities. Suppliers need to be aware of these. Customers are simply not interested in how things get done, they just want to be sure that they actually do get done, to time, to quality and to price, preferably from contact with polite, helpful people in clean and attractive premises.

What are the thresholds within which customers decide if an organisation is getting things done right?

On a theoretical scoreboard with an arbitrary scale that goes from one to 10 points, let us assume that customers are invited to score their rate of satisfaction with the levels of service they receive in given key areas. Seven might be the lowest acceptable level for all customers in all of these key areas, if the customer is to be satisfied. Nine might be the level at which the customer is delighted. Unless the company scores at least seven and not more than nine *in every area*, the customer is either dissatisfied because his minimum expected level of service is not being met somewhere, or the company is wasting resources by doing better than is necessary to delight the customer.

Suppose that you and your competitor both score an average of seven, it might be imagined that you are on an equal footing. That is a false assumption, unless you both score sevens across the board. If seven is the minimum and nine the best that is needed and either party scores below seven for any key aspect, and higher than average for another key aspect, they fail to achieve all basic minimum satisfaction levels and *must* improve. They are on dangerous ground. The company that scores sevens across the board meets basic satisfaction levels, and there is room to improve up to nine, the measure of delight. This company is safe, but, as they sometimes say in school reports, 'Can do better, if they try.'

Thus, from the theoretical boundary figures suggested, it is clear that there is a threshold below which a company cannot afford to fall, on any key issue. There is a narrow band, however, between this lower threshold and the best performance threshold to be aimed at. Companies should gear their performance targets to this band. The closer to nine they score, the more likely it is that customers will find delight.

Companies that want to measure key values must *constantly* monitor how targeted customers perceive value. All the measures for improvement are wasted if they do not improve the customers' perceptions of service quality received. The only people to know for sure whether their expectations have been met or exceeded are the customers. Companies who want to know how well they are meeting customer requirements must keep on asking. One can never know the answer to a question before it has been asked. The more one deals with a customer, the more one grows familiar with what satisfies and what delights, but one should always keep asking and always act according to the answers.

The retention index is a gap analysis tool designed to measure a company's ability to retain customers derived from their customer

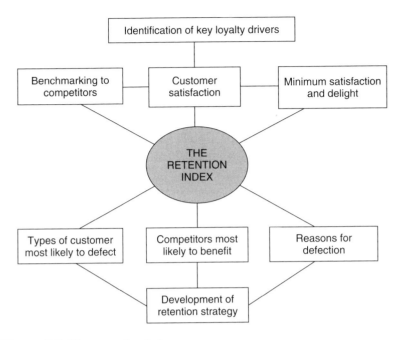

Figure 7.2 The retention index
Source: Suntook, F. and Total Research Strategic Marketing Services (2001) *The Lifebelt: the Definitive Guide to Managing Customer Retention*. Chichester: John Wiley & sons Ltd

satisfaction performance (Figure 7.2). The retention index compares the levels of customer satisfaction between a company and its competitors and quantifies a customer's minimum satisfaction levels, (below which he is likely to defect) and delight levels (above which the supplier is exceeding expectations).

Managers are judge and jury

Managers provide the means by which the measures are taken and determine the methods – reports, survey results, sales figures, employee and customer turnover, absenteeism data, faulty manufactures etc. – by which the results are judged. With managers lies the opportunity to adjust what is being done until it matches what customers want. As we have seen, there are many methods by which measurements can be made, many processes and areas of business activity to be measured, and many uses to which results obtained from measurement can be put. They will vary from company to company, but have the same basic outcome requirement. They must answer the questions:

- Is this improving the perceived value desired by those customers who matter most to the company?
- Is the action necessary?
- Is it cost-effective?
- Is the company within the boundaries of customer satisfaction and delight with this action?

Beginning with the customer, the practical steps to be taken are with measurements concerned with customer focus. There is vital information to be deduced from the activities of frontline people. These staff should log carefully the ways in which they spend their time. The details should specifically include time spent on customer contacts and the outcomes, whether these contacts are by telephone, letter or in person. The information will show how time is spent by individuals, and its profitability. Where there is need for retraining, this will also be evident. It will also indicate how customers contact the company, what their queries, comments and complaints concern and how they are being handled. Measurement makes information available to those who can influence the way in which things happen. This links comfortably with processes, employee involvement, training and continuous improvement. We have already looked at how training and appraisal are linked, and that investment in people is another process to be measured for success against cost-effectiveness. This applies as much to frontline staff as to all employees.

   With these factors in mind, a suitable format for the daily logs for frontline staff, in particular, should be carefully designed by management, and completed logs should be handed in every week, at least. The sooner problems and potential problems are discovered, the sooner they can be resolved, before they become catastrophic. This is true of all aspects of a business, of course, but most sensitive where direct contact is had with external customers. The more people who need to be involved in effecting changes, the faster the dissemination of information should be. Managers need to decide early on how frequently the various data has to be provided to them, and they should ensure that this timetable is upheld by those whose duty it is to compile the data and reports.

Loyalty measurement factors represent a list of beneficial measures which, if used within a service excellence programme, will supply an early warning of trouble, or confirm the success of customer retention strategies.

Who needs to know what?

As we saw from the EFQM particulars given above, managers have a comprehensive responsibility for the means, methods of gathering, and *dissemination* of information. Managers should ensure that information derived from data is universally distributed within the company, so that teams and line managers can tackle problem areas, improve training programmes and extend coaching sessions. The information will also encourage those employees who are performing well, so that they should feel fulfilled and eager to strive harder yet.

Customer and employee satisfaction measurements should form part of the company's information-gathering systems. Of particular value to management are data on complaints. All complaints have an origin. Pacification of an irate customer is valueless, unless the cause of the complaint is located and removed. Proper logs and careful study of these will reveal what might otherwise be deliberately hidden.

By passing information derived from measurement from top management to supervisors, we can see that line managers and teams, the people in the 'hot spots', know when and where to improve or re-engineer processes, establish where benchmarks are not being reached, discover where training expansion or alteration is called for. Such measurement also establishes how completely employees are involved in the service quality activities. It will pinpoint whether the focus of the organisation is still on the customers, or whether it has shifted towards fiscally focused results.

Managers and shareholders have also to consider the budgetary implications of what is done within the organisation, so that cost-effectiveness is a major consideration of all service quality improvements. It is right, therefore, to cost all activities and measure their outcome against allotted budget and expected return.

In all the plethora of talk about customer and employee satisfaction, let us remember that companies are in business to make a return for their investors, to generate profits for expansion and to pay and retain excellent employees in accordance with their value to the organisation and its competitors. That is the motivation behind any business. Part of the struggle for excellence is to remember that profit is the key to the future, and profit derives from satisfied and loyal customers.

Measurement and response to change

When major changes have to take place within an organisation, to meet and take account of external influences, data that are accurate, comprehensive and bang up to date facilitate decision making. Global marketing is one such novel change that has moved off the horizon and into every organisation in the past few years. The increasing accessibility of Internet marketing and the fierceness of competition to woo and win customers called for some drastic responses from the business sector. The viability of some strategies has been called into question. Money has been lost. For example, women's web pages, based on the old magazine concepts, aimed at the new female net users, have proved rather more expensive to run than the income they generate. Whether, as the market expands, this will always be true remains to be measured over time. Companies considering the implications of major changes, such as Internet marketing, have to decide when and how to respond to what, in this case anyway, is likely to be an inevitable tide in marketing and purchasing behaviours.

Difficult management decisions, then, depend heavily on measurements of existing customer behaviour, defection rates, service requirements, marketing and implementation costs. The costs, profits and expansion/contraction prognoses must be measured (calculated) on the basis of quantifiable facts. Only up-to-date, accurate information accurately guides decision making. This brings us to processes, how and what to measure and why.

Production processes

At their most basic, production processes can be measured for accuracy, productivity, unit costs, timeliness and backlogs. There are established formulae for each of these measurements. Supervisory staff check the accuracy of individuals and units by observation and by inspection. Daily logs should be kept for manufacturing accuracy, and individuals should be checked for their standard of work, on a regular basis. Every item that comes out of production with a defect is time and money wasted. Every bottleneck leaves some employees waiting, idle and frustrated.

The number of hours required to produce a unit, multiplied by the average hourly wage (plus overtime, bonuses etc.), divided by the number of units of work completed, is the formula by which unit cost is calculated. Productivity is the number of units produced over a given time. Where similar work is done in different locations, and there is a difference in productivity or unit cost that cannot be explained by some temporary circumstance, managers are led to investigate whether it is a staffing problem, a training problem, or has to do with the work environment, or something else, that can be adjusted for improvement. Constant measurement and comparison will quickly show bottlenecks or other matters that require attention. Apart from the effect it might have on price and availability, productivity and unit cost considerations are of little concern to the customer. If goods are delivered late, however, the customer is disappointed. If it becomes a habit, the customer will seek an alternative supplier.

Timeliness is a matter that customers everywhere consider to be of key importance. It is to do with the length of time it takes to process a job from start to finish. Customers, as individuals, are impatient. They want the goods as soon as possible. Companies, in their turn, like to see the customer's payment going into the bank without delay. Slowness of execution creates dissatisfaction in the customer and can lead to cash-flow difficulties for the company. Information about timeliness and its measurement is easily furnished from the data in a company's computer, but there should be shopfloor logs from which individual activities can be watched and assessed. The computer does not know what is actually happening; it only knows what it is told. One small delay in a production line can do irreparable damage.

It is worth considering a typical situation that happens in companies of all sizes and how a look at the measurements might suggest a solution. Every winter, there is an outbreak of coughs and colds among staff. The smallest team, and the least visible from within the organisation because they work away from the main premises, might happen to be delivery drivers. If several of the company's delivery drivers are laid low by influenza every winter, it will impact upon a key area – timeliness.

Someone has to take responsibility for hiring temporary drivers, or passing the work to outside carriers, in order to keep to the delivery schedule. This person should be able to give statistics on how much it costs to make alternative arrangements and to justify decisions taken. It would be part of the ongoing measurement processes that include absenteeism as well as the financial returns.

From the figures supplied, what might management decide to do? They could decide to offer drivers anti-influenza injections every autumn. As an incentive, this might be linked to a small 'health' bonus. How would the value of the decision be measured?

Let us assume that injection costs £5 per person, takes five minutes to give, and the incentive bonus is £20 per person. It would be simple to multiply these figures by the number of drivers, compare the answer to the cost of the alternative solutions and make a decision. There are other questions that this exercise throws up. What would it be worth in customer satisfaction? What would it be worth in employee satisfaction? What would it have cost in sickness pay, as well as the cost of hiring alternative carriers, had the old seasonal infections been allowed to continue? Would the idea of injections against influenza have occurred to anybody, if the company had not measured everything carefully and made regular comparisons of data? If it works for delivery drivers and is cost-effective, why not provide protection for everybody in the company? These apparently minor matters are shown to be highly significant when detected from measurements and cost comparisons.

Repeat measurements

That was a simple problem to solve, once it had been identified. The derived improvement in service to customers would be very clear, but it should still be checked back with them and with the drivers. Anti-influenza injections alone might not have been enough to ensure timeliness in the winter, when bad roads and weather conditions also affect delivery times. It might yet be necessary to look again, to see whether the dispatcher could do better by planning more and shorter journeys, with drivers setting out earlier in the day and using routes that are possibly longer, but less subject to weather disruption. If that is still not found to be enough, the tyres on delivery vehicles could be changed at the onset of winter, to give better grip in ice and snow. This illustrates the accumulation of small forward steps that can be made by continuous measurement and back-checking of something apparently simple and straightforward.

We have seen the effects of lack of timeliness. When the flow of orders is slowed, for any reason, and timeliness is affected, cash flow suffers, customer satisfaction levels drop. Is timeliness affected, not by delivery problems, but because there is a backlog in the workflow process? What caused it? How can it be overcome quickly? Whose task would that be? Where the answers are not known, because the questions have never been asked, measurement will suggest that the time has come to deal with them. The only reason to measure anything, remember, is so that action can be taken. No action should be taken without justification. Measurement furnishes the justification and directs the action. Action taken should be cost-effective and the cost-effectiveness of the action should be measurable.

Mention has already been made in this book about the need for flexibility, to adapt to and anticipate changes. Change affects all the areas in the second circle of the life belt. There is nothing in a company that cannot usefully be measured. If there is, it is superfluous and should be abandoned. There is an old expression about having belt and braces protection. It implies always double-checking what is done. Once a defect or lack is uncovered and remedied, managers should go back to source and ensure that all is now back on track, and check at customer level whether an improvement has been noticed where there was a perceived problem. They should look out for opportunities to make further improvement, step by step, and check each step as it is made.

This type of customer-reaction-to-changes measurement will ask:

- Is the customer making repeat purchases?
- Is customer activity with the company increasing?
- Is there a wider range of goods or services being purchased?
- Has there been an increase in the number of referrals?
- What percentage of the business total is due to this customer, or segment of customers?

Asking these questions, in what ever way is appropriate to the organisation and its customer base, as a routine and not simply to check the effect of any improvement steps that have been taken, will confirm current levels of customer appreciation of what the company offers. Regular comparison of the answers will quickly show where there is a failure to satisfy. The management task, in that case, is to identify what is wrong, rectify it and check again. It is no use bolting the stable door once the horse has gone.

The successful company builds an impregnable prison wall around its customers. It wants them to remain permanently captive. Managers should always have at their fingertips the actual value of their best customers, on a monthly, yearly and life-time calculation. This information belongs to all the staff. They form the impregnable wall and serve as prison warders. They deserve to know the penalty for losing prisoners.

Improved performance raises expectations

In the same manner as repeated reference to the customer for information about satisfaction levels provides useful input to guide other aspects of company activity, study of processes offers opportunity for action for product improvement. There is no economic reason to improve product or service beyond what customers actually want. However, product and service must meet expectations. The better an organisation performs, the higher the expectations customers have for future performance. Customers who purchase regularly expect that standards will rise over time. Car buyers, for example, expect to find enhancements to all the product features they already appreciate, every time they trade in an old car and buy a new one. To exceed or to fall below expectations in any of these is not cost-effective. Brand loyalty flies out of the window with falling standards. Again, it pays to watch what your competitors are doing. If they are offering improved products and tempting your customers with them, it is time for you to take action.

Similarly, study of service delivery also throws up areas for improvement in attitude, competence and all the attributes that are needed for top-class service quality provision. How well is the competition handling this and are you better or worse than them?

Once again, there is a direct correlation between what an organisation does to improve service quality and the customers' perception of quality service, the so-called customer value definition, so that ongoing measurement and analysis of results facilitates decision making and budget allocation. Everything that is done in a company should relate back directly to how it impinges upon and influences the key areas that matter most to customers. Organisations are complicated organisms and require strong management if they are to perform well. Careful control of even apparently trivial things like stationery wastage, accumulation of rubbish in offices and conservation of electricity can lead to efficiency savings and create a more pleasant working environment. These in turn affect employees and make their lives easier and more agreeable.

Thus, we can see how important it is to understand what customers, internal and external, value most, before a start is made on any service quality improvements. It cannot be emphasised too often that action must follow measurement. The results must be studied and compared with the same dimensions when measured previously, to highlight trends as well as target achievement or otherwise. The more an organisation does for its customers, internal as well as external, the more it will be expected to do. There is no room for a single backward step anywhere.

If feedback from customers is to be of maximum value, companies need also to discover where and why they scored well. If things are not broken, they do not need to be fixed. They still require a regular check-up, however. Areas in a company's service provision where things are being done that provide customer satisfaction and delight should also be carefully explored. There might be ways to adapt the successful strategy to other processes, to increase performance quality.

The motto attached to customer surveys should be, 'If you ask customers about their satisfaction with what you offer, they will expect improvement forthwith.' If you embark on a costly survey, make sure you are ready and able to implement any changes customers tell you are wanted. Once surveys are started, they should address customer value and satisfaction. Data should be collected from as many sources as possible within the confines of budget. Information gathered should then be sorted according to product, market, segment, individual customers and individual customer value dimension. The database should be constructed to show, by regular comparison with past data, what trends are happening. Finally, the data should be integrated with data gathered from other sources, such as competitor's offering, and likely changes due to other external circumstances.

Simple formats for report forms will make them easy to use. Time will not be wasted by managers who have to complete them, and the reports will be delivered punctually. If the forms are too complicated, managers will look for excuses for late or non-completion. Equally, simple forms with as many as possible common features applicable to all departments make the task of analysis easier and faster. The point behind them, as we have said, is the action they trigger.

The type of survey used on external customers applies just as well to internal customers. To get maximum value for the wages paid to people and the training they are given, people need to derive value from working within the company and be satisfied with what they do and with what is provided for them. This, as we know, motivates them to perform better and take pleasure in helping the company to live up to its service culture. Organisations that spend money on cultivation of customers and employees wish to conserve both. Competitors are always seeking to ensnare both. In this book, we have spoken of internal and external customers. Much of what applies to the one is equally applicable to the other, particularly in respect of measurement.

At Hewlett Packard, customer satisfaction is measured in a number of ways. What they do is not necessarily applicable to other companies, but their approach is interesting and valuable.

1. *The classical survey of existing customers, competitors' customers and non-customers.* This seeks a rating on particular aspects of customer satisfaction and a weighting of those aspects, that is, a satisfaction rating and an importance rating.
2. *Process performance online measurement.* Typically, when a product or service is delivered to a customer, Hewlett Packard will carry out a brief telephone survey: Did the product arrive on time? Did it work as expected? Were the installation engineers polite and knowledgeable?
3. *Complaints process.* Complaints are logged, and the management teams review the frequency and type of complaint. What are the common complaints; caused by what organisation or product, or by which process being broken? Resources are deployed to solve those problems.
4. *Relationship measurement.* This is based more on feeling than on hard data, with an executive talking to a CEO or a board member of another company: This measurement is carried out with major customers. Hewlett Packard interviews 20 of its management team, sending a structured set of questions in advance. Customers generally don't mind giving their time for that.
5. *Comparative surveys from markets researchers.* The company subscribes to independent market studies.
6. *Project quality teams with customers.* These are teams set up to tackle specific problems with customer companies.
7. *Partnership programme with selected customers.* There is formal measurement of the relationship with, for example, a jointly shared scorecard showing how well Hewlett Packard is doing and what is delivered.

It is evident from this type of measurement study, that Hewlett Packard regards partnership with its customers as very important.

In *Beyond Better Products: Capturing Value in Customer Retention*, by Mark Vandenbosch and Niraj Dawar (2002) the authors warn that eroding competitive leads are the result of forces that are equalising companies' ability to innovate: the increasingly rapid and free flow of information and knowledge, the movement to global standards and the advent of open markets for components and technologies. They go on to explain how companies can devise coping strategies and make money.

When product improvements can be matched quickly by competitors, companies have only two remaining levers available to influence purchase decisions: they can reduce customers' interaction costs, or make the purchase and subsequent product ownership a less risky proposition. To increase their customers' sense of expected gain from a transaction, companies can reconfigure their activities to lower buyers' interaction costs and perceived risk. *Products* must be combined with other elements before customers can realise their full value. Companies can avoid the need to be wholly responsible for customer tasks altogether. A trusted supplier can turn itself into a market maker for many *products* and services that it does not actually produce, and make money in the process. Companies often have to collaborate with other organisations to help 'form the future'; in other words, to shape businesses and *products* that will change the way commerce happens. An example of this collaboration is found in the personal computer, which usually comes packaged with a bundle of the latest software.

Summary

In summary, there is no aspect of what an organisation does that cannot be measured against quantifiable facts, to produce information upon which subsequent action can be taken in order to improve the offering to customers. There is no valid reason not to measure.

The final arbiter of success is the economic health of the company and the forecast value of its intellectual and customer-based assets. Intellectual assets are well-trained, competent, motivated employees with long service and long-term aspirations within the organisation. The long-term financial assets are, of course, derived from loyal customers, who wish for a long and mutually beneficial relationship with the organisation. It can appear to be expensive, or a waste of time, to measure, measure and measure again, and to act to adjust each measured process over and over, but without this repetitive and constant vigilance and subsequent action for improvement, success itself cannot be measured properly.

Measurement essentially belongs to management. Each part of the business needs to be measured by the person with authority over a specific department, its employees, systems and processes. Various methods of measuring have been proposed, all of them valid, all of them requiring a profound understanding of how a business functions, and all of them providing a close-up of failures and successes.

Comprehensive measurement, consistently applied, offers a new view of the company, and it sometimes happens that some measurements incidentally focus on other aspects of company activity, as with the SECOR survey on customer lifecycle. The skill lies in choosing what to measure, and making a case for choosing that rather than something else. Having defined what is to be measured, the how and when often become self-evident.

With what is often a long chain of hands through which a product or service passes before it reaches the end user, dialogue and measurement need to encompass the full length of the chain, as the Hewlett Packard organisation, in its relationship measurements, understands. The SECOR survey takes this supply chain into consideration, too, and suggests measurements to cover employee attitudes and behaviours in the four major sectors on which the survey is based. It used to be thought that customer retention was the key to profitability and growth. Nowadays, it is fashionable to take a new approach, which is summed up by asking whether customers would recommend the company to a friend, agree strongly that the company deserves their loyalty, and how likely it is that they will continue to purchase products and services from the company. The new motto, to replace, 'The customer is king,' might now be, 'The net promoter customer is king'.

As it applies to the management objective of raising profitability in the organisation, all the actions taken to achieve excellence have to be repeated endlessly, to improve employees' performance, streamline processes and move customer expectations onwards and upwards, ahead of the competition.

The days have gone when almost all potential customers slowly scoured advertisements, shop windows and other sales outlets for the goods of their choice. The Internet provides a ready means whereby instant comparisons of price and availability between competing organisations, followed by purchasing decisions, may be made. As with many purchases, of major items in particular, price and availability, coupled with the good name of the producer or supplier, are what govern these decisions. The Internet is a useful marketplace for the cash rich and time poor. To sell here requires very swift, accurate service and delivery. This new element in customer relationship management for profitability underlines all that has been said about measurement. It makes it vital to measure against competitors, and to stay ahead in the battle for customers.

8

Continuous Improvement

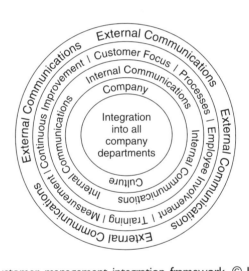

Figure 8.0 Customer management integration framework. © John A. Murphy 2005

On 10 April 1899, President Theodore Roosevelt, in a speech at the Hamilton Club, said, 'I wish to preach, not the doctrine of ignoble ease, but the doctrine of the strenuous life.'

To keep a business up to scratch certainly makes for a strenuous life. With one eye on the competition, the other on the whole organisation, no business and no management can expect to enjoy ignoble ease. The trick is to learn to enjoy the activity, instead.

Initially, all service quality improvements are expensive of management time and company finances. The same is true of the systems and processes for measurement of their success. The whole concept is analogous to a man running before an avalanche; he dare not stop for fear of being overtaken and overwhelmed. Thus, these initiatives should carry the following:

HAZARD WARNING

The more service quality improvements you give your customers, the more they will expect.

Customers, like spoilt children, will not often thank you for what you give, but if you cut down on it, they will quickly register their annoyance. Unless you are prepared for this, you might doubt the wisdom of seeking to make continuous improvements. If there is any one of your competitors who can do better than you, watch your customers carefully. They will be perfectly cognisant of what is available for them elsewhere and anxious to chase the advantage. That is the consequence of *not* working for continuous improvement.

There are two compelling reasons for making continuous improvement a priority and they are these: your competitors recognise it as essential; and, you might never catch up with them if you slacken control. Serious competitors, in any field of activity, are constantly in training to be the best in the game, and the winner is the one who trains hardest and to best effect.

This chapter looks at the whole subject of continuous improvement, and considers why and how to sustain the momentum. It also looks at benchmarking, the way in which industry standards are set, and against which individual organisations', teams' and employees' performances will be judged. All is far from doom and gloom. This chapter takes a positive attitude to the whole subject, and it is pivotal in understanding how customers can be retained. The customer service integration framework shows how continuous improvement sits alongside and completes the circle of key factors that lie at the heart of an excellence culture.

Continuous improvement starts with planning and operating processes. This leads to identification of required inputs and evaluation of outputs. From here, performance is examined and processes and inputs modified as necessary to achieve better performance. The key principles for continuous improvement are: focus on the customer; understand the process; involve the people, *not just once, but always*. Thus, everything that is done must be for greater customer satisfaction. Processes must be fully comprehended, and the means provided to enable them to be performed without unnecessary delays, or waste of time, materials and labour. This also involves subcontractors and outside suppliers of goods and services. These people should also understand and be willing to comply with the organisation's aims and objectives. Everybody in and connected with the organisation should be pulling in the same direction. The philosophy of continuous improvement must, of necessity, become a way of life for the organisation, both within and peripherally. It is very much a cultural issue.

Advantages of continuous improvement

Continuous improvement is the route to greater customer satisfaction. The search for continuous improvement uncovers limitless opportunities. Once started on the infinite upward spiral, people become obsessed with the idea of continuous improvement. It is an exceptionally powerful people motivator. It drives the organisation that understands this beyond seeking to give satisfaction and on towards provision of incredible customer service. It puts bars across the prison windows. Customers may look out, but they are unable to walk out.

Teamwork takes the strain

When we discussed teams and the way in which they take given areas of responsibility and make them their own, we suggested that problem solving was no longer used as an excuse for nothing being done.

Instead, it became a challenge, a stimulant, something exciting and interesting, to be tackled with alacrity and without fear, for the benefit of the next customer, internal or external. What did we mean by taking this view of problem solving? Has it anything to do with continuous improvements?

Problems become opportunities

Problems are caused by something affecting the smooth progress of an operation, with an ultimate adverse effect upon customers. They might be mechanical, personal, environmental, external, internal, monumental or microscopic problems. They all step in the way of progress towards the longed-for Nirvana of perfect service. In this light, we can see how each problem is an opportunity to do better. A problem solved, no matter how small, is another inch forward on the upward spiral.

In any organisation, employees take their example from managers. In their booklet, *The Handbook for Leaders: 24 Lessons for Extraordinary Leadership*, Zenger and Folkman say, 'Great leaders are not defined by the absence of weakness, but rather by the presence of clear strengths. The key to developing great leadership is to build strengths.'

They further emphasise the way in which great leaders improve productivity, reduce turnover, enhance customer service and create high levels of commitment among employees. The better the leaders, the better the results in all these areas, and these results are achieved consistently. It follows from this that continuous improvement starts with the leadership of a company. Any weaknesses at the top will be reflected down the line. Great leaders are superb motivators, and motivated people enjoy seeking new ways to make improvements. If the pattern of behaviour is right, attitudes come right, and the appropriate character is formed. This is as true of the leadership as it is of the team.

David Freemantle, in *The BIZ: Little Things that Make a Big Difference to Team Motivation and Leadership*, makes the same points and says that the great leader always makes time for and takes a personal interest in employees, and always sets the best example with everything said and done. The motivation for this is employee happiness, and is not profit-based. It builds great teams and great teams seek continuously to improve what they do for the organisation.

People engaged in teams that have the secret of working together in harmony and unity of purpose can rid an organisation of problems. Better than this, they can identify and comprehend problems fast. As a group, they can bring concentrated brainpower to the task; they share the responsibility of finding a solution, and the satisfaction of removing a spanner from the works. Teams define improvement opportunities, review the information and prepare action plans, document these action plans, investigate the process, implement the changes and verify the success of the action taken.

Does the website require updating? Is there an equipment problem? Are supplies coming in late? The answer might be yes, but it will not be so for long, in an organisation devoted to continuous improvement. Continuously improving systems, processes and employees' ability to handle them, resolve problems, or anticipate them before they actually happen. Does management properly and fairly acknowledge the improvement in employee skills and actions? This recognition process is part of the overall continuous improvement strategy. To keep employees keen to serve, they require recompense for their efforts. The success of teams should be broadcast throughout the organisation, to share their expertise and to applaud the teams that excel.

Every problem, therefore, should be seen not simply as something to be removed, but as an opportunity to improve some aspect of the work processes, always with the customer in the forefront of the thinking. The employees who work under an empowered team system enjoy the challenges and respond cheerfully to them, because their efforts can be measured and acclaimed. Thus, there is a double benefit to be derived from problems. Employees enjoy higher levels of job satisfaction by being able to think and act for themselves in the analysis and solving of them. Instead of an organisation employing hundreds of individuals, under the teamwork system, the number of working units is reduced to the number of teams. As the teams meld into a cohesive whole, the organisation begins to operate after the fashion of a one-man band. One man knows what to do and does it.

In this situation, the old blame and excuse culture, that bedevils so many organisations, cannot exist. Passing the buck becomes incomprehensible when teams and amalgamations of teams take responsibility for their own actions. If the organisation acts as a whole, strikes also become unnecessary and cease to happen. The secret is total involvement of every person and process within the organisation in the ongoing improvement battle. This should be backed up by continuous measurement, always against the ultimate scale of customer appreciation and satisfaction, and with one eye always on the competition.

Improvement means shared information and ideas

We have seen how important it is for information to be shared with everyone. The more any person understands of a given situation, the more likely they are to agree with the actions taken, and this applies to work situations as much as it applies in any sphere. The same sharing principle applies to benefits. The organisation will feel a benefit from its improvements, as customers stay longer and refer future customers. As the financial benefits filter through, management has a duty to share them with those who have helped to create them.

Rewards come from hard work

In commerce, there are three inter-related factors in operation: goods or services, vendors and purchasers. The merchant does business for the rewards it brings. If he works alone, he knows every detail of the business and of his customers' requirements. He exploits this knowledge; he keeps all the profits, takes all the risks, and does all the work. In a large organisation, the same relationships between goods and services, vendors and purchasers are valid. The organisation replaces the single merchant, but all else remains as before. This explains why it is important to share information freely, if employees are to be encouraged to work as hard as the single operator. The more informed and united in purpose teams are, the safer the future outlook.

How does one start a service quality initiative and then keep it going forward?

If one imagines the situation before a quality improvement initiative gets off the ground, it appears as if there is nothing that does not require change of some sort, and the prospect of reaching even part of the goal is dismal. This is true enough. An organisation that has grasped the necessary truth about customers, and the need to imprison them, probably will have to change everything. In our customer management integration framework lies the secret of how to tackle the global changes within an organisation.

We began with the way in which we define the most valuable customers, and spoke of the new way in which to view them as having a life-time value, providing they can be tied to the organisation. Having understood this, we also saw how to mark out those types of customers whom the organisation can best serve. Next, we saw that customers can tell organisations everything they need to know about their own expectations, desires, needs and satisfactions.

Armed with the customers' 'shopping list', we moved to look at how best to fulfil it. This entailed a look at all sorts of processes: manufacturing, training, employee involvement and empowerment, the building of trust and the process by which a comprehensive series of measures is made of the worth of what has been accomplished. The key to moving the quality initiatives forwards lies with the trained and authorised teams. Without this solidly built foundation to bear the weight of the change, it will be sluggish and piecemeal. Having set it in motion, it is not so difficult to keep it moving. Let it come to a halt and it becomes much harder to start it again and catch up with competitors.

Suddenly, we discern that the whole quality improvement initiative exercise is just another process. As previously discussed, the whole organisation is the ideal team that runs it, from top management to most junior employee. The improvement begins with the organisation's leadership. Leaders determine policy and strategy. Leaders employ people capable of implementing the policy and strategy and taking it forward. The right people make partnerships, build cohesive teams and become resources. Best leaders formulate the right policy and strategy, employ the right people, facilitate the construction of partnerships and resources, and devise processes to permit smooth implementation. The success is the satisfaction enjoyed by the organisation's team and shared with its customers. Its profitability aspects can be measured in terms of *customer results, people results, society results* and *key performance results.* Figure 8.1 explains how the combination of these factors achieves excellence.

Teams take time to form and need time to discover how best to run themselves efficiently. At a formative stage, they have need of extra help and support, as we have already mentioned in an earlier chapter. They need milestones with which to chart their progress, and encouragement to keep forging ahead.

Once the continuous improvement machine is up and running, it has its own momentum to roll it forward. The three key principles: customer focus, understanding the process and employee commitment, apply equally to administrative functions, accounting procedures, personnel deployment, pricing policies, distribution systems, advertising, packaging, even the way in which the premises are utilised. Improvement should be evenly distributed throughout all work processes, and

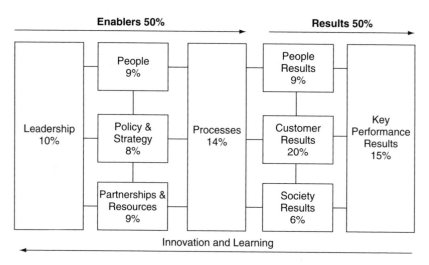

Figure 8.1 The business excellence mode/EFQM excellence model
Source: ® 1999 EFQM. The model is a registered trademark of the EFQM

measurements should show whether this is so. A chain is as strong as its weakest link, and no part of what is done within an organisation can be allowed to slip behind in the service quality improvement spiral.

We have mentioned the word trust before. Mutual trust between employees and management, between individual team members, and between different teams has to be cultivated and sustained. If people are to respond positively to challenges and feel motivated to pursue relentlessly the service quality improvement goals of an organisation, they need to be shown appreciation, given praise when it is due, be offered continuous opportunities to improve and extend themselves. They need to know that management has confidence in them. There is no upper limit for this employee enhancement, any more than there is a finite level of quality improvement at which an organisation can give a sigh of relief and rest on its laurels. The goal posts are always moving.

To reassure managers who doubt whether it is worth the trouble, there is always the accountant, who can point to the improving profits. Of course, if things do go wrong and problems remain unsolved, the buck stops at the desk of the chief executive officer, but relentless pursuit of the right strategy and the right objectives means that the CEO need have no fear. Neither need his fellow managers worry. A well-founded organisational culture; a base of carefully selected and fully informed customers; trained, competent and enthusiastic employees; cost-effective processes and all the rest of the changes made will ensure that the result of the continuous improvement effort will be beneficial to employees, to customers, to shareholders and to managers. It will become a way of life for all employees and managers. Continuous measurement of every aspect of the organisation will indicate how well the continuous improvements are working. Customers will come to expect it and make favourable comparisons, measuring the organisation against competitor suppliers. New customers will be drawn into the organisation.

It might be worth a digression here to look at British Airways, whose chief executive, Bob Ayling, in November 1999, announced further catastrophic losses. He spoke about how the company has slimmed down its running costs and is now turning to pricing policies, aircraft, staff and training and, last in his list, customers. When Sir

Colin Marshall ran this company, he had already done everything necessary to drag it back from the brink and customers had returned in droves. The trouble with staffing shortages in the summer of 2004 led to a further loss of confidence in the minds of travellers. When British Airways forgot about continuous improvement and the wishes of its customers, the weight of the company dragged it downhill. Now, sadly, it has to struggle all the way back to where it stood a decade ago. It will be less easy this time, due to competitor airlines having learned and remembered the lessons Sir Colin Marshall taught. Customers, who used the airline because they expected quality, for which they were willing to pay extra, have turned away because their expectations were not met.

One problem of British Airways is an object lesson in change management. Where smaller airlines were very careful about the customers they chose to attract, with a view to finding the extra dollar or pound per flight, British Airways made a drastic mistake in capturing an insufficient customer base, and alienating, by its pricing and staffing strategy, many potential customers. These customers went to other airlines, because they offered what passengers wanted. There was insufficient profit left in the organisation to match the product to customer expectations.

Keep outside suppliers of goods and services up to scratch

So far, in passing only, we have mentioned suppliers and suggested that they should be brought into a quality improvement programme. Unless this is done early, manufacturing defects and consequent delays in production might well result from the use of faulty, bought-in components. There might equally be problems with using outside carriers, designers, advertising companies etc. Where an organisation relies for any part of its provision on outside companies, these should be drawn into the organisational culture and expected to deliver to the same high and improving standards as the organisation wants for its own goods and services. It needs to be made perfectly clear that this will be part of any ongoing arrangements and that failure to meet standards will terminate the connection.

Shopping in the global marketplace

Ten years ago, many aspects of marketing were taken for granted. Today, a whole new set of problems, or benefits, depending upon how one reacts to them, have burst onto the scene. The euro currency, for the first time, enables companies to shop around for components, raw materials, even for manufacturers; and price transparency allows them to compare what is on offer. European legislation ensures that it is safe to trade with our European neighbours. The Internet information highway lets us shop faster and further afield than ever. Many companies have seen the benefits of the unified European currency system and open frontiers. Quality standards have been set across the EU countries. The EFQM system of improving and measuring service quality and all other aspects of excellence in business ensures a level playing field. The standards of product and service quality set in one country in the EU is recognised and accepted in all the others. As this market grows, so the availability of quality product and service grows.

In terms of what we know about customer retention as the only way ahead for modern businesses, trouble will always be noticed first at customer level. If the original segments of customers are abandoned, and new segments adopted without the long, detailed consultation process that defines their expectations, nothing else matters. Since all processes are geared to serve the defined and understood customers, change of segment requires a redefinition of the whole of the business. British Airways and Marks & Spencer are two examples of companies who forgot about the needs and expectations of the customer base they had originally chosen. Both assumed that they had no further need to improve. Both stopped measuring customer satisfaction levels effectively. For both companies, keen-eyed competitors were waiting, like ravening wolves, to snap up their abandoned customers. Ten years ago, British Airways and Marks & Spencer would have been used as examples of best practice. Now, we see them as examples of what happens when hard lessons are forgotten.

What has been said here about the supply chain applies equally to the delivery chain. If the producer takes every step to ensure that all is well within the organisation, buys the best components and raw materials, and yet allows the service or products to be delivered to its end users by organisations without an excellence culture, much of the original company's efforts are wasted. The links in the chain from manufacturer, or service provider, to consumer must be brought to the same level of service excellence as that expected in the main organisation. Untrained frontline employees, transit damage and late deliveries are all too common and always detrimental to an organisation's reputation. The list of possible hazards when the producer loses control of product is endless. The need for continuous improvement, to match that of the parent organisation, is self-evident.

Ethical distortion of customer segments

Measurement of customer satisfaction will quickly start to reveal anomalies in what was once a stable customer base, when global shopping for cheaper supplies becomes accepted by organisations anxious to lower prices. There will be some organisations who decide that they can no longer ignore price differences, and who will go abroad for their supplies. Organisations who follow the route of cheapness will take with them those customers for whom price is a prime consideration.

There will be other customers, however, who do not wish to exploit workers in less fortunate countries, who will refuse to countenance those who do so. These will adhere to organisations that ignore what is on offer elsewhere and remain loyal to their suppliers. New questions will be asked of customers, about their feelings on the choices of chasing cheapness without regard for the consequences to others, or on taking an ethical stance for as long as they can. Similarly, how major organisations react to what their suppliers do in this respect will determine their loyalty to those suppliers. Some will expect bought-in supplies to become cheaper. Others will find it necessary to probe more deeply into sources and consider ethical issues. Whether it is an organisation that makes choices about its suppliers, or customers for the products and services provided by the organisation, loyalty is the key issue.

In time, of course, more and more organisations might see from their measurements and reports that they are losing customers, for one reason or another. They will need to re-examine what is failing, and have to take tough decisions. When price becomes a serious issue for too many customers, organisations and suppliers who wish to stay in business have to look at the options available to them. They will need to check their processes and systems again, to see if they can cut costs without harming the integrity of their service quality culture or alienating their shareholders. This is the only alternative to putting a noose around their own necks, which is what happens if an organisation has to start its service culture and improvement battle right back at the foot of the spiral, while its competitors are still firmly on track.

Within Europe, where there are a common currency and common legislation, together with reasonably stable governments, it is safe to shop around. When the whole world is the market stall, with fluctuating currencies, rampant inflation here, deflation there, governments toppling and dictatorships arising, there will always be an element of risk. Add to this the ethical sensitivities of many customers, and the very strong sentiments they feel, and the global market becomes a powder keg into which one does not venture lightly in search of cheapness. The expansion of trade and industry in China is already impacting on world steel and fuel supplies and prices. Cheap labour in underdeveloped economies is sucking employment away from the west, and many famous names have already succumbed to the lure of cheap labour and moved production and call centres out of Europe. More will follow.

This should be enough to warn of the vital importance of measurement and continuous improvement of all the internal processes, of customers' attitudes and levels of satisfaction. Suppliers are a part of the organisation's public face. World politics are the storm clouds that threaten national economies. There is nothing that can be left to chance now. Watch must be kept on everything that touches an organisation, and notice taken of what competitors are doing and how what they do affects their customers. This brings us to benchmarks.

Benchmarks

The original use of this word came from the work of the surveyor and meant a mark made on a stationary object of previously determined position and elevation, and used as a reference point in tidal observations and surveys. It came into more general use with the meaning of a standard or reference point against which something is measured. In these present times, with legislation, national, international and, specifically, European, benchmarks are as subject to change as the tides they were once used to measure.

What is the value of having fixed points by which to measure, when everything we have said about service quality improvements hinges on this being a continuous process? Benchmarks can be moved further up the mountain, the measurements can always be adjusted accordingly.

Benchmarks fall into four basic categories: internal, competitive, functional and generic. The application of benchmarking will develop in an organisation that focuses on continuous improvement. The benefits of benchmarking are many. It creates a better understanding of the current position. It brings about a better sensitivity to changing customer needs. It encourages innovation, develops realistic stretch goals and establishes realistic action plans.

Cynics may argue that the cost, in terms of money and labour, is prohibitive. Benchmarking, according to data from the American Productivity and Quality Center's International Benchmarking Clearinghouse, suggests that an average benchmarking study takes six months to complete, occupies more than a quarter of the team members' time and costs around £50,000. The same study gave the answer that the average return was five times the cost of the study, in terms of reduced costs, increased sales, greater customer retention and enhanced market share.

Internal benchmarks

Internal benchmarks are used to make a comparison of internal operations and processes. Feedback from competitive benchmarks is sometimes useful in finding ways to improve internal operations and processes.

Competitive benchmarks

Competitive benchmarks, in the simplest terms, refer to comparisons with competitors. As improvements are made and organisations progress towards excellence, competitive benchmarks will become a measurement against the best in class. Due to continuous improvement strategies of the field leaders, benchmarks soon find themselves falling just on the threshold of satisfaction. As one organisation devises ways to lever its offering over that threshold and nearer to the line that defines the level of delight, other organisations in the same field will follow, possibly overtake, and the benchmarks move with them. The European Union, common currency and, through the Internet, globalisation, will affect benchmarks, as new laws are passed and new quality standards set. Leaders in any field of product or service provision try to go far ahead of existing benchmarks.

Functional benchmarks

Functional benchmarks are those used for comparison of similar functions within the same broad industry, or industry leaders.

Generic benchmarks

Generic benchmarks are used for comparisons of business processes or functions that are very similar, regardless of the type of industry. They can be used to set standards to measure processes, performance of product, for standards of training, for surveys of customers, for throughput from machines, productivity of employees, for unit costs of products. Any organisation can set its own benchmarks, against which it measures its own performance. Some processes are difficult to benchmark, by their nature. There are many things benchmarks can do, however.

Benchmarks can be used to identify key target areas for improvement. They identify best practice in this area by any business. They enable a company to compare its own practice against the best in class. Benchmarks also identify new practices, used by others, which would take the organisation beyond the benchmark. They enable new practices to be implemented. Benchmarking is a continuous exercise, with the targets always moving higher up the service quality spiral.

In seeking for new ways to offer customers satisfaction, benchmarks might cover product or service consistency, correct and timely delivery, and correct billing. Internally, levels of waste, rejects or errors, costs of operation and staff turnover might be targets for benchmarks.

The regular application of competitive benchmarks provides an organisation with competitive advantage as a result of improving productivity and quality. From this, it is clear that no business is too small to benefit from benchmarking. As the title of this book makes clear, its theme is the profitability of maximising management of customer retention. Businesses that do not use competitive benchmarking in order to improve existing processes or develop better ones, in the ongoing search for improvement, are unlikely to survive for long.

The practice of benchmarking should change the perspectives of executives and managers, help organisations to compare themselves with those of world class, challenge current practices and processes, and create improved goals and practices for the organisation.

New ideas can come from the comparison of one organisation's methods with those of another. Much time and money can be saved by this form of input. There is no disgrace in taking over the best ideas and innovations of a competitor. Proper use of benchmarking will often lead to an open exchange of ideas and techniques, to mutual advantage, even with fiercely competing organisations.

Benchmarking is easy to do. It is based on common sense and is a practical process to implement. It is a foolhardy organisation that imagines it can cope well without it. It has become a key component of service quality provision.

In customer terms, it means meeting and exceeding requirements for service, quality, performance and satisfaction. In process terms, it means going for zero defects, zero waste, and getting things right at the first attempt, in manufacturing and service environments. For employees, it provides the means to take ownership of their work and their customers, act decisively, innovate and, through training and coaching, become expert at solving problems. From management, it demands commitment, resources and planning.

The benchmarking tool

Introduction of the benchmark as a tool of management formalises the way in which managers and employees understand requirements and processes. It puts a sharper focus on what can be achieved. It facilitates the continuous search for examples of improved practices and processes from outside the organisation. In terms of continuous improvement, benchmarks help to show the way ahead. Without them, the organisation might well begin to lose its way, or decide that it has gone as far as it can with improved service quality.

Many organisations are initially enthusiastic for cultural change, people battle to overcome problems, the teams form and work hard together, but it is not always easy to keep the enthusiasm burning, once the easier tasks have been performed and the major changes put into place. Competitive benchmarking is a spur to further endeavour. If others are getting there, it is not for you to fall behind. What one organisation can do by way of improvements to an already good situation, you can do, and must do, better. If any organisation is not shown to be deriving advantage from its quality improvement efforts, benchmarking the steps taken and analysis of what this reveals will show up the defects.

It might be that certain key business processes are being overlooked. Is the management structure in need of reorganisation? Have proper teams been set up and trained to cope with new product or service development? Are frontline staff fully empowered to deal directly with customer complaints and grievances?

The better a company is at achieving its service quality ideal state, the greater the need to watch for what its very best competitors are doing and to benchmark against them. Benchmarking keeps an organisation's attention on what is happening outside, and stops it from becoming too introspective. It also provides a constant feedback on performance, which helps to ensure that the continuation of improvement is sustained.

As organisations move along the road to service quality, there will be certain changes in tactics that come with development. In the early stage, organisations benchmark against direct competitors. As they improve in what they are achieving, they benchmark against best in class and certain world-class organisations. When they become world-class companies, they benchmark customer service, distribution, and product development against other world-class organisations. In terms of quality improvement, world-class organisations continue to measure and document service quality improvement in the ways they have always used, dragging the benchmarks forward.

Benchmarking, in essence, comprises four steps:

- planning;
- data collection and research;
- analysis;
- implementation and review.

A general overview of these four steps is given below.

- **Planning**. Management must be committed to benchmarking. Key issues for the business must be determined. What to benchmark must be decided. Parameters for the study must be clearly defined. The staff to carry out the task have to be selected, and the study has to be planned.
- **Data collection and research**. Each process to be benchmarked should be analysed and documented internally. Identify potential benchmarking partners. Prepare interview and data exchange documentation. Carry out visits and collect data.
- **Analysis**. Normalise the data, using appropriate statistical methods. Define the gap between current performance and benchmarked performance. Determine causes of the gap and identify what needs to be done to close them. Set targets to close gaps and exceed best performance. Adapt and refine revised practices. Examine ways to

adapt processes, replace them, or incorporate new ideas in order to improve performance to meet new targets.

- **Implementation and review**. Communicate the new plan and obtain approval. Establish an implementation team. Produce implementation plan. Implement changes in line with the plan. Review performance and adjust the benchmark. Continue to benchmark. Continue to seek improvements. It is good to look beyond competitors in the same field. Other companies, with different products and services, will share many processes with one another and have useful ideas and suggestions that might be adopted.

An organisation is ready for benchmarking if:

- Processes have been documented with measures to understand performance.
- Employees understand the processes that are related to their own work.
- Direct customer interactions, feedback or studies about customers influence decisions taken about products and services.
- Problems are solved by teams.
- Employees demonstrate by words and deeds that they understand the organisation's mission, vision and values.
- Senior executives sponsor and actively support quality improvement projects.
- The organisation demonstrates by words and deeds that continuous improvement is part of the culture.
- Commitment to change is articulated in the organisation's strategic plan.

Field leaders and their recipe for success

Field leaders in any industry always say the same sort of thing when describing the recipe for their successes. The EFQM awards prizes to organisations that it recognises as leaders in the service quality field.

World-class organisations, those who are recognised as leaders in the field, score highly on 10 strategic performance measures. They are what we have already discussed in detail and are these:

1. Senior management made a commitment and circulated it in writing throughout the organisation, to create a world-class organisation.
2. Strategy and business objectives are customer-centred, regularly reviewed and updated, and widely communicated within the organisation.
3. Management's leadership style encourages people to use their initiative, manage themselves and their processes, and accept personal responsibility for satisfying their customers.
4. The supply of qualified, competent and flexible people is sufficient to meet operational demands, changes and contingencies.
5. Utilisation of resources is as good as, or better than, the best of the competition.
6. Productivity, unit costs and flexibility are as good as, or better than, the best of the competition.
7. Customers rate the quality of products and services highly in relation to those of major competitors.
8. Employees express a high degree of satisfaction with the way they are managed and deployed.
9. The local community is satisfied with the company's impact on environmental and safety matters and its involvement in community activities.
10. Investors are satisfied with the company's business results which are as good as, or better than, the best of the competition.

How does one measure continuous improvement?

Organisations, small and large, continually need to measure the effect of improvements made. Organisations should measure improvement against customer reaction and increasing profitability. They should also measure improvement against the best that other organisations are doing. This leads to steps being sought to take an organisation ahead of the benchmarks, and become the benchmark for others. There is a carefully engineered and comprehensive system available from the EFQM excellence model (see Figure 8.1).

The EFQM excellence model offers suggestions for evaluation and measurement and explains how to use them. One is the *pathfinder card* and the other is the *RADAR scoring matrix*. The pathfinder card is designed to assist in the identification of improvement opportunities through self-assessment and to help build improvement plans. It is a series of questions designed to be answered quickly while undertaking a self-assessment. This tool can be used at either criterion or sub-criterion level. The pathfinder card, in the main, reflects the RADAR logic that is at the heart of the EFQM excellence model. It should be used as a guide to organisations on what steps need to be considered on the route to excellence.

To use the pathfinder card, a criterion or sub-criterion should be selected and the questions from the relevant results or enablers section (shown below) applied. Improvement activity should be focused on areas where gaps are identified. For example, the results might indicate that the organisation does not have targets for a particular group of stakeholders.

Results
Do the results:

- Cover all appropriate stakeholders?
- Measure all the relevant approaches and deployment of approaches using both perception and performance indicators?
- Show positive trends or sustained good performance? If yes, for how long?
- Have targets? If yes, are the targets achieved?
- Have comparisons with others, for example competitors, industry averages, or best in class?
- Compare well with others?
- Show a cause and effect link to approaches?
- Measure a balanced set of factors for both now and in the future?
- Give a holistic picture?

Enablers
Approach
Is the approach:

- Soundly based?
- Focused on stakeholder needs?

- Supporting policy and strategy?
- Linked with other appropriate approaches?
- Sustainable?
- Innovative?
- Flexible?
- Measurable?

Deployment
Is the deployment of the approach:

- Implemented in all potential areas across the organisation?
- Implemented to its full potential/capability?
- Achieving all the planned benefits?
- Systematic?
- Understood and accepted by all stakeholders?
- Measurable?

Assessment and review
Is the approach and its deployment:

- Measured for effectiveness regularly?
- Providing learning opportunities?
- Benchmarked with others, e.g. competitors, industry averages or best in class?
- Improved based on the output from learning and performance measures?

RADAR scoring matrix

This is the evaluation method used to score applications for the European Quality Award. It can be used, too, by organisations that wish to use a score for benchmarking or other purposes. Basically, there are nine criteria, each given a predetermined matrix weight, established in 1991, and now widely accepted across Europe. The matrix weights are shown in Table 8.1.

Generally, each sub-criterion is allocated weight within that criterion, for example 1a attracts 25% of the points allocated to criterion 1.

Table 8.1 Matrix weights of RADAR scoring matrix

Criterion	Score
1. Leadership	10%
2. People	9%
3. Policy and strategy	8%
4. Partnerships and resources	9%
5. Processes	14%
6. People results	9%
7. Customer results	20%
8. Society results	6%
9. Key performance results	15%

There are three exceptions. Sub-criterion 6a takes 75% of the points allocated to criterion 6 (Customer results), while sub-criterion 6b takes 25%. Sub-criterion 7a takes 75% of the points allocated to criterion 7 (People results), while sub-criterion 7b takes 25%. Sub-criterion 8a takes 25% of the points allocated to criterion 8 (Society results), while sub-criterion 8b takes 75%.

The first step to scoring is to use the RADAR scoring matrix to allocate a percentage score to each sub-criterion. This is achieved by considering each of the elements and attributes of the matrix for each of the sub-criteria in the model. In the preceding chapter, we detailed criteria 6, 7 and 9. Criterion 8 (Society results) deals with what an organisation is achieving in relation to local, national and international society as appropriate. As with criteria 6, 7 and 9, this also has sub-criteria based on perception measures and performance indicators.

The EFQM excellence model provides an example of the type of sheet that would be used for scoring the matrix, and shows how to summarise for analysis of the total results. What the EFQM has aimed to provide with its excellence model is a unified approach to looking at what is done within organisations, to enable fair and just comparisons to be made between different types of organisation, with different employee numbers, processes and customers. This was done to help to improve performance throughout Europe and to set clear parameters by which the performances of contenders for the EFQM's own awards would be adjudicated.

The most important judge of improvement is always the customer, internal and external. Regular meetings between line managers, or leaders of process management teams, with a set agenda, seem to furnish a useful strategy. Internal customers know what is happening in their own process. They know whether they have been able to make improvements, solve problems, or whether things have happened with which they were not equipped to cope. The agenda of such regular meetings should cover the spectrum of what might have gone right and what has gone wrong. If there is a coaching or a training need, this will come to light. If the team is not united, or if it is overloaded, or where there is a problem that seems intractable or just temporary, this type of meeting will expose it. It can be useful to allow employees to let off steam, particularly when they have been under pressure for a long period, when dealing with extra orders, coping with process problems, pacifying difficult customers, or learning to use new equipment, for example.

Frontline staff reports and daily duty logs will bring to light areas where improvement might proceed faster, or where it is simply not happening, and provide answers about why this is so. These are the people who will get feedback if there is a problem in production or distribution, administration or something else that customers dislike.

Nothing succeeds like success

Organisations who put all their thrust into continuous improvement expect to succeed. Customers who are given improved and continuously improving service quality want more of the same. When they are given it, they tell others. Customers who think highly enough of an organisation's offering to recommend it to others will usually expand the range of goods and services they purchase. As they expand the range, so they become less and less inclined to make comparisons with what other organisations have to offer. There is no need for them to shop around. They have what they want. They become lazy and complacent.

In this lethargic condition, price and competitors' offerings cease to matter to them. They no longer require bombardment with expensive marketing. They now cost nothing to retain, except this improving service quality. The prison gate has slammed firmly shut on them. If the gate is not manned and the locks maintained, the prisoners will find ways to escape. If they quietly accept what is offered, without complaint, the organisation will have all the proof of success it could desire.

Cost-effective captivity

Not only does continuous improvement bring loyal, captive customers; it brings savings in marketing costs and in customer recruitment. What applies to loyal external customers also applies to loyal internal ones. Internal customers stay longer in their posts, serving customers who have become familiar to them and whose whims and fancies they understand and can satisfy. There are savings here, too. No longer is it necessary to calculate the cost of catering for an employee churn of up to 25% a year. The longer the employees remain in place, the cheaper the training programmes, the less the administrative costs of hiring and firing, of team building and of recruitment. If a team loses one member, the team-building process might have to start again from scratch, while the newcomer is integrated. If this happens too often, the whole ethos of teamwork might be lost.

Success is measured in satisfaction and loyalty. The satisfied employees seek to work for ongoing improvement, for the satisfaction they derive from it. As the continuous improvements accumulate and customers perceive them, come to accept and then to expect them, so they grow in loyalty and bring in new customers by referral. Employees derive satisfaction by giving satisfaction and remain longer with the organisation. The financial benefits of such a continuous improvement pattern can be used to reward internal customers with higher salaries and promotion prospects, and external customers with improved service quality. Where price becomes an issue for customers, the extra profits can be used to make *price improvements*.

Summary

In summary, everything we have examined in previous chapters has brought us thus far. The way to continue along the road towards profitable customer-retention management is by following the guidelines set out at the beginning of the programme for a new organisational culture, and using the system of measurement advocated by the current EFQM excellence model. The model will be reviewed periodically, to incorporate anything that might have been overlooked. EFQM also knows that it has to look for continuous improvements, if it is to keep its position in the European business world. It will take account of changes happening in and around Europe and globally.

A valuable tool to help with continuous improvement is benchmarking. This applies to everything an organisation does, and makes a fair comparison with similar processes, companies, activities and against competitors.

Nothing radically new is needed by organisations that have adopted the advice offered by the EFQM excellence model. It is only necessary to do more and more of the same. Every process and every system should be checked against what customers want and will want, and measured, logged, reported and discussed. Where an opportunity exists for any improvement, no matter how small, it should be taken, and then checked and measured again. One small step sometimes shows how other small steps could move things along some distance. This truth applies to everything an organisation does, not just the production and administrative processes. We have to remember that customer expectations rise in line with an organisation's continuous improvements, and continuous measurement is essential, if the organisation is to keep one step ahead of what the customer expects to receive.

There is plenty of guidance about what to do right. There are fewer specific warnings about what sorts of behaviours to avoid. It is not always best policy, for example, to place emphasis on the cost of goods and services an organisation buys in, especially if the cheapness is accompanied by unforeseeable perils that could interrupt supply, and by ethical considerations that are unacceptable to some customers. It is better to strive for continuously improving service quality from tried and tested suppliers as well as within the organisation itself. Organisations should maintain their customer base intact and satisfied, and rely on these customers to act as missionaries for them and their service culture. Once an organisation embarks on a proven service quality programme and maintains and improves it by constant vigilance, it knows where it is heading. Any change that might affect a substantial part of the established customer base is not to be undertaken lightly.

An organisation that benchmarks against its competitors and keeps a watch on benchmarks set by the best in the field has the ammunition to win the continuous improvement war. To keep it measuring and improving, great leadership provides the motivation, means and methods to employ.

In time, as global marketing is expanded and tested, the advantages and disadvantages of changes can be compared and measured against accepted and understood benchmarks, and rational decisions can be taken. It would be poor strategy to impoverish the home market by increasing unemployment, for example. This will lead to higher taxes, fewer and less valuable sales, uncertainty about the future for thousands of employees and a slow disintegration of everything that successful organisations have worked so hard to build. The temptation to go down this route has proved irresistible to many well-known companies already, and more are thinking about it. Some have come to regret succumbing to the lure and are busy reversing their strategies. There is such a thing as being too cheap, and if it is at the expense of service quality, the prognosis for the future is dismal indeed. In this connection there is loyalty to consider: loyalty to suppliers, to customers and to employees, and the importance to them of their moral and environmental considerations.

If an organisation feels itself irrevocably driven to seek cheap supplies, it needs to begin at the beginning, by redefining its customer base, and redesigning its processes. No longer will it be able to set the rules for suppliers, assume a stream of supplies will be available when wanted. It cannot even know from week to week exactly what its supplies will cost. In the world of unpredictables, it is always safest to be loyal to what one knows and has tested. *Organisations are customers, too.* What they want for themselves they must offer their customers. What applies here to suppliers applies also to the workforce and the cost of employing and training it. Cheapness is not usually an appropriate goal. We have already established that top quality goods and services, at a known price and readily available when required, are basic requirements of every customer. Once any of these is no longer secure, there is trouble ahead for the organisation. Continuous improvement means offering much more than the basics. Benchmarking helps to keep organisations on track and allows them to equate one action with another, and see how other organisations have fared.

Improvement and continuous improvement is spurred by great leadership creating great teams and a highly motivated, properly trained and empowered workforce. The first push always comes from the top; the momentum to keep it going comes from motivated people all along the line.

If world-class organisations find it a viable strategy to strive for continuous improvement, it has to be a valid endeavour for every organisation. Every company has a chance to join the ranks of the leaders in its field. There is an old proverb that says, 'Success is never blamed'.

9
Communications

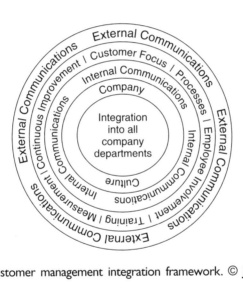

Figure 9.0 Customer management integration framework. © John A. Murphy 2005

We understand many things when we use the verb 'to communicate'; from a unilateral transmission of information or ideas from one person or group to another, to an exchange between individuals and groups of individuals. The methods employed to communicate are many and varied; they are also increasing to such an extent that many people are exhausted by information overload. When this occurs, the information is transmitted but not properly received. In the business sense, when this happens, something must be done to refine the process of communication, unilateral and multilateral, to its bare minimum so that it might be heard and comprehended accurately.

Before starting to develop the subject of communications, it might be salutary to mention an article about workaholics published in the *Observer* newspaper a while ago, in which the author, Richard Reeves, without providing his sources, claimed that an average British executive receives 190 messages, of one sort or another, during a working day, and four executives out of 10 are only able to work for an average of 10 minutes without interruption. It seems astonishing that such harassed people achieve anything constructive in their working days. The message here is that all forms of workplace communication need to be controlled, simplified and streamlined.

Week by week, new methods of communication are presented to the public, all of them based on information technology (IT). The sophistication in technology, however, is impacting adversely on communication by the spoken word. The almost universal use of text messaging, especially by the younger generation, is damaging the grammatical base of languages upon which comprehension of communication depends.

The avalanche of information to which modern people are subjected, aggravated by universal use of the latest IT equipment, is probably more than human minds, engaged upon a job of work, can absorb properly. Similarly, everyone, from executive, process team member, customer, supplier or jobseeker, can only handle so much 'communication'. So, before looking at effective communications, it is probably worth thinking about *what needs to be communicated, how, why, when, from whom and to whom.*

The starting point for discussion of communication, so far as this book is concerned, has to be the way in which the organisation's culture and mission are communicated to every employee and every supplier. It is a message, set by consistent example, from the most senior executive. It should be clear, simple, exciting and challenging. It belongs to everyone. It should be constantly reiterated, by everything else that is said and done within the organisation. It is intended to motivate. It should stimulate personal development. The company's culture is the most important message to be communicated.

Everything else that is done within the organisation should repeat the message that the aim is excellence; the culture is one of continuing improvement. The purpose of training should be aimed towards the same goals and repeat the message. Communication should constantly remind people that the happiness and satisfaction of the customer and of themselves is paramount.

Above all else, communication of the service culture should be an infection that causes a pandemic. Unless it catches the interest of every person in the organisation, it cannot thrive. One can talk about it, write memos and bulletins about it, report it in newsletters and magazines and write interminable instructions on how to achieve it, but what falls on deaf ears remains uncommunicated.

On a more specific level, in the context of the job itself, managers who wish to communicate with others about work must first ensure that the employees fully understand the aspects of their personal sphere of work that make a major impact on the organisation in general. If they do not do this, they cannot enter into a useful and productive dialogue with others. If people are not interested in what is being communicated or discussed, because they do not understand it, or they think that is has nothing to do with them, time is wasted by the communicator and the non-listeners.

First, there is the actual job. Employees benefit from knowing precisely what their own job entails, to whom they are answerable, and what part the work that each person does contributes to the total job. Employees need to know exactly where the work comes from and what happens to it when they have finished their stage of it. Workers should also have a good idea of their own work targets, how well they are being met and by what standards they are judged. Communication on matters of working environment, payment and promotion also plays a vital role in the attitudes employees have to their task.

Also related to the actual job are other issues of interest to employees. They find it helpful to know whether and how they can influence costs, and what safety standards are to be met. If changes are to be made, people need to be told what they will be and why they are necessary. Lastly, people should be able to say what the priorities in their work will be for the coming month.

Apart from the details stipulated in a person's contract of employment, other information that is of more than passing interest to employees might be about how one obtains promotion and how supervisory staff are selected. People might also want to discover how wage levels are set and on what basis bonuses are awarded.

The answers to all these types of questions were requested and given, at some time, by someone. Thus, to avoid repetition and misunderstanding, there should be an opportunity to think about these matters and find a way to formulate them clearly. After this, it is possible to communicate them to those who are affected by them. These questions are important to employees and should be dealt with openly and honestly, by those who formulated the answers to them. The more that employees know and understand about job and job-related issues, the more likely they are to stop worrying about them and concentrate on doing the job itself.

There are three basic ways in which to communicate in industry. A manager or supervisor communicates with others face to face. They may communicate by means of an intermediary: a staff representative, or a shop steward, or someone who represents other workers in a group. Then, there is the mass communication by way of noticeboards, newsletters, intranet, email, text messaging, and so on. Each is useful in certain circumstances. None is universally satisfactory.

Despite advances in technology, the use of noticeboards to communicate matters affecting everybody can be useful. The noticeboards must be situated where employees gather and have time to study the notices. This indicates a staff canteen, or at the entrance to the works, or office. Notices should not be left until they turn yellow with age. Someone should ensure that they are updated regularly. Safety notices and other long-standing notices belong in permanent spots, where they act as reminders. One noticeboard is far from sufficient for this type of communication.

Public address systems are mainly of use in an emergency. If workers are bombarded with verbal instructions, often in competition with the noise of machinery, telephones ringing and general hubbub, there will always be people who cannot hear them and others who will not listen. Newsletters are not ideal for passing work-related messages to staff. They are good to show off successes, introduce new products and new faces on the board of management, and to give background and general information on pension improvements, or new premises and similar matters.

Communication can be a response, or it can call for a response

When communication calls for a response, it covers the replies to letters, memos, telephone calls and emails, the answers given to questions asked directly, dealing with complaints or suggestions, responding to training and anything at all where there was a trigger action.

One of the most difficult skills to acquire is the art of imparting and exchanging information in such a way that it is effective and appreciated by both parties. Tone of voice can mitigate a reprimand, for example, and there is no offence taken or given. The written word, if this should cause offence, will be read time and again, and cannot be unwritten. Care, therefore, should be taken to ensure that those who correspond with or speak to others on behalf of the organisation know how to do this without giving offence. To those whose duties include responsibility for verbal and written communications, training should be given as necessary.

Some organisations use multiple-choice reply forms to deal with run-of-the-mill letters, but this is a very impersonal way to answer customers, and although it is intended to save office time, it does not engender good customer relationships. In the same way, the telephone system of multiple-choice selection between many departments by pressing certain keyboard buttons, while it suits the organisation and saves time, can totally frustrate anyone who is hard of hearing, whose fingers are injured or arthritic, or someone who is blind.

Top management should always pass communication down the line by way of face-to-face discussion with the next tier of managers, who, in their turn, will take it to the next tier down. The safest and fastest way to communicate is for top management to allow the next level down a chance to talk it through and clarify any anomalies before taking the message further down the line. Although management time is expensive, it is productive when controlled use is made of it. Too many subsequent queries and interruptions are time-wasters.

Top management needs training in communication skills, not just as much as other employees, but far more so. It is top management that recognises and rewards these skills in others. It is crucial, therefore, that top management understands and can use those same skills. If information is to pass downwards, in writing and verbally, to reach all parts of an organisation, purpose, clarity and simplicity of message are essential.

David Ewing, editor of *Harvard Business Review*, recognises and highlights management communication as the number-one problem in business today. While technology has advanced in leaps and bounds, he adds, managers' and academics' understanding of the substance of the process has not.

In their (2004) book, *Business Communication for Managers: An Advanced Approach*, John M. Penrose *et al.* tackle the matter of communication from the point of view of business management training, and lament the fact that colleges too often sacrifice basic skills, such as writing and speaking. A survey they made of 100 executives in *Fortune 500* companies revealed that oral presentation, memo writing, basic grammar, and informational and analytical report writing need more attention than they receive at present. Another study of executives in *Fortune 500* companies extended the important communication skills required to include external communication and technical applications.

The book discusses five communication skills areas considered by the authors to be critical for the advanced business communication graduate. Foundations of communication (written, oral, social and business listening, and informational reading); social communication; technological communication; employment communication; and organisational communication.

Of the skills considered to be necessary, *visual skills* form a part. It is not in dispute that visual aids reinforce a message and enhance a presentation. The advantage of the visual element of a message is in the speed with which it is absorbed. Visual communication subdivides into four basic skills: literacy, numeracy, articulacy and graphicacy. Another skill, technical literacy, is coming into the vocabulary of communication skills. The latter encompasses the ability to make appropriate use of technological tools in an information society.

Proficiency in *written skills* calls for the ability to write with clarity, precision, brevity and force of logic. These aspects apply equally to long and short report writing, progress reports and analytical reports. If a company uses a translation service, these skills are paramount. Poor translation of user handbooks or technical manuals can cause endless time wasting, mistakes and annoyance to their users.

Articulacy, the ability to use spoken forms of communication, is required in many interpersonal situations, and yet insufficient emphasis is given to training in this skill. It is required in face-to-face discussions, telephone conversations, informal group discussions, formal group meetings, interviews and formal presentations. In this form of communication there are many ways of distorting the message. Body language, differences in the sexes, prejudices and other unrelated factors can influence the way in which a verbal message is delivered and how it is received.

Another side to this articulacy skill is the way in which it is useful during interviews, when seeking employment, or promotion. Any manager, who has interviewed a tongue-tied candidate for a position, will know how difficult it is to make a fair assessment of that person, and how easy it is to select instead the articulate applicant. Once people have achieved this skill, it stays with them throughout their career, facilitating promotion and easing their way to better things.

Listening skill is reciprocal to verbal communication skill. Most research, according to the authors mentioned above, indicates that we do not listen well. Failure to listen correctly results in a communication breakdown between speaker and top management, supervisor or other team member. The speaker desires the listener to respond in order to judge that what is said is being heard. Good listening skills enhance work performance and the quality of employees' personal lives. Many training programmes ignore communication skills, and listening skill especially. Proper listening technique helps in mutual understanding of the message to be conveyed, since any unclear elements in the message will be highlighted by the listener and can then be clarified to the satisfaction of both parties to the exchange.

Literacy is too often overlooked because it is expected that the skill will be present in the workforce. For reading to be effective, it has to be followed by comprehension if the communication is to fulfil its purpose. To be bombarded by written material, all day long, sometimes blunts critical analysis of the messages it contains. There are ways in which employees can be trained to analyse, sift and deal with all the written communications that come to them. The authors recommend the following:

1. Think about the title of the manuscript, if it has one. What does it suggest regarding the content? Is it a comprehensive article ('A Thorough Discussion of…'); a historical or documentary review ('A Review of…); an organisation of existing information; ('A Taxonomy of…'); a position statement ('The School Board's Failing Marks'); or persuasion to action ('A Proposal to…')?
2. Get a feel for the whole package. This might come from a table of contents, which should be scrutinised for major sections and amount of space devoted to each of them. If there is an abstract, or executive summary, certainly read it and reread it. However, be aware that it may not fairly represent the article. Keep an open and critical mind. If you find no table of contents or abstract, page through the article and pay attention to sections, headings and subheadings. Note also the relative space given to the sections.
3. Now – finally – read the text. First, read it quickly for an overall feel for the content. You then will need to reread for deeper understanding of the content. Others prefer their first reading to be careful, slow and methodical. With either technique, consider highlighting (to capture your reactions) or annotating (which combines underlining, or highlighting, but add margin notes that interpret or react to the keyed phrases). Annotation is the more valuable approach if you need a thorough analysis of a complex message. You might want to generate your own system of highlighter colours or pencilled circles, underlines, brackets or arrows to represent places of confusion, disagreement, importance or summary.
4. Examine tables, graphs or other illustrations and think about how they complement or supplement the text. You might also challenge them to see if they misrepresent data.
5. Compare the message to other known information and challenge its assumptions and arguments. One approach for testing arguments is the 'ABC test' that asks, is the information appropriate, is the support believable, and is the support consistent and complete?

Following these steps should help you to read more critically and with greater understanding and comprehension. It may be more memorable, as well. The strategic process of reading case situations will help you polish this skill area.

Most of us have opened a box containing a new piece of technical equipment, with which we are unfamiliar, and have turned to the handbook, looking for instructions, only to discover that it is incomprehensible. This might be down to a bad translation, or due to poor use of English grammar. Literacy skills, then, are not just important in passing information from person to person within an organisation. Handbooks determine whether the customer uses the new equipment, or, regretfully, puts it away and forgets about it. In the field of translation, there is no room for anything but the best.

Graphicacy is invaluable when combining text and illustrative material for teaching and for sales purposes, as in a lecture using OHP slides, or in devising advertising, even in creating an organisation's logo. Not everyone can learn this, which is more a gift than something learnt, but in combination with the rest, it makes a powerful communication tool of management.

Once top management has grasped the principles behind these skills and learnt them, they should be able to incorporate them into the communications cycle of the framework. From the top comes vertical and horizontal communication across teams and departments, and to the top flows feedback from internal and external customers.

Top managers have a very simple method open to them to check how communications are working. They step out of the office, go down to the people whose work is affected by the communication, and chat to them about what they were told and whether it makes sense. This is known as walking the job. A manager with eyes to see and ears to hear can learn much from such an exercise. The more often this is done, the better the manager understands the job of others, and from this, the better he understands his own task. Of course, communication covers a broad canvas. It starts with customers, as our master diagram of the customer management integration framework shows.

Once a service excellence culture is in place, and people are beginning to understand the changes that are well under way, it is time for an examination of the exchange between customers and the organisation and between the organisation and supplier organisations. Communication between these will decide what needs to be communicated internally.

In the customer management integration diagram, which represents an organisation with an established service excellence culture already in place, communication commences with an information exchange between customers and the organisation providing goods or services. The contact with a new customer will probably start with an approach to the organisation, either as a result of referral or the impact made by advertising. It will be followed up with personal or written contact. In a previous chapter, we examined how information about customer needs might be accumulated. From this information, advertising and marketing initiatives are designed. Again, it must be mentioned that all in the supply chain, from raw material source to end user, require communication from the main organisation.

An organisation will also need to communicate with customers after a sale has been completed. There will be information about and with the product or service, to explain how it works, what it contains, what it aims to provide, and so on. Labelling, instructions for use, for care and repair, guarantees and after-sales service information come with almost every product. With certain services, advance information needs to be communicated to a user. When someone goes to hospital, for example, they may be told what to bring with them and what the treatment comprises. Customers wishing to add components to existing equipment need to know whether the new is compatible with the old.

User surveys, focus groups and questionnaires, as well as feedback filtered through frontline employees facilitate two-way communication by allowing the customer to have input, before and after a purchase has been made. The measure of success with this form of communication comes by way of further purchases, over a broader range of products or services, and from referrals.

Management has an ongoing role

Customer input, as we have seen, shapes product design, processes, delivery and innovation. It is the motivator of employee behaviour, skill and involvement. All of these reflect the ability of management to interpret customer input. So, from the first exchange of information with customers, management needs to be very much involved, if a valuable source of information is to be exploited. Management reacts to customers. Customers react to service excellence and product excellence. Employees are told what is required and should be supported while they do the job. They, in their turn, react to information that comes back from satisfied, or dissatisfied, customers.

While the organisation bent upon radical changes accumulates information about the desires and fancies of its customers, customers themselves are, at first, unaware of the cultural upheaval about to take place. Management, at this stage, is preparing to design the new service quality culture that will guide the change process. They set the example and make the rules. At this time, other managers are informed about the role they have to play, and chief executives lead the way by regulation and example. The customer cannot, as yet, be given any communication concerning the way ahead.

As the new service quality culture seeps down through the organisation, new patterns emerge. Teams are formed, processes are redesigned, and people become interested, motivated and challenged. They develop their skills and learn to enjoy pulling together for desired objectives. The type of communication that passes between people at this time is tightly focused. It keeps attention fixed on the customer. It discovers ways in which to do things better. It generates overall improvements. People skills are enhanced and job satisfaction accelerates. It only happens when communications are handled skilfully.

After the message has percolated to every corner of the organisation and people have agreed the objectives, interesting developments occur. Customers begin to notice improvements. It is a natural outcome of what has been done inside the organisation. As feedback from outside starts to reveal that an impact has been made upon customer perception, managers are able to confirm that there is communication taking place with customers about the new service culture. At this point, the organisation is in a position to communicate formally its new service excellence successes externally.

Leadership is the key

As the chief executive heads the organisation, the lead for all changes and the prime example for all behaviours must originate with this person, who should, ideally, have ownership of the communications role in the framework. He or she must have a very clear grasp, therefore, of what the customer wants, will want and might find irresistible. Only then can the unequivocal message of service excellence be transmitted down the line. Every manager, team leader and supervisor needs the skill to interpret incoming information, and communicate information to others. If training is required, training should be provided. Messengers need to be taught how to communicate effectively, clearly and concisely. They also ought to be able to decide whether the message has been properly received.

Communication is a dialogue. People might be informed about something, but unless they hear the message, it has not been communicated. Those who communicate should evoke a response. Almost everyone has encountered the society bore, the person who can talk without interruption, but who does not expect the listener to respond. There is no place for the bore in the workplace. If there is something to be said, it should have a purpose and fall on receptive ears. What is communicated should be to the point.

This failure of people to comprehend communications, if not spotted and dealt with swiftly, alienates. This applies to external customers as much as to internal people. Customers are impatient. Having made a purchase, they want to use the product. If their desires are thwarted by incomprehensible or overcomplicated documentation, they might accidentally damage the product, decide that it is not fit for their purpose, demand a refund and go elsewhere. As well as with the supply of products, this situation occurs with financial services, with health services, with any services that are documented in any way.

Poor communication is both damaging and unfair to employees

Employees become frustrated and their motivation is damaged, when they cannot understand communications and, therefore, find it impossible to implement them. Until communications are firmly controlled and subjected to rigorous examination and measurement, an organisation cannot know whether failure in processes, training, customer focus, employee involvement, or continuous improvement efforts, is due to poor communication somewhere within the system. Poor communication throws all other measurements into doubt. Appraisal and target setting would produce unjust results for employees who receive unclear communications.

What are communications?

They are messages from people to other people. Communications bombard us all, at work, at leisure and when we are travelling. There are advertisements on billboards, on television and radio, in magazines and newspapers, in shops and restaurants, in buses, trains and taxicabs, and on our computer screens. There is the email and the (now almost defunct) fax machine to bring us information, and we have the postman and the insurance salesperson. If we belong to a club, we probably get newsletters. Organisations for which we work have house magazines, bulletin boards, noticeboards, safety regulations, and instructions on how to behave in the event of fire; there are internal and external telephones, memos, mail and the human voice. Trainers have videos, overhead projectors, photographic slides, demonstrations and tape recorders to deliver information and seek feedback.

In the days before technology overtook the workplace, people spoke to one another, or wrote letters. Both forms of communication required answers. It was ill mannered to ignore either the spoken word or the letter. During the Second World War, when newsprint was at a premium, newspaper reporters, with so much news to impart, were forced to select only the most essential news items and précis them down to what amounted to an extended headline. The daily newspaper of those days comprised four or eight pages. Constraints leading to such brevity would have been good training for a modern manager, who sometimes tends to verbosity.

There are many ways in which people perceive communication. In the face-to-face situation, body language is the most impressive way to pass a message. The tone of voice adds a considerable impact, but the words themselves assume a very minor role. Communication by telephone, on the other hand, is mainly by tone of voice. The verbal element is still relatively minor by comparison.

Commonly, we still exchange information by speaking or writing to people and listening to, or encouraging written replies from, people. To avoid mental burnout, recipients of communications filter out what is unimportant, or irrelevant, and try to deal with the essentials. A person under pressure tends to deal with what can be accomplished easily and quickly, and saves the rest for a more opportune moment, when there is time to spare. What is not easily absorbed and understood will probably be shelved until later. What is shelved is usually overlooked.

Many large organisations use staff representative committees or union shop stewards to pass on communications from management. These people often have considerable influence over their colleagues and are in a good position to scotch any rumours. Rumour is the dangerous way in which misinformation is spread, or genuine information without the back up of the reasons behind it. Both types of information are potentially troublesome. However, one cannot hunt with the hounds and run with the hare. The use of such intermediaries needs to be done with care and the messengers must be fully cognisant of *and in sympathy* with management thinking if they are to broadcast it fairly.

Body language also sends messages

People have a need to play a part in dialogue that is part of communication. It is human nature to want the opportunity and encouragement to communicate with and respond to other people. Those who are denied a chance to provide input, use body language to show emotions that they are unable to verbalise. Watchful leaders and managers need to understand this language as fully as the spoken word. Frontline staff, too, should receive training in how to read the body language of customers. Body language often conveys a far deeper message than mere words. Like the tone of voice used, body language can fortify or nullify a communication. People can always tell whether someone is listening carefully, or is bored and distracted, or disagrees with what is being said. Listeners, too, can often make a fair assessment of how convinced the speaker is of the truth of what is being said. In the work situation, with colleagues and customers, body language is so revealing that its complexities need to be understood by all communicators.

There are, then, apparent difficulties about handling communications with precision, but closer examination of the subject indicates that this is not quite true. When management designs a communications system for use within an organisation, and to communicate with customers, it should follow the same rules employed for re-engineering processes. Always the customer, internal and external, is the guiding factor. The communication 'product' should be exactly what is needed, easy to use and only delivered at the right time to the right user/s. People should be properly trained to communicate and properly informed about what the task is, or the exact nature of the communication.

Is every communication necessary?

If we think about this, it becomes obvious that some communications are not necessary, or not yet. In business, where proper use of time is important and the customer is critically important, communications should be as much part of the business process as everything else should. In the light of processes, we can ask the same questions we asked about production and service delivery processes. First, define the types of communication that are essential to create customer happiness in such a way that it engenders employee happiness.

- What are the key factors about communication within, to and from an organisation?
- From whom do communications come?
- To whom are the communications addressed?
- What purpose do they serve?
- Are they essential?
- When are they most efficacious?

- How do they improve the current situation?
- Do these communications expect a reply/response?
- Is this the best time to communicate?
- Can we measure their effectiveness?

When management stops to consider the communication process within their organisation, it is helpful to remember that certain types of communication, coupled with training, can motivate and stimulate people, encourage personal development and bring advantages to the organisation. In top-down communication, the communicator must speak with knowledge and authority, if people are to absorb the messages delivered. The language used must be appropriate to the person being given the communication. When the communicator is a trainer, the lessons should be clear and sculpted to the needs of the trainee.

Managers, supervisors and team leaders might communicate by words, written instructions and by demonstration, as appropriate. There should be a quick way for employees to pass information back up the hierarchy, between team members and across teams. Technical information about processes should, ideally, be available on tap, to be accessed as needed.

Make it easy for two-way communications

Apart from the fact that poorly constructed communications turn customers towards the competition, communications that are poorly understood within an organisation work against the coordinated efforts of teams and managers. Every communication has to be comprehended by and be useful to the recipient. It has also to be necessary and timely. Communication of information should be pervasive and elicit some sort of response. This might be in the form of action, reaction or resistance, as well as verbal or written.

Where there is doubt about the wisdom or usefulness of a piece of information that provokes resistance, time is wasted while the matter is thrashed out. A problem is revealed. It has to be investigated. It might be to do with a lack of feedback from the team to management about the process concerned rather than with the communication itself. Managers who are not told something are in the same difficulty as employees down the line who are not told something.

Managers, team leaders and supervisors should certainly provide the means for employees to communicate with them and with others, and should encourage listening as well as informing. If teams are properly empowered, their side of the communication dialogue is as important as the leader's. In the same way as top-down information is communicated, there should be a recognised and easy method by which managers, team leaders and supervisors receive information from those over whom they have authority and can pass it back to the top, when necessary. Unless this facility exists, time and effort will be wasted in lengthy arguments, and goodwill can quickly evaporate.

If certain times are set aside for discussion and exchange of information, at every level, people will know when they can air matters that bother them. The work pattern will not be disrupted and input from colleagues will probably make resolution of problems easier and faster. The frequency of such meetings will vary, of course, from one organisation to another. Once the timetable is established, it should be kept.

To the rest of the world, we are foreigners

We live in a multicultural society and trade with countries worldwide. It is probably stating the obvious to mention that these factors necessitate the use of languages other than Standard English, or even US English, both in dealings with employees and customers. Multinational companies spend considerable sums in language training and in cultural awareness programmes, to enable smooth communication with others. Thus, this consideration has to be remembered when organisations explore trade expansion, or have multinational customers and multi-ethnic employee bases.

The Post Office publishes helpful books about foreign trade, currencies, holidays and other useful points, but it takes in-depth knowledge of language and culture if one is to trade abroad successfully, even within the European Common Market. In formulating communication strategy, the customer and supplier require organisations to 'speak their language'. A small example of this is found in Belgium, where on 31 October, All Souls Night or Halloween, Belgian families purchase large flowerpots of chrysanthemums. They call these 'Dead Flowers' and place them on family graves. It would be embarrassing, then, to take a pot of these chrysanthemums to a Belgian hostess, when she invites you to attend a Halloween dinner party.

To deal with religious and ethnic minorities in the workplace requires proper representation of all such groups, and understanding of their religious and dietary peculiarities. This means informing canteen staff about what food is acceptable. It means that managers should know when religious holidays fall, and let team leaders know in advance, so that employees can be organised to cover for absentees.

Where uniform is mandatory, a decision must be made about how far ethnic minority wishes can be allowed to override company regulations. This is for management to decide and for line managers to explain and enforce. Employees who have a problem require to be told who took the decisions and why. Not all employees are racially tolerant, and concessions to minority groups can give rise to resentment, but trouble must be nipped in the bud. The way companies deal with these highly sensitive issues is one area where proper communication, two-way and easy to understand, is critical.

In times of high unemployment, many organisations took the view that, if one wanted to be employed, one swallowed the whole package on offer, and showed due gratitude. Companies who behaved fairly and tried to understand the feelings of their ethnic and religious minorities reaped the reward of loyalty and avoided trouble when unemployment levels fell and there was greater employment choice.

Effective internal communication

There are certain basic guidelines for effective internal communication. These, like all improvements and changes, start with the chief executive:

- Lead from the top. *If the chief executive and his board of directors are not committed, it is unlikely to succeed.*
- Conduct an audit. *Like all good marketing, it is necessary to understand what the target market thinks and needs.*

- Communication is a two-way exchange. *Listening is harder than talking. Even harder is proving that you have listened.*
- Do not get mesmerised by media. *Internal communications is not the same as the production of an employee magazine or video. Choice of communication channel should be determined by the message and the circumstances.*
- Face to face is best. *Employees usually prefer to hear the news from their own managers and supervisors.*
- Only communicate when you have something to say. *If the top management is unclear about where the business is going, why, and what the role of the employees in this future will be, it has little of substance to communicate.*
- Constantly measure how well the messages are being received, and how staff view the process of communication.
- Honesty is the best policy.
- If your external and internal messages do not coincide and reinforce each other, you have a problem. If they do, you may have a competitive edge.
- Communications is an integral part of the management process. It is never an afterthought.

Monitor the effectiveness of communication

As with everything we have looked at so far, the exchange of information, and all communications, with and from external customers, internal customers and suppliers, requires constant monitoring, measurement and evaluation, to ensure that it is effective, necessary, timely and properly targeted. Extra information, revealed through effective communication, is valuable for the continuous improvement strategy.

Team briefings

The team as the work unit has already been examined in this book. Now, as we think about communications, it is worth examining how a team-briefing session relates to communication. The leader would probably begin by asking each member of the team to give a brief report on progress and problems encountered since the last session. It is useful for the leader to have in her hand a written list of the targets set at a previous meeting, and a list of any problems currently under review. The past has to be cleared from the agenda before anything new comes on stream. The leader will be making a report on how the team is faring and whether improvement in output is measured. This report will be passed to the team before it goes up the hierarchy. For this reason, it has to be discussed openly with those whom it concerns.

The leader would encourage input to any discussion from all team members, and watch for signs of tension and stress. If anything seems to be affecting the unity of the team, the leader needs to be able to spot and identify this. It usually indicates that there is a people problem. It will be necessary to get to the bottom of it, before passing on. Leaders are usually responsible in some measure for the well being of team members. Interpersonal friction destroys harmony in the team, and it is advisable to investigate the cause at once, by one-to-one interviews, if this seems to be called for. If it is a process problem, it might instead call for a brainstorming session, with the leader as conductor and observer.

The leader has the task of explaining anything that will affect the team. This would range from small things like filling in the holiday rota forms to the impending arrival of new equipment. In a well-run organisation, there should be no surprises. If there is unanimity of purpose and the unexpected happens, teams will adapt and accommo-date to the new circumstances. Wherever there are problems with something new or unexpected, unless these are temporary, resolvable and of short duration, the leader should report them to management. At the same time, the official team response to all relevant communi-cations concerning the issue must be obtained. It is then an occasion when the team leader should ask for advice from further up the chain of command.

Leaders also instigate training sessions, sometimes perform coaching and generally monitor teams' progress. To do this effectively and fairly requires leaders to be able to give clear, simple, concise instruction and to facilitate teams and team members to participate fully and freely in all aspects of dialogue. This type of communication requires formal training. Some people are naturally good communicators. Others have knowledge but lack the ability to share it. It is a skill that can be taught and practised.

Any form of communication, from whatever source, is one of two types. It is either part of a process and can be slotted neatly into the time and work rhythms, or it is uncontrolled. Customers' personal presence, letters, telephone calls and emails fall into the latter category. Steps could be taken to make dealing with these the responsibility of certain employees. People might be empowered to deal with the run-of-the-mill communications, and decide what should be passed up the hierarchy of management.

Non-office-based employees, such as salespeople and delivery staff, should be given specified times for making contact. This enables them to be monitored, ensures that they are not left waiting for attention and keeps them in regular contact with head office. If they are in difficulties, they can be helped quickly. If there is anything they need to know, there is a given opportunity to tell them. Drivers do not appreciate having to pull off the motorway to take a call on a mobile telephone.

This is a category of employee who has no access to the company noticeboards. They require to be briefed in a regular and systematic way about everything that affects them. How this is done depends upon the company and how often the salespeople and drivers come to the headquarters. Urgent matters can be passed on verbally at the daily contact times, but reinforced with a written version to be handed over along with any written information on less urgent matters, when these people come in, or when they bring their expenses sheets to the accounts people.

When management wants to inform employees of anything, it should be done in a formal and recognised manner. For matters of ongoing relevance, copies of the notice should be handed to each person by his/her supervisor, line manager or team leader. People do not like notices tucked into pay packets or sent to their homes. They feel that this is an intrusion into their privacy and it is often deeply resented.

Internal emails are not always the best method for blanket communications from management to employees. They are sometimes suitable for passing information to a small handful of people and can sometimes be a secure way to send out confidential material. Verbal communication should only be used in day-to-day matters. Where important information is distributed verbally, it is advisable to back it up by a written version and ensure that every person concerned has a copy for future reference. Verbal messages can easily be distorted in the delivery process.

Personal pagers are useful to communicate with people who work outdoors, or whose work takes them from department to department, but they are only useful to call someone to a telephone, or to another location. They should not be used to communicate the type of information that requires written back up or as a substitute for a face-to-face meeting.

We need to think of communication as part of an information-exchange process for continuous improvement. Unlike most processes, the exchange of information is not quantifiable in quite the same way as the other subjects we have discussed. It is far more arbitrary and the ways to deal with it are manifold. However, it obeys the main rules of all processes: it should enhance customer satisfaction with improved service quality. Internal customers are accessible in different ways from external customers, but communication with both is two-way, if it is to be effective. To find out how well it works, originators should meet with the people for whom the communication was ultimately intended. The managers can ask them directly what they understood of it and whether it made them change anything about the way they work. They should also be able to tell from regular reports whether improvements have occurred as a result of recent communications.

Certain basic rules emerge, when organisations think seriously about communication. They need to communicate effectively, avoid information overload, jargon, baffling language and misleading small print. They should look for ways to measure how effective communications are, and how to make sure every person, internal and external to the organisation, is best served with the necessary information exchange mechanism. Too little information and communication is worse than too much. One cannot blame the employee who disobeys a regulation, if that employee was never informed of it.

Keep it simple

Whether the communication is between customers and the organisation, or between people within the organisation, it should be easy to understand. Small print and convoluted language are barriers to understanding. Can you read and understand the small print on an application form for a credit card, a mortgage or other financial service?

Simple, straightforward language is what works inside an organisation and between an organisation and its customers and suppliers. This applies particularly pertinently when it comes to handbooks, instruction leaflets and to lists of ingredients in foods and pharmaceuticals. It is also highly relevant in financial services, where the devil lies often in the faint-coloured, small print.

People cannot respond to something they have only partly understood. Failure to employ simple language and give clear instructions to external customers makes extra work for after-sales and technical support staff, who have to deal with enquiries. In certain instances it can be dangerous to health, as when someone has a nut or other allergy and is unable to read the list of ingredients contained in an item of food.

Failures in communication from organisation to customers that lead to critical feedback from customers, internal as well as external, can be corrected. After-sales and service staff, when they have proper report systems in place, pass information concerning the problem back to management. They, in turn, communicate it to the originator. This person makes the necessary alterations, puts it back into circulation and asks for customer reaction. This situation often arises when a new product comes on stream. Computer software is one example where the product is contained on a small compact disk, but the handbook is a hefty tome. If there is a problem in comprehending the instructions, the customer will never buy software from that organisation again.

Failures in communication, from the top down and from below up, can be detected from absentee reports, staff turnover, process bottlenecks, customer complaints, errors and rising unit costs. The better the reporting system, the faster communication and processing errors can be detected and corrected. People who are content and who understand the purpose behind what they do, make fewer mistakes, are absent less frequently, have less inclination to look closely at the job market and are called on to deal with fewer complaints from customers.

Keep the door open to doubters

When information is passed down the line, there should always be an open door to the office of the originator for doubters to enter, in order to discuss the problem and clear the air. Much information begins as a written memorandum from the top to managers. They might pass it along verbally, and explain any anomalies or misunderstandings. Unless those who receive written information have every encouragement to challenge and question, or ask for explanations, they cannot give an honest rendering to others. Neither can they implement the instruction or utilise the information correctly. Properly constructed communications do not invite challenge or discussion.

Executives who complain that they are interrupted every 10 minutes have to look at their communications arrangements and see what can be done to ease the flow of their own workload. It is usually unnecessary to deal with a regular stream of communications throughout the day. The first task would be to take a close look at how communications are written and distributed. Although the executive's door should be open to managers with problems, it should not be necessary for managers to have problems arising from communications directly. Simple instructions and information supplied in clear, simple language, explicit and to the point will avoid the need for most queries.

The way in which staff are deployed and the responsibilities they are given should provide everyone with breathing space. Timetables for communication sessions, regular, scheduled meetings, and enough employees to do the work of the organisation are what are needed. Too many organisations are still of the opinion that a cut in the workforce can be absorbed by asking those who remain to work harder, or longer. The customer is not part of this equation. When employees are shed, service quality falls and customers begin to look to competitors for better service quality. Communications begin to miss their targets and time is wasted in seeking clarification.

Why is it more important to cut costs than to improve profitability? Is there better value for customers when an executive is harassed and exhausted by trivia? Is time better spent when he works as an enabler for others? If more staff are required for the smooth running of an organisation, they should be engaged. If communications become a troublesome burden on the desks of senior people, they have the power to hire help. They should ask why they are interrupted so often. They should enquire whether customers perceive the problem. Nothing that destroys the satisfactory relationship with established customers is good business sense. It is better to employ more staff, monitor things carefully and have time for the exchange of information and for executives to analyse the product and effect of communication.

To replace top managers is extremely costly. Properly managed, communications show up fault lines in the organisation. They enable steps to be taken to remedy problems before staff grow discontented and customers drift away. Executives and managers who are overburdened until they become sick can be very costly to replace. They find it increasingly difficult to motivate others when they no longer feel motivated themselves. As the spiral for continuous improvement rises, so the reverse is true. As things come unstitched, the organisation will spiral downwards, and to hasten its slide, the laws of gravitational pull apply.

Summary

The same criteria that apply to process measurements can be used to monitor and control effective communication and set up training procedures to ensure that communicators are competent and skilful. To begin, the service excellence culture has to be communicated to all employees. Next, it is necessary to sort out what types of communication happen between external customers and the company, and appoint people to deal with these. This will involve post room people, telephonists, sales staff and so on. Then, a reporting system should be devised, to ensure that vital information derived from such internal/external communication goes where it can be best utilised.

Internally, communication should be targeted at the person for whom it is of use. It should be delivered according to a recognised pattern, so as to avoid interruptions to work flow and to ensure a listening audience. Too many managers feel that it is better to bury employees in information. This has the opposite effect from that desired. People make use of the wastepaper basket, filling it with unread material, useful and useless. A busy person, given information at the wrong moment, will not hear it, or read it. The information might well be vitally important. If the CEO has the time and inclination to do so, a great deal of useful information is to be gleaned by examination of the contents of the organisation's wastepaper baskets before they are emptied by the janitorial staff. Are written communications finding their way, unread, out of the office or off the factory floor?

Lines of communication should be laid down, so that the communicator is recognised as having the authority to communicate. This avoids the need for people to double check with others. The desire to double check indicates that something is not quite right with the communication system. It wastes executives' time, when they have to confirm or refute information.

Information exchanged between team members will usually be on an *ad hoc* basis, especially when it concerns a process understood by the whole team. However, when such an exchange produces something of value beyond the team, it should be formally passed up the line, for management to distribute according to the established system. This authenticates it and makes it acceptable to others.

Apart from information and communication directly related to customers, or to the technical performance of tasks, there is information about employee performance to be communicated. When a team performs exceptionally well, this can be broadcast throughout the organisation, to encourage the team and to inspire others. Where this is not done, the team itself should certainly receive praise and reward. When someone falls below standard, a private, face-to-face meeting with a team leader, line manager or supervisor is called for. There is often something to account for falling standards. Sometimes it can be work-related and eliminated. If it is personal or a health problem, senior management should be asked to decide what steps to take. This, of course, is a confidential communication. It is not necessarily best handled in writing, at least initially.

If a team falls below standard, and the leader cannot discover the cause, the matter should be communicated up the line. The team leader might be the cause, or it could be one of a number of other matters, possibly unrelated to the team's own area of responsibility, that give rise to a problem. Leaders should be encouraged to be honest and open with management and with teams about failures as well as about successes. Hidden problems have a habit of growing. An airing is generally hygienic and leads to a cure. The source of the problem might well lie outside the boundaries of the team that experiences it.

Management action in communications falls into four general compartments. The first covers the market and entails independent market research, in all its various forms. The second deals with external perception surveys, and this means not only the way in which external customers view the company, but the way in which competitors view it, since their perceptions of their business rivals govern their own strategies.

The last two categories requiring consistent management action are in the field of continuous customer surveys and employee surveys. The data gathered from all four action areas mentioned should be disseminated throughout the company, so that all employees know whom they serve and why it is important to the customer that things are done in the way that they are.

There is a skill in communicating; for it to be fully effective, the communication engages both the communicator and the party to whom the communication is addressed, in one of the many forms available today. Between the parties to a communication there is a potentially dangerous gap of misunderstanding, and it happens when the message is imprecise, or the audience is, mentally, otherwise engaged, or is resistant to the message. Training can hone the skills necessary to the communicator, appropriate to the messages to be conveyed and the method by which they are passed on. Routine times should be set aside for regular and routine communications to be made, so that the recipients are able to concentrate.

Once a communication has been delivered, the communicator is advised to check that it has been comprehended. Not hearing it or not understanding it properly are worse than not having it at all. Misunderstandings can lead to discontent, rumour and trouble. Communication is a vital way in which all parts of the framework are kept in touch and informed. It is, therefore, worth time and money to ensure that it is performed properly, at all times, on all subjects, between all parties. Like everything else, communication can be and should be subjected to continuous improvement.

Culture

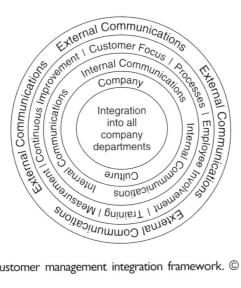

Figure 10.0 Customer management integration framework. © John A. Murphy 2005

What exactly do we mean by corporate culture?

We use the word 'culture' in many contexts, and it is, perhaps, sensible for us to define it precisely, before thinking about how it applies to an organisation determined on maximising customer retention and profitability.

The Readers' Digest Universal Dictionary offers several definitions of the word, some of which are omitted here because they refer to it in the context of biology, although, even that definition might be applicable in this book. The main relevant definitions are:

1. *Social and intellectual information.* This definition is relevant to COMMUNICATION.
2. *The totality of socially transmitted behaviour patterns, arts, beliefs, institutions, and all other products of human work and thought characteristic of a community or population.* In the work situation, this applies to TRAINING and PROCESS ENGINEERING.
3. *A style of social and artistic expression peculiar to a society or class.* Everyone engaged in an organisation forms part of EMPLOYEE INVOLVEMENT.
4. *Intellectual artistic activity.* This definition encompasses PROCESSES AND SYSTEMS.
5. *Intellectual and social refinements resulting from such activity.* EMPLOYEE MOTIVATION AND INVOLVEMENT are embraced by this definition.
6. *Cultivation of the soil: tillage.* In the business sense, this would cover CONTINUOUS IMPROVEMENT.
7. *Breeding of animals and growing of plants to produce improved stock.* MEASUREMENT is involved in this farming application, as it is in the business context.

With a little imagination, one can easily see how all these definitions apply to the sections within the customer management integration framework, and we are able to appreciate how they combine to produce what we refer to as the culture of an organisation. The biological definition of 'a culture': a micro-organism grown in a Petri dish, under carefully controlled conditions, applies equally to a business culture, which also flourishes and grows, but only if it is in the right conditions, and is subjected to continuous inspection and attention.

Ashby and Pell (2001) advise executives where to begin the process. They say that, before an organisational culture can be changed, it must be analysed and assessed. It is necessary to understand the current culture and to determine what problems exist and how seriously they affect productivity, quality of product or service, morale of the workers and the overall efficiency of the organisation.

The discovery of penicillin was a moment of serendipity. The right conditions for it to grow were in place. There was an expert on hand to recognise the antibiotic properties and to see their potential. Organisations also benefit from similar situations, if they go about it in the best way possible and have defined their goal.

Hussey (1998) provides, in diagrammatic form, a pattern of the elements that comprise a company, and shows how they interconnect back to the top. The impact points that Hussey indicates begin with change decision – at the top. This links to information systems, culture, decision processes, control systems, reward systems, structure, people, and tasks. Each one connects to every other one. Thus, each has to be assessed at the start of the change process. The customer management integration framework, shown at the beginning of this chapter, illustrates the same interconnectivity between culture and all other facets of organisational structure.

Beginning to develop a culture

The chief executive, having analysed and assessed the organisation and thought about how any proposed change will ripple down and out through and from the organisation, starts the culture development process by determining an objective for the organisation. This is a vision of the future of the company and relates to the way in which profitability is achieved and improved by enhancing levels of customer satisfaction and retention. It is, at this stage, theoretical. Before it can be advanced, certain other matters must be considered, involving the core values of the company. The culture grows out of these core values, once they have been absorbed and become integrated into all aspects of company activity.

Once decided upon, core values must become inherent, sacrosanct, never to be compromised. It is the first step in the rest of the organisation's life. Having begun the process, failure to complete and continue it amounts to catastrophe. A promise broken is trust destroyed. An organisation's culture will develop to inform every activity undertaken by all employees. The second step, then, will be for the chief executive to make a written record of these core values and where he sees them leading. Thirdly, he must consider how to involve all members of staff in embedding them into the daily work patterns and customer management, and this he does by means of clear and appropriate communication to all levels of employee.

Next, he has to inform the board of directors and the major shareholders of his vision and his plans for the company. He has to persuade them what steps must be taken, and he needs also to explain their significance in monetary terms. These plans for change on a major scale will come at a price, and this has to be settled at the outset, since it can make or mar the project, if funding becomes a problem at a later stage. There is no gain without pain, as the proverb warns, but what gain and for what pain might shareholders expect? Beyond initially approving and facilitating the development of core values, the shareholders usually have little to do with their eventual implementation in company activity. They judge their success absolutely in terms of profitability.

There will be some that ask, 'Why do we need to develop a culture? Aren't we doing all right without one?' This question can be countered by reminding the interrogator about competitors whose businesses are expanding rapidly and whose profits are growing faster than their own. These expanding companies already have core values and are forming, or have already formed, a culture that leads to extra profitability by providing customer satisfaction through excellence, and they are reaping the rewards in the form of customer retention and in their increased profits. It makes economic sense, therefore, to keep one eye on competitors.

The next tier of management now has to become attached to the vision, and enthused by it, and to infect the rest of the workforce with the same missionary zeal that they have. If managers truly share the vision, they will be able to apply core values to their own areas of responsibility in terms that are unequivocal, succinct and readily comprehended. To do this, they must show employees the benefits of adopting the new culture wholeheartedly. There are many ways in which employees might benefit from employment in a thrusting and visionary organisation. These benefits, as we saw in previous chapters, come in the form of job satisfaction, a better working environment and tangible rewards. People who enjoy their work and feel that their employer is interested in them, willing to help them develop their skills, and allows them responsibility and reasonable autonomy, will not look elsewhere for employment.

Employee retention is one easily measurable way to increase profitability by adopting a culture for excellence. Satisfied employees are more productive, because they look for ways to improve the systems and processes for which they have responsibility, and this also improves profitability in a way that can be measured. Happy employees will radiate enthusiasm for what they do, and this is contagious, so that new ideas and innovative practices seep laterally through the organisation as well as floating to the top and sinking to the bottom of the hierarchy.

As employees become infected and enthused, they will quickly begin to see how they can share their enthusiasm with colleagues and customers, and become a part of the process of change.

In his book, *Who Says Elephants Can't Dance?* Gerstner, former CEO of IBM, said, 'I came to see, in my time at IBM, that culture isn't just one aspect of the game – it *is* the game. In the end, an organisation is nothing more than the collective capacity of its people to create value.'

The same author gives other examples of the benefits of developing a strong culture, which, he says, almost always reinforce those elements that make an institution great. Management, he warns, does not change culture. Management invites the workforce itself to change culture. He quotes successful executives, referring to personal experience of culture development. One makes it a high priority to promote and reward executives who embrace the new culture. Another said that he measured the success of his culture initiative in terms of customer satisfaction and shareholder value.

In answer to questions about why it is necessary to find a company vision, formulate core values and drive towards a successful culture, there is a general consensus of opinion. No company is a success, financially or otherwise, without satisfied customers. Development of a strong company culture, therefore, has proved to be beneficial in terms of profitability linked to customer satisfaction and retention. The following example shows how the trickle-down process works in practice.

Top management
A top manager in a new or young company develops and attempts to implement a vision/philosophy and/or a business strategy.

Organisational behaviour
Implementation works. People behave in ways that are guided by the philosophy and strategy.

Results
The firm succeeds by most measures and that success continues over a period of years.

Culture
A culture emerges that reflects the vision and strategy and the experience people had in implementing them.

Source: Hellriegel, Slocum and Woodman (1995) *Organisational Behaviour*, p. 469.

Ashby and Pell, in their work, *Embracing Excellence*, reinforce the Hellriegel *et al.* proposition when they state that organisational culture is not limited to what is written in a formal statement. Much of what *becomes* culture develops slowly and imperceptibly over time and becomes ingrained in the behaviour of everybody in the organisation. They also say that there is a direct relationship between the employee retention rate and the corporate culture of an organisation. If employees are convinced that the company is truly concerned about quality, they will make every effort to produce quality work.

Think Christmas pudding

Everyone recognises a Christmas pudding, and yet, the recipe for making it varies from cook to cook. However, the basic ingredients are much the same and the end results are similar. We all recognise one when we see it, and the same is true of a well-constructed and successful culture within an organisation.

It is useful to investigate how some of the best companies formulate their recipes for success. A number of companies, such as HSBC and Colgate-Palmolive ensure that they live their values by linking them to their remuneration system. Colgate-Palmolive maintains that, by living its values of caring, global teamwork and continuous improvement, people develop a sense that they are part of the Colgate team, working together towards a common goal.

Colgate-Palmolive has identified a set of behaviours that reflect its ability to live the values. The behaviours provide examples of what managers will see when people are what they call 'managing with respect'. Each employee is assessed on these behaviours during performance reviews.

The company's booklet explaining the basis upon which employees are assessed is headed *Personal Leadership – Everyday, Everywhere, At Every Level. Defining and Understanding Global Leadership at Colgate-Palmolive.*

MANAGING WITH RESPECT

The logo says, 'COLGATE. Becoming the Best Place to Work'. The sections inside are the following guides to behaviour and assessment:

Communicate effectively

Expressing ideas clearly and simply; listening to others; creating an environment where people are comfortable expressing their ideas; promoting the timely and ongoing flow of information to others.

Behaviours indicating strength:
- Spends as much time listening as talking.
- Keeps people well informed of plans, goals and objectives of the company, department and the organisation.
- Provides clear understanding of job priorities and performance expectations.

- Asks for opinions and ideas on important issues.
- Shares information openly.
- Encourages others to say what's on their minds.
- Clearly and simply expresses ideas and concepts.

Behaviours indicating development need:
- Fails to get quickly to the point when speaking.
- Tends to withhold information from others.
- Does not listen well.
- Fails to achieve mutual understanding.
- Fails to respond to non-verbal cue.
- Does not set clear goals or performance expectations.

Give and Seek Feedback
Developing all Colgate people by giving and seeking constructive, specific feedback.

Behaviours indicating strength:
- Shows interest in the development of others.
- Gives informal feedback and coaching to perform better.
- Creates an environment where others can learn from their mistakes.
- Seeks to understand personal impact by asking for feedback from others.
- Changes and adopts new behaviour as a result of learning and feedback.

Behaviours indicating development need:
- Has an unrealistic understanding of personal strengths and limitations.
- Gives little feedback to others.
- Acts defensively when feedback is given.
- Neglects to recognise good work.

Value Unique Contributions

Valuing and recognising the contributions and good work of others; respecting individuality; involving others in making decisions and establishing priorities.

Behaviours indicating strength:
- Recognises and appreciates good work.
- Provides opportunities for people to use their skills and abilities.
- Gives people the freedom and autonomy to get their work done.
- Cares about people as individuals.
- Provides opportunity to have impact on decision making and direction of work group.
- Rewards high, average and low performers differently.

Behaviours indicating development need:
- Fails to delegate authority to get the work done.
- Does not value and respect differences.
- Shows little concern for the well-being of others.
- Takes for granted the hard work and extra effort of others.
- Neglects to involve or inform others about issues that impact them.

Promote Teamwork

Creating a commitment to common goals; resolving conflict in a positive way.

Behaviours indicating strength:
- Displays teamwork in getting work done.
- Encourages people to work as a team.
- Anticipates and facilitates resolution of conflict.
- Facilitates a sense of belonging to the organisation and the company.

Behaviours indicating development need:
- Is preoccupied with protecting turf.
- Puts personal agenda before the best interests of the business.
- Is insensitive to the priorities and issues of other departments and organisations.
- Avoids personal conflict.
- Shows partiality by not treating all team members equally.

Set the Example
Setting a positive example for conducting business in an ethical manner; managing stress; creating a pleasant and balanced work environment.

Behaviours indicating strength:
- Stays positive and confident in face of stress and uncertainty.
- Demonstrates ethical, professional behaviour in all interactions.
- Creates a casual, and pleasant work environment.
- Encourages and supports work/life balance.
- Embraces change positively taking personal responsibility for its success.

Behaviours indicating development need:
- Preaches rather than practices Colgate values.
- Neglects to put issues on the table in a candid and open way.
- Is insensitive and indifferent to personal situations and work/life balance.
- Interrupts and cancels meetings.

When a manager conducts a performance review with an employee, the form used deals specifically with the five sectors on Managing with Respect principles of Valuing Colgate People mentioned above. They are concerned with how well the employee:

1. Communicates effectively.
2. Gives and seeks feedback.
3. Values the unique contributions of others.

4. Promotes teamwork.
5. Sets the example.

Marks are given in descending order, from 1 = Exceptional to 4 = Below expectations. These marks indicate the overall performance rating, considering achievement of all objectives, use of competencies in achieving performance results, and principles of valuing people.

Use of a standard formula for assessments is seen as fair and just, since it obviates prejudice and is, therefore, acceptable to employees and managers alike. Unless this fairness pertains to all employee involvement, there will be resistance to change.

Hussey, in *How to Be Better at Managing Change* (1998), referred to this when he said that resistance emerges when there is a threat to something the individual values, for example, job loss or demotion, resentment at an imposed change, lack of trust in leaders, belief that change is wrong, personal animosity.

Ashby and Pell, in *Embracing Excellence* (2001), also refer to this, but in a positive way, when they define the features of a great organisational culture as:

 1. An almost missionary zeal.
 2. A sense of pride, sincerity and cooperation.
 3. An attitude of *constructive discontent* (continuous improvement).
 4. A value-based mind-set and management style.
 5. An emphasis on creativity and innovation.
 6. A focus on building role models, not just leaders.
 7. A sense of high expectations and professional standards.
 8. A fair, commensurate compensation and incentive programme.
 9. A habit of celebrating success.
10. Adhering to the golden rule.

It is an interesting exercise for executives and employees to rate their own companies, with marks out of 10, for each of the foregoing features.

Several experts in the business world have tackled the subject of resistance to change. Lewis *et al.* (1995) use Lewin's three phases of the planned change process to illustrate the way in which the change process works (see Figure 10.1).

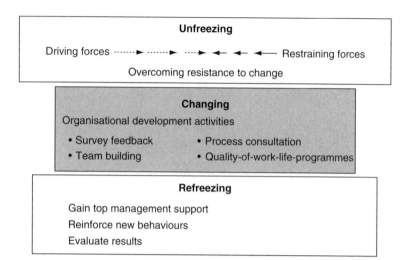

Figure 10.1 Lewin's three phases of the planned change process
Source: Lewis, P.S., Goodman, S.H. and Fandt, P.M. (1995) *Management Challenges in the 21st Century*, South-Western, p. 364

Hussey suggests four ways to deal with resistance by using communications. Effective communication, he says, helps to reduce resistance by ensuring that the change is fully understood. It helps people to realise that the organisation has given some thought to them. It ensures that everyone understands and this will reduce resistance, as, for example, when there is a widespread awareness of a crisis. Managing people's expectations is important.

He goes on to suggest an *easier approach* to the leadership of fundamental change. The steps he advocates are interconnected and consist of:

1. Envision
2. Activate
3. Support
4. Implement
5. Ensure
6. Recognise

Hussey's easier approach to fundamental change

Step 1 – Envisioning

A vision, he says, represents a total view of what the organisation is trying to become at some point in the future. The components of good vision are: emotional appeal; credibility; challenge; internal integrity; and it should relate to the past, present and future.

Step 2 – Activation

- Demonstrate your own beliefs in the vision – remember that judgements are formed not on what you say, but on how you behave.
- Extend personal contact as far as possible.
- Workshops of key people are a valuable way of building commitment.
- Ensure that there are opportunities for two-way communication.
- Use the everyday meetings to emphasise the message.
- Seek out examples of success that reinforce the vision.
- Select your team members with care – be willing to empower the team, so that it can make a genuine contribution.
- Audit the nature and content of internal training.

Steps 3–6 – Support, Implement, Ensure and Recognise

Express confidence in subordinates and peers involved in the change; provide coaching to help them to overcome difficulties; ensure that key people are properly empowered; be empathetic to people's situations, and use praise and sincere thanks.

Rule books

In a successful culture, rule books are for idiots, cultural concepts are for the properly motivated. Of course, rules are necessary for reference, when an employee is temporarily out of his or her depth in an unexpected situation, or to resolve disputes over action to be taken. Blind adherence to the rule book, however, is a lazy employee's way to avoid using any initiative.

Rule books are of value as a reminder of what is expected. They should not be treated as a lifeboat for the non-swimmer. If employees cling to the rule book, that is clear evidence of the need for more training, or for a change of occupation. All employees have to function within the rules, but should be able to bend them to suit individual circumstances, especially when it is a question of offering customer satisfaction. This applies to internal as well as external customers. This type of initiative should be encouraged throughout the organisation, not permitted for some employees and forbidden to others.

N.G. Bailey, a major engineering company in the UK, adopted an excellence culture a few years go, and has been refining and polishing the implementation of its core values ever since. In the company's own words, it recognises exactly what its company values are.

- *People: our most valuable resource.* We will continue to invest in our future by attracting, developing, involving, motivating, retaining and rewarding highly competent, committed and creative people who are the best in their areas of expertise.
- *Partnership: commitment to all our stakeholders.* We will be totally responsive to, and strive to exceed the expectations of, all our stakeholders – everybody who has an interest in our business – working safely and consistently with responsible environmental practices.
- *Performance: high quality, creative solutions.* We will respond to rapidly changing markets with entrepreneurial, innovative solutions that deliver exceptional value to our customers and partners, helping them to maximise their success.

- *Pre-eminence: long-term devotion to be the best.* We will create a continuously improving working environment, supported by strong leadership, which promotes openness, trust, communication, teamwork, empowerment, loyalty and job satisfaction.

Growing and sustaining a customer-focused culture

Paul R. Sparrow, Professor of International Human Resource Management at Manchester Business School, produced a research proposal entitled *Growing and sustaining a customer focused culture* (2004), in which he mentioned some of the methods used by companies to link employee behaviour and reward to business performance. Citing Asda as an example, he speaks of the work it has done on flexible working and the way this links to business performance. The company claims that its initiatives can be linked to a £4 million reduction in the cost of absenteeism, the retention of staff and is an inducement tool for recruitment.

He refers also to Woolworths, which has recently introduced company-wide targets to measure employee engagement, as part of its efforts to become an employer of choice. It has begun to change the way it uses its employee surveys, and the new surveys are conducted twice a year against a series of statements that are focused around employee engagement. Tesco, he says, uses segmentation to analyse its employees. As a result of this analysis, staff were placed into one of five categories, in a bid to be more receptive to employees' needs. To study the link between morale scores and improvements in other areas, Tesco's staff are surveyed twice a year.

Paul Sparrow mentions that a number of building societies began to examine the qualities that need to be conveyed to customers. These included: *responsiveness* – readiness to provide a service; *competence* – having knowledge and skills to deliver a service; *access* – approachability and ease of control; *courtesy* – explicit politeness; *respect* – consideration and friendliness; *communication* – keeping the customer informed in language that he/she can understand; *listening* – understanding – making the effort to appreciate customer needs; and *reliability* – performance and dependability.

Studies in the retail sector demonstrate that staff need to internalise the concept of service excellence, which means be committed to it and have a good understanding of its principles. They need, also, to have the confidence to deal with problems and have sufficient job autonomy to exercise personal judgement. Role models, in this case their line managers and the organisation, have to demonstrate appropriate behaviour. Role modelling requires support from the boss and the supervisor, who must themselves show a personal commitment to service. Top management has to convince staff that the organisation is consistent and genuine about its commitment to customer service. One way in which this is done is during the selection and recruitment process, when new staff are hired for customer service qualities. Somehow, the human resources manager must decide what is implied by the need for employees to live the firm's values, and hire accordingly.

Sparrow does not mention specifically the relationship between reward and customer service derived from commitment. The retail sector is notorious for low wages and high staff turnover. It takes something extra to win hearts and minds in this field. The original motivation for a person accepting employment is a basic need for the remuneration expected. Even with low pay, fair dealing and honesty create mutual trust between employer and employee. This is a good basis for the development of employee commitment, but good results should be rewarded fairly and honestly.

All too often, shop staff are expected to work longer hours than they are contracted to work, for no extra pay, and this elicits a negative response as far as the company and its aspirations are concerned.

Patrick M. Lencioni, in his article, *Make Your Values Mean Something* (2002), cites the four corporate values of Enron mentioned earlier.

History showed that the company failed to live up to a single one of them. Empty value statements, Lencioni reminds us, are meaningless. They create cynical and dispirited employees, alienate customers and undermine managerial credibility. He refers to the *Fortune* 100 companies, 80% of which touted their values publicly – values that stood for nothing. Values can set a company apart from the competition by clarifying its identity and serving as a rallying point for employees. Too often, executives mistake other kinds of values for core values.

*   *Core values* are the deeply ingrained principles that guide all of a company's actions; they serve as its cornerstones.
*   *Aspirational values* are those that a company needs to succeed in the future but currently lacks.

Lencioni says that 55% of all *Fortune* 100 companies claimed integrity is a core value, 49% espoused customer satisfaction and 40% touted teamwork. He points out that, although these are unarguably good qualities, they hardly provide a blueprint for employee behaviour. Siebel, on the other hand, has a list of values, topped by *professionalism*, which set it apart from the 'frivolous' cultures of many technology companies. Siebel's employees are not allowed to eat at their desks, nor can they decorate their office walls with more than one or two photographs. These prohibitions distinguish Siebel from competitors and give prospective and current employees a clear understanding that, to succeed, they must act professionally at all times.

It is impossible for a new employee to spend a week with this company without realising that customer satisfaction is a core value. All the artwork on the walls comes from the customers' annual reports, and all the conference rooms are named after customers. Even bonuses and compensation packages are awarded on the basis of customer satisfaction surveys conducted by an outside auditor.

> **If you are not willing to accept the pain real values incur, don't bother going to the trouble of formulating a values statement.**

Too many executives choose, after they have decided to embark on a values initiative, to hand it all to the human resources department. HR formulates employee surveys and holds lots of meetings, to gather input and build consensus. The author reminds us that this is precisely the wrong approach.

> Value initiatives have nothing to do with building consensus – they're about imposing a set of fundamental, strategically sound beliefs on a broad group of people.

Values initiatives

Lencioni says small teams that include the CEO, any founders who are still with the company and a handful of key employees, drive the best value efforts. Like a fine wine, a good values programme is never rushed. Executives should discuss values over a number of months; they should consider and reconsider how the standards will play out within their corridors.

Integration

Core values next have to be integrated into every employee-related process, hiring methods, performance management systems, criteria for promotions and rewards.

Comergent, a young e-business company, has successfully created a strong culture around dependability, dedication and self-motivation by integrating these core values into every system that directly touches employees. Job candidates, from receptionist to vice presidents, are screened not only for their skills and experiences but also for their fit with the company's values. During interviews, Jean Kovacs and her staff ask frank questions about workload expectations and past accomplishments. To test their self-motivation and dedication, for example, she asks candidates to describe something they've accomplished that other people thought would be impossible.

After employees arrive at Comergent, they are reminded again and again that the company's values are more than just words. People are evaluated against the core values, and when it comes time to award stock, bonuses and salary increases, Kovacs and her team again use the values statement as a metric. Even the decision to let someone go is driven by values.

Another example of a values-driven organisation is Nordstrom. It constantly reminds employees of its core value of customer service. During orientation, rather than receiving a detailed handbook describing how to deliver great service to customers, new employees are told elaborate stories recounting the lengths to which fellow employees have gone in order to wow its clientele.

Wal-Mart, the retail giant, constantly stresses its core values of excellence, customer service and respect to employees.

From these examples of core values we have a selection of ingredients with which to make the recognisable Christmas pudding of a culture that satisfies employees and customers alike.

Trust

We mentioned trust with respect to low paid employees at the beginning of this chapter. N. G. Bailey has trust incorporated into its list of core values, under the heading: Pre-eminence: long-term devotion to be the best. Like the word culture, trust has a multiplicity of meanings. For now, the most applicable definition of trust is a firm reliance on the integrity, ability, or character of a person or thing; confident belief, faith.

Robert Galford and Anne Siebold Drapeau, in an article entitled 'The enemies of trust', in the *Harvard Business Review* of February 2003, adapted from their book, *The Trusted Leader* (Free Press, 2003), discuss the difficulty of pinning down trust in an organisation. According to these authors, the term organisational trust means different things to different people. They mention the three different kinds of trust covered by organisational trust. The first is *strategic trust* – the trust employees have in the people running the show to make the right strategic decisions. Do top managers have the vision and competence to set the right course, allocate resources intelligently, fulfil the mission, and help the company to succeed? If this area of trust is missing from the organisation, there is nothing that can replace it.

The second type of trust is *personal trust* – the trust employees have in their own managers. Do managers treat employees fairly? Do they consider employees' needs when they make decisions about the business, and do they put the company's needs ahead of their own desires? This type of trust is complicated by many factors, not least of which is the complexity of human nature.

The third type is *organisational trust* – the trust people have, not in any individual, but in the company itself. Are processes well designed, consistent and fair? Does the company make good on its promises?

An established body of research demonstrates the links between trust and corporate performance.

The building blocks of trust are old-fashioned managerial virtues like consistency, clear communication and a willingness to tackle awkward questions.

The enemies of trust are manifold and ubiquitous. They can come in the guise of a person, the manager, for instance, who habitually expresses contempt for top management. It can be knit into the fabric of the organisation: a culture that punishes dissent or buries conflict. Some enemies of trust are overt. You promise that this will be the last lay-off, and subsequently more people are laid off. Other enemies are covert. A conversation you thought was private is repeated and then grossly distorted by the rumour mill. Any act of bad management erodes trust, and the list of enemies could be endless. The authors of the article say, however, that there are common features leading to breakdown of trust, which are explained in the following pages.

Inconsistent messages

These can occur anywhere in an organisation, from senior managers down, and are one of the fastest-moving destroyers of trust. They can occur externally, in the way an organisation communicates with its customers or other stakeholders. Either way, the repercussions are significant. A manager who makes promises to employees and then casually breaks them, when it comes time for him to conduct performance reviews, meets confused and sceptical staff. It happens, too, that senior executives often communicate inconsistent messages and priorities to various parts of the organisation, and this leads inevitability to misunderstanding and confusion.

The antidotes to inconsistent messages are straightforward, if not always easy to implement. Think through your priorities. Before you broadcast them, articulate them to yourself, or to a trusted adviser, to ensure that they are coherent and that you are being honest with people instead of making unrealistic commitments. Make sure your managerial team communicates a consistent message. Reserve the big-bang announcements for truly major initiatives.

Inconsistent standards

If an individual manager or the company plays favourites, their trust will be eroded. Employees keep score – relentlessly. Imagine what would be the consequence of the CEO taking the new vice president of marketing out to lunch when he was promoted two months ago but failing to do so when a new head of IT was appointed last week. There might be legitimate reasons for the CEO's inconsistent behaviour, but the IT executive and the people around him/her will jump to the least-flattering, least-legitimate conclusion.

There is the case where the company's star performer is allowed to bend the rules while everyone else is expected to toe the line. In order to keep him, you, as an executive, may think it's worthwhile to let the most talented employee live by different rules. The problem is that your calculation doesn't take into account the cynicism you engender in the rest of the organisation.

Misplaced benevolence

Managers know they have to do something about the employee who regularly steals, cheats or humiliates co-workers. However, most problematic behaviour is subtler than that, and most managers have a hard time addressing it. There can be few organisations without at least one person who is so out of his class that his colleagues ask themselves why his supervisors don't do something. They learn to work around him, but it is not easy. The supervisor is reluctant to punish him because he is not harming anyone or anything on purpose. That kind of incompetence destroys value and destroys all three kinds of trust.

Another type that is found too frequently is the person with a negative attitude to everything. They might have been passed over for promotion, or feel that they have been unfairly treated in the matter of salary or bonus. While they do not directly sabotage the organisation, they see the downside of everything. Two results can follow a person of this type. Colleagues grow tired of the negativity, or they catch it themselves.

The last type is the one who behaves appallingly and gets away with it because of his technical competence. Extremely ambitious people also sometimes behave in this way, destroying teamwork by putting their own agendas ahead of the organisation's interests. Is this person so valuable to the company that his behaviour has to be tolerated? It is a problem that managers cannot side-step.

Sometimes, problematic employees can be transferred to more suitable jobs, or they can be coached or trained, or surrounded by people who will help them to improve. Sometimes, the only way to resolve their problem is to let them go. The longer they are allowed to continue with their bad behaviour, the more everyone else feels the effects, and blames you.

False feedback

When an incompetent or otherwise unsuitable person is dismissed, managers often face wrongful dismissal hearings. The sacked person points to performance reviews and says how good they are. The problem about these is that they are lies. It is difficult to be honest about a person's shortcomings when sitting face to face with them at review times. If you are not honest, you will find your hands tied when you want to get rid of unsuitable employees, and those people who deserve praise will feel aggrieved and demoralised by receiving the same praise and marks as the useless person. If you don't hear their complaint, its effect will be felt in a lower quality of work from the competent employees.

Failure to trust others

Managers who cannot bring themselves to trust others also find it impossible to delegate work, or have to fence it round with so many directives that the person to whom the task is given feels insulted at not having autonomy. This type of manager is often overburdened and needs help to carry the workload. Failure to delegate, when he has the opportunity, robs him of any sympathy from his superiors and isolates him from those under his control. The best of these employees will not tolerate his behaviour and will quickly find employment elsewhere.

Stress and its impact on satisfaction

A modern and increasing problem in the workplace is stress, the root causes of which are often to be traced back to lack of trust in the competence of managers to secure the future of the business, and line managers to apportion work fairly, and who fail to pick up signals that indicate a personal problem with a given employee. In turn, there arises the fear that the employment is insecure. Line managers, who show favouritism to some, induce stress in others due to lack of overt signs of appreciation and lack of empowerment; other workers are stressed by their perception of lack of advancement opportunities. Stress, however engendered, results in miserable employees, increased absenteeism and long and often unproductive working hours. Stress is a poison that quickly permeates the whole workforce, as the weaker succumb to illness and exhaustion, and add to the burden of those who must bear the extra workload. Understanding the causes of stress, and its management, are skills that should be acquired by management before the poison spreads too far and erodes loyalty and satisfaction among employees as well as customers. The outcome, otherwise, is loss of profit.

The decline in customer satisfaction

In spite of all that has been said and written about organisational culture, development for the enhancement of customer and employee satisfaction and loyalty, things are still going awry on both fronts. Sparrow and Cooper (2003), made a graph of some MORI data, gathered since 1969, of British public attitudes. The graph relates to the percentage of the British population agreeing that large firms help make things better for those who buy their products and services. It indicates a slow drop from a peak that began to decline in 1981–2, peaked again, briefly, and then showed a sharp drop in those who agree, over a period commencing in 1984, and continuing the downward trend until 2003. Why is this the case?

Some interesting and relevant questions formed the topics for discussion at a CMLG Workshop held in September 2004. They help to highlight possible reasons for the decline in customer satisfaction that were indicated in the MORI data. Note that these topics deal with frontline staff, perhaps the very people who might be expected to have most job satisfaction, once they have been trained appropriately. For many organisations, the term frontline staff, meaning those who actually meet the end user at the moment of purchase, can be misleading, due to the long chain of people who handle products and services before they arrive at the last customer. However, we have stated earlier that a culture grows organically, once the right plants have been put into the right garden. One might as well start with the frontline people, because they make the most impact outside the organisation. For the sake of this exercise, the customer is the person to whom the product or service passes next.

Topic 1 – Coaching and developing frontline staff

- What are your frontline staff equivalents?
- What impact does their demeanour and behaviour have on your customers?
- Is this impact directly measurable or anecdotal?
- What programmes have you put in place to improve the customer experience with frontline staff?
- What worked for you and what didn't?
- Have your customers noticed any difference? How has this been expressed?

- Have any improvements been measurable? If so, how?
- What are the three most important things you should consider when coaching and developing frontline staff?

Topic 2 – Embedding customer focused culture in the organisation

- Are most of your customer contacts relationships or encounters?
- How do you balance personalised service versus consistent application of the rules?
- What steps have you taken to embed behaviours to ensure that all activities are customer driven?
- What has worked, what hasn't?
- How do you see contact centres evolving in the future? What value/how relevant is a relationship management centre for you?
- What steps have you taken/are you planning to make your people key stakeholders in the business?
- What are the three most important considerations for embedding customer-focused culture in the organisation?

In considering the first set of questions, senior management sometimes fails to see what happens at grass roots level. For instance, a very well-known carrier of heavy goods insisted that all its drivers wear full uniform at all times, and sent spies to filling stations along their routes, to check up on them. The thinking behind this was to preserve and enforce the presentation of a businesslike image. The upshot was a huge staff turnover in hot weather, when the uniform was inappropriate to the season. It was the spying activity, however, that angered employees most. Once again, it was a question of trust destroyed.

The answers to the second set of questions will depend on the type of business, the spread of its customers, and its present level of profitability, reflected in the mirror of its competitors' businesses. An architect will have far more scope to build a contact relationship with a customer than a business that manufactures electrical cable, or printing ink, for example. On one hand, the architect may not need to build this sort of close relationship, if the customer is a one-off client; whereas the supplier of ink or cable will probably have a standing customer base, and would want to make every effort to keep and expand it. All types of business, if they devise and grow the appropriate culture for them, will benefit in the long term. Each company is aware that mistakes are costly. The architect's mistake could signal the end of a promising career. The cable manufacturer's mistake might, at worst, result in loss of life.

It is worth thinking here about the rest of a company's employees, how their jobs, behaviours and skills fit into the culture, and whether they affect it well or adversely. Is it worth expending as much time and money on them as on frontline staff? Is this the same question we ask when we think about customer segregation and which customers to favour and which to treat as casuals? Not exactly.

Rachel's Dairy, a major supplier of high-quality yoghurt and dairy products, has added a new element to its highly successful company culture. The demographic changes in the European population have significantly altered the balance in age groups, so that those aged over 60 now outnumber children under 18. To continue to regard anyone over the age of 35 as already too old to employ and train, is self-evidently a nonsense, in view of the drain on manpower due to retirement of women at age 60 and men at age 65. The workforce, at this rate, is diminishing too swiftly to enable the economy to continue to flourish.

Too many companies tend to view older workers as having time-limited value, and of being incapable of retraining or further self-improvement. Rachel's Dairy takes the opposite view, has no upper age limit inherent in its recruitment procedures, and positively encourages its people to remain in place until they feel like retiring. All training opportunities available to younger people are offered equally to the older employees. The result has been that men and women with a long work record elsewhere have found new satisfaction, job security and appreciation with the company, and are able to use and improve skills honed over many years. Rachel's Dairy has discovered a treasure trove in its older workers and does not regret its approach to ageism. Its success in the marketplace is a tribute to its ethos and culture.

In connection with the age of a workforce is the prevalence of stress, a new and high-profile cause of unhappiness and illness. The older workforce is generally more stable, less troubled by family break-up following divorce or separation; has less debt, having paid off most or all of any mortgage, and is more reluctant than younger workers to incur credit card debt. It does not suffer the financial consequences following on from contributing to the cost of higher education, which is, in turn, succeeded by later entry into the job and housing market. These older workers are, generally, in much better health than workers of one generation back in time, and their ability to work into their seventies and beyond can be considerable. If they work longer, their retirement pensions will be increased.

These many influencing factors usually mean that younger workers, sometimes overeducated for the job vacancies available to them, marry and start their families later in life, and both partners need to work, to meet all their financial commitments. The size of family is limited by financial and biological constraints as well as housing need. Stress is often most evident in the younger workforce, due to these factors. Older workers grew up with security of employment as a given, learnt their skills on the job and gave loyalty to their employers in return. They were less influenced by global communications, television and magazine advertising and peer pressure than the younger generations.

Older workers assumed that their pensions would keep them in comfortable retirement. That this has proved to be a false hope forces younger employees to consider how much they can afford to add to any pension they presently anticipate receiving. For far too many young householders, the sums do not add up, even before thinking about extra pension contributions. Thus, we see that education and housing costs, the price in money and in status of having, rearing and educating children when both parents must work, as well as the cost of providing an adequate pension for themselves, are certain to prove stressful to younger workers.

A new phenomenon that makes for stress in the older workforce is the reluctance of grown-up offspring to leave the family home because the cost of making a home for themselves is prohibitive. Rapidly rising house prices are the root cause here. This has nothing to do with what an employer does for the workforce, in almost all companies. However, a good employer understands these many pressures and does all things possible to ameliorate the stress to which they give rise. Anything, from a cheap mortgage to a child-minding facility, is useful.

This warning comes after these provisions have been put in place: there will be no gratitude. These moves by the organisation simply make it possible for workers to stay in post, rather than take frequent time off to cope with outside pressures. They are of benefit to the company in greater measure than they are to the workers. No two employees have the same set of problems. If employers are to manage stress, it all comes back to *listening* to what individual employees are saying, and doing something helpful. Communication is the key to stress management, in most cases and in most organisations.

There will never be another generation of workers to match those that are retiring now, or have retired within the past 20 years. They knew poverty in post-war Britain, and were not part of the get-rich-quick consumerism that pertains today. They enjoyed free education, a free health service and, in most instances, cheap rented housing in the public sector or low interest mortgages on reasonably priced properties. They regarded their jobs as jobs for life, and they gave their all to their employers. The trades unions helped to bring about material benefits in working conditions and pay. The older workers saw their savings vanish in the inflationary spiral of the 1970s, and they are feeling the shortfall in their pensions, so that they are often unable to help their offspring on their way. Care of the elderly sometimes means that the family home must be sold to pay for this service, which deprives the next generation of its inheritance. For younger workers with elderly parents, this is also a potential cloud on the horizon and a common cause of stress.

D. Guest, and N. Conway, in their paper entitled *Pressure at Work, and the Psychological Contract* (2002), maintain that deterioration in psychological contract is restricted to around 25% of the workforce, mainly the less educated and those in peripheral jobs. Additionally, 36% of employees claimed to believe their employer has no concern for their job satisfaction or welfare, and only 37% believe that their main goals in life are work-related. These statistics pertain, regardless of the size of firm, tenure, type of job, education etc.

With so many factors contributing to stress in the workforce, it is worth examining some of the reasons for these statistics, and to consider how they might be altered for the better. Everybody has problems of one sort or another. It is how we deal with them and the help we receive that either makes for stress, or helps us to cope. In essence, trust in the organisation engenders loyalty of the workforce. Some things cause trust to decay.

Galford and Drapeau (2003) deal with aspects of trust and the causes of its loss. They explain what enemies of trust are and how to vanquish them.

Elephants in the parlour

There are situations so painful or politically charged that it is easier to pretend they don't exist. Things happen in an organisation about which everyone gossips and yet no official explanation or confirmation is forthcoming. Someone might have left abruptly and the matter is not mentioned in the staff meeting next day. Rumour is dangerous. It is better to bring such matters out into the open, and answer questions honestly. If matters of confidentiality are involved that inhibit full discussion, it is better to apologise for hedging your reply and give the reason why you cannot say anything more. One sure way to damage trust in you is if employees suspect that you are trying to conceal something.

Rumours in a vacuum

When a company is in the throes of a complex initiative, such as a new product launch, there are ample opportunities for a breakdown of trust. Employees will know that something is happening, and if they do not know the full story, they will over-interpret any information that comes their way. Rumours will circulate; most of them will be negative. To counter this, try to put yourself in the employees' shoes and see what you can tell them about the situation, why it needs attention and, if you don't know yet what is to be the outcome, tell them so. It is best to be as honest as you can under the circumstances pertaining at the time. Not all initiatives come to fruition; not all are successful and some have to be abandoned before they are in place. Lack of knowledge makes for lack of trust. People begin to feel that their jobs are under threat. People fear change. Information counters rumour.

Consistent corporate under-performance

If a company regularly fails to meet expectations set by its senior management, trust erodes rapidly. Employees begin to fear that they will be laid off and this forces them to concentrate less on the organisation and more on their own position and future. Top management has been unrealistic when setting its goals, or has failed to communicate them properly. The answer, if it is not already too late to correct the situation, is to revise expectations and communicate to all employees why you are doing what you are doing. The more people understand about what lies behind expectations, the more likely they are to continue to trust you and the company, even in tough times.

Trust in tumultuous times

However vigilant you are about maintaining trust, the day comes when something emerges, like a prospective take-over, merger or other cause of upheaval. People feel the tension in the air and immediately become spies, eavesdropping on conversations, intercepting emails and memos, desperate for information about how their lives might be affected by the changes taking place. It is not always possible to say too much in the early stages of these organisational earthquakes, and the authors advise you not to speculate until you can also inform about the future of the business. This is when you must try to see things from the point of view of your employees, people with mortgages to pay, children to rear and educate; debts to pay, holidays booked. If you can reassure them honestly, without saying anything that turns out to be over-optimistic or patently untrue, communicate and restore confidence and trust.

Summary

A mighty oak tree grows from a small acorn that is planted in the right place for it to develop. The culture of a great organisation grows organically from its core values. Culture is not capable of being invented and implemented. Core values, having been chosen by the CEO (preferably in consultation with staff) and approved by top management, are immutable and universally applicable throughout the organisation. As they are accepted and absorbed into everyday work practices, they begin to develop into the culture.

Core values start with a vision of the future that belongs to the CEO, who thinks about where he wants to see the company in future years. He has to consider how these core values might best be integrated into all of the company's processes and systems, and be understood and accepted by every employee, in order to realise that vision.

Having resolved what he wants and how he might achieve it, the CEO next has to persuade those who will fund and support his initiative. Opposition from directors and shareholders should be countered by a reminder of what competitors are doing and how their success is measured in terms of profitability derived from customer satisfaction and retention.

The next tier of management has to be infected with enthusiasm for the initiative and brought to an understanding of how it will affect and benefit them as individuals and their teams. They will examine their processes and systems, and communicate with other departments, to share information and ideas; new training schemes will be provided, to answer newly discovered shortcomings in skill levels.

The enthusiasm filters down through all levels of the organisation and involves every employee. As a consequence, people begin to derive enjoyment and satisfaction from their tasks, and readily accept more responsibility. This leads to new innovation and ideas. People stay in post longer and become ambassadors for the organisation. The cost of retaining staff, being considerably less than the cost of recruitment and training, brings increased profitability.

Employee review becomes targeted at specific goals. It is a tool for assessing the integrity of training and recruitment, and for measuring how well the core values are assimilated down the line. It defines what is expected of every person, and it removes an opportunity for personal antagonisms to influence reports.

Top management needs to keep the core values to the forefront in all future planning, and remain committed to nurturing them. The day never comes when a CEO can sit back and tell himself that he now has a perfect culture and need do nothing more about it. Like tomorrow, culture never quite arrives. It is always just one step away from his grasp and he must never stop reaching out for it.

To keep employees enthused, their efforts must be honestly and fairly rewarded. Some organisations strive to be one of the best employers, and this is a valuable target, but it can be taken too far, and the customer's interest sometimes takes second place. Happy employees are good for an organisation; and happy customers, who stay loyal, are worth all the effort put in to attracting and binding them to the organisation.

Management must always project total confidence in the company's core values and use every opportunity to demonstrate this. Management meetings, staff conferences, training sessions and other events offer a chance to reinforce the message. Progress should be linked to recognition and reward.

The whole structure of an organisation is based on mutual trust and recognition of worth. The final requirement in an excellence initiative, therefore, is the growth and maintenance of trust. This means trust in top management to keep the organisation steady and on course, and for employees and customers to be confident that the course is worth following. Employees trust managers and supervisors who treat them even-handedly and fairly, reward them appropriately, and deal punctiliously with those who do not conform, rather than allow them to damage teamwork and undermine individual effort. Nobody likes to carry the workload of a lazy or incompetent colleague, or of someone who is regularly absent due to problems outside the workplace, or to suffer someone who refuses to work as part of the team. Personnel problems must be tackled promptly, and be dealt with fairly and reasonably, where possible. If they prove intractable, the employee either has to face up to them or resign.

Middle managers and supervisors also have to ensure that the processes and systems over which they have control are non-controversial and are seen to be the best there are. They should be subjected to constant review and measurement.

The final point about building a culture for the future is that the person who devised the core values must be the person who oversees the enactment. He understands what he wants and nobody else does. Nobody else cares, either, until the wheels start to turn effectively and the profits begin to flow.

It is at this stage, when profits increase and the organisation has begun to undermine its competitors, that danger lurks, waiting for the attention of the helmsman to wander, and his hand on the tiller to lose its firm grip.

A growing culture, like a growing child, needs constant direction, example, guidance and care from the people in charge of it. The same is true of employees in a successful organisation, who expect all this

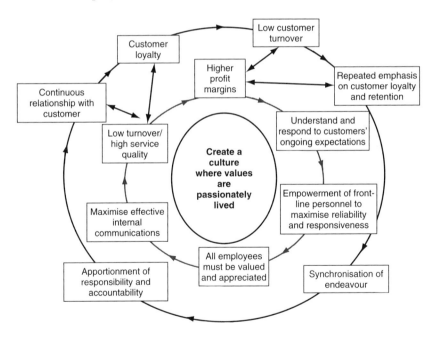

Figure 10.2 The cycle of success
Source: Professor John A Murphy 2005

nurture, and a reasonable financial and job-satisfaction reward, as well as thanks and praise, for their contribution to the organisation's increasing profitability.

Cycle of success

The overall philosophy and logic outlined in Chapters 3–10 can be encapsulated diagramatically in the cycle of success shown in Figure 10.2. Whether the goal is higher profits or low customer turnover, it can be achieved through fully understanding the *ongoing* expectations of customers and mobilising empowered and valued employees to build lasting relationships. Central to maximising the consistent realisation of these expectations is the creating of a culture where core values are passionately lived.

Case Study 1
Alfred McAlpine Business Services Limited

Area of business excellence

As a service business, Alfred McAlpine Business Services recognise that the value they deliver comes directly from the skills, capabilities and can-do attitude of their employees. To remain at the leading edge of customer service excellence, they have embarked upon a focused human resource strategy to consistently attract, develop and retain the best people available and provide them with the motivation, skills and tools to continuously improve their services and delivery. To achieve this consistently, they have had to overcome the challenge of establishing a culture of delivering high levels of service across an organisation that has a large number of employees who directly face customers in their daily roles, and many working from mobile or remote locations without day-to-day managerial contact. They believe that it is their service focus that has enabled them to build enduring and successful relationships with their progressive client base.

Background

Business Services is part of the UK-based Alfred McAlpine plc Group and employs around 3000 of the group's 8500 staff. Alfred McAlpine is a service business with a strong focus on the built environment. Business Services provides facilities and asset management, information systems and workplace advisory services. Business Services generated £270.2 million of Alfred McAlpine's £931 million turnover in the last period, and created £17.4 million of Alfred McAlpine's £38.2 million profit. Business Services serve approximately 80 customers; blue-chip businesses in various sectors such as financial (e.g. Nationwide Building Society, HBOS) and professional services (e.g. Land Securities), healthcare, technology and infrastructure (e.g. EDS, BAA) and major public bodies such as the MoD.

Business activity

The business has four key areas of activity: facilities and asset management, information systems and workplace compliance. It has been providing integrated facilities management services to some of the world's leading organisations for nearly 30 years. Facilities management is defined by the organisation as a process of adding value to their clients' business – taking pressure off them, so they can take care of their clients. This involves managing and maintaining buildings and the services provided within them. They are involved with their clients in planning how they make best use of their space to support their business operations; they run help-desks and reception areas; they implement moves and changes, refurbishments and fit-outs; they maintain the mechanical, electrical and information technologies that are embedded in buildings and are critical to continuing operations; and they manage the provision of services such as catering, cleaning and security.

Supporting its facilities management activities, Business Services provides advisory services on workplace compliance, IT services and asset management services covering the financing and provision of vehicles, plant and temporary accommodation. Business Services has built up a strong reputation for consistently delivering these services in working environments that are critical to the ongoing success of their clients. In most cases, they are relied upon by their clients to provide safeguards against building or engineering failures that would cause major disruption within their business.

Structure

Business Services has structured its business to meet the specific needs of its clients in the various markets that they operate. For example, the skills and resources needed to manage and maintain the infrastructure in a busy international airport would vary greatly from that of a major banking organisation's data centres. The market-focused structure that Business Services has created reflects these variations in demand, and allows each part of the business to offer flexible, bespoke solutions that meet the specialist requirements of each sector. Due to the critical nature of the services it provides, Business Services delivers the main engineering functions (such as mechanical, electrical and building fabric engineering) in-house through its own highly skilled workforce.

- The Corporate Business Unit provides facilities management services to clients in the financial services, legal, professional, property management, insurance services and media markets. It employs nearly 800 people, and operates throughout the UK, providing services in head office buildings, IT/data centres and branch networks. Services to head office buildings are usually provided through Alfred McAlpine teams that are resident in the client's buildings, and a mobile maintenance team provides support services to smaller buildings and branches.
- Technology and Infrastructure provide facilities management services and integrated business solutions to a range of market sectors, including aviation, technology, energy, retail and water.
- Government and Health delivers a wide range of services to public and private sector clients throughout the UK, including the defence industry, many local government authorities and the health-care sector. These services range from strategic property

solutions, traditional facilities management, electrical and mechanical installation to the maintenance of specialist equipment and building services.

In support of the three market-focused businesses, the Business Services structure also incorporates dedicated specialist operations in the fields of IT services, workplace advisory services and asset management.

- Information Systems is a UK-wide service organisation that helps meet business objectives through a new generation of IT services. With major business partners, including Microsoft, BT and Cisco, it provides advice, services and optimum customer care.
- The Workplace Advisory Services Business helps clients address the full range of health, safety, environmental and technical compliance issues faced in an ever-changing operating and legislative working environment. Areas of expertise include health and safety, construction safety, asbestos, disability, occupational health, fire, water hygiene and environmental consultancy.
- Asset Management is made up of three constituent parts: Facilities Management provide tailored solutions to meet specific customer requirements within the quarrying, landfill and bulk materials handling sectors, as well as major civil engineering construction sites throughout the UK; Fleet Services manage more than 4000 vehicles, from company cars to commercial and specialist vehicles for municipal applications, including access platforms, traffic management vehicles and highway gritters; Temporary Accommodation Services serve a wide range of sectors such as sport and leisure, pharmaceuticals, health, building and construction, operating a fleet of more than 800 units, which range from Jackleg units, modular building systems, secure anti-vandal units and fully self-contained welfare units.

Aims and aspirations

The mission of Alfred McAlpine Business Services is to be a stimulating, challenging and rewarding place to work, and to deliver strong business performance for their clients and stakeholders. They believe that having a positive culture is the essential foundation of high-quality customer service. Everyone in the business is encouraged to take the extra steps required to turn ordinary service into exceptional service. It demands that they take responsibility for their own actions, and concentrates on building high-quality business relationships. This culture of excellence in service is built on the foundation of five key values: passion, honesty, collaboration, winning and enjoyment. They value people who are passionate about their work and about doing the very best job for their customers. They demand honesty in dealing with each other and external stakeholders. People who listen and explore new ideas and create new value through collaboration are valued by the company, as are people who are committed to creating success for themselves, the company, and their customers. Finally, they value job satisfaction, recognising that staff that enjoy what they do put more in – and get more out.

Success

The organisation has achieved success through recognition that employees are its only asset, and its culture is focused on service excellence and commitment to collaborative working, both inside the organisation and with its clients. A recent illustration of this was members of the facilities management team based within their client's, Sainsbury's, premises actually leaving their desks and normal roles for three days during the peak Christmas rush and working in a hands-on role, full nine-hour shifts, unloading deliveries, stacking shelves and answering shopper queries. The have-a-go attitude of their employees leads to many instances where employees have gone above and beyond the call of duty to help out a client when called upon. Clients are continually delighted by the manner in which their services are delivered. A culture of delivering exceptional customer service is encouraged, through peer nomination, by rewarding staff for their actions with a variety of attractive rewards, including experiential rewards such as Red Letter Day and leisure vouchers, and an annual customer-service awards dinner. Employees are extremely proud of the reputation for delivering excellent service and consistently demonstrate new ways to maintain and enhance it through their behaviour and interactions with clients. Their customer-focused culture has become well established throughout the organisation over many years.

Employee involvement

Involvement and feedback from employees is a fundamental part of Business Services' strategy. Employees are engaged at every level through a number of different routes. Internal communication audits are conducted every quarter. Samples of employees are interviewed and asked for their feedback on the effectiveness of internal communication channels. These reveal an overwhelming preference for face-to-face communication. Employee forums are held on a quarterly basis and are made up of elected employee representatives, through which all employees have the opportunity to influence management decision making. The results of the MORI-managed Alfred McAlpine plc annual employee survey are studied very closely, and any significant issues are identified and addressed. The use of MORI ensures that comparison can be made with results of other companies. Recognising the importance that non-customer-facing support services (e.g. finance or HR) can have on the ability of front-line employees to deliver service excellence, an annual internal services conference is held. This conference aims to stimulate new thinking about internal service improvements, to communicate people's role within the organisation as a whole, and to focus on defining and improving overall customer service. An outcome of the initial internal services conference has been the creation of a range of internal service work streams, involving volunteers from across the business, to meet on a regular basis and focus on topics raised at the conference. These groups implement approved changes and discuss topics such as internal processes and procedures and their effectiveness, and report back, with suggestions, to Business Services' directors on a dedicated customer service board. Finally, communication with all staff and sharing of their knowledge is achieved via 'Revelation'; Business Services' recently developed, central knowledge-management, web-accessed, database system. The system provides a single, secure platform for the distribution, storage and management of company information. It replaced all existing, disparate systems, inherited from a number of companies, and provides a resource for the sharing of information, ideas, opinions, developments and best practice.

Structured development

The Customer Service Board is made up of directors from throughout the business, with responsibility for each of the different operating areas and support functions. Its core objective is improvement of external and internal service levels. By involving employees from throughout the business in work streams, the Customer Service Board is making improvements in the following key areas:

- Training – customer service training, accredited through the Institute of Customer Service, is available to all employees, and their participation is actively encouraged. All training activities are coordinated through Business Services' training 'Academy', in order to manage staff development proactively and to ensure that everything is done in line with the overall vision and strategy of the company. Each individual's training requirements and career development are planned carefully through a People Development Programme (PDP).
- Performance measurement and management – a customer experience measurement system identifies how teams are performing against customer expectations, and provides quantitative information to allow managers to manage service levels actively.
- Internal services – the performance of internal teams is measured and managed in the same way as customer-facing teams.
- Communication – open interaction between employees, customers and leading exponents of customer service best practice is achieved through regular forums, conferences and bulletins.

Measurable impact

Compliance, contractual performance and financial performance are all rigorously managed within the industry. The opportunity for differentiation arises in the measurement and control of customer service. Recognising this, Business Services has become a Founder Council Member of the Institute of Customer Service (ICS), a non-profit-making, employer-led, professional body focusing on service research and individual development. This membership enables Business Services to benchmark its customer service approach against other leading organisations and personnel, providing access to continually updated knowledge and good practice. The ICS awards, focusing on Communications, Solutions and Innovations, are designed to encourage customer-facing staff to develop their skills and competencies and to be recognised for this. Membership of the ICS has given Business Services the opportunity to be assessed against a rigorous model of customer-focused, service excellence, best practice. This is a model that examines all aspects of a business – from customers, processes and employees, to leadership, culture and agility. The Customer Service Board aims to maximise the benefits of ICS membership by engaging in three key customer-focused activities. Business Services host regular customer and supply chain forums to discuss relevant business topics. Secondly, many Business Services employees are working towards the ICS accredited awards. Finally, the Customer Service Board is continually developing a comprehensive and transferable framework for the measurement and management of customer satisfaction. Business Services' customer experience survey measures satisfaction, and places importance on 10 key elements of service, from professionalism to ability to add value. Customers are asked to rate their satisfaction with different service elements and say how important each one is to them. The gap between importance and satisfaction is then measured, to ensure that the organisation is delivering in the areas that matter most to each client. This 'gap' is reported frequently (from monthly management meetings right up to the board of Business Services). The whole process is backed up by regular communication with and feedback to the client and, where necessary, by detailed action plans and time scales.

Another key measurable adopted by Business Services is 'Investors in People' (IIP) accreditation. IIP is a national standard of good practice for training and development of people to achieve business goals. It provides a national framework for improving business performance and competitiveness, through a planned approach to setting and communicating business objectives, and developing people to meet these objectives. To demonstrate commitment to generating a culture of continuous improvement, Business Services has chosen to be assessed for re-accreditation every 12 months rather than the standard three years. The rigorous re-accreditation process involves an audit of procedures from an independent assessor. Business Services first achieved IIP accreditation in 1997, and has successfully maintained people development standards to date.

Benefits

Investor in People status brings public recognition for achievements measured against a rigorous national standard. ICS and IIP membership helps Business Services to attract the best quality people. This is reflected in its most recent customer experience survey, which shows that its clients rate the best aspect of its service to be its people and its ability to deliver results. Alfred McAlpine's latest annual staff survey figures reported an employee satisfaction rating at Alfred McAlpine of 80%; a 4% rise on the previous year and well ahead of the 69% UK norm (source: MORI). The survey indicated that the major sources of job satisfaction were their strong safety culture, the positive working environment, and the freedom and information they give people to perform their roles. Staff also appreciated the energy and team working, involvement of the directors at site level, and being valued and recognised.

Conclusions

As a result of the customer-focused culture of the organisation, Business Services is able to make the unusual claim that it has never lost a customer for non-performance. This has been achieved through its performance in four key areas. Firstly, the organisation places a strong emphasis on the people factor, with its development of employee recognition. Secondly, Business Services encourages its staff to develop relationships with customers by looking for opportunities to be truly engaged with the customer; something highlighted by the example of its employees' actions at Sainsbury's. They see all client relationships as partnerships. Thirdly, Business Services is focused on generating value for the organisation from benchmarking opportunities, and also has a strong drive to achieve compliance in all areas of its business. Finally, Business Services has facilitated the development of all its strategies through embracing an overriding culture of excellence throughout the organisation.

Case Study 2
Centrica

Area of business excellence

The Centrica-owned company, British Gas, has restructured its business from a structure based around what different sectors of the organisation did, to one focused on providing a seamless interaction experience, aiming to provide what its individual customers want, consistently.

Background

British Gas is an energy, communications and home services supplier, which is part of the Centrica group. In 2003, its operating profit was £206 million. It currently has 28,500 staff, serving approximately 12 million gas and 6 million electricity customers.

Aims and aspirations

At the start of 2001, British Gas consisted of three separate businesses: energy, telecommunications and home services, each with a separate management structure, location and legacy system. Historically, this fragmented structure had been allowed to exist because, in the newly competitive energy market, British Gas had focused simply on aggressive volume targets, to satisfy demands from the City for market share. More recently, British Gas has recognised that this structure and focus is not the best economic solution. The customers who suffered the most were the most valuable, multiple-product holders. For them, moving house might involve more than five telephone calls and over 25 pieces of communication. Customers were not treated according to their value to the company. This meant that, while a low-value service care customer might receive a same-day response service visit, a high-value customer might be left waiting for days. British Gas decided to focus on the opportunity offered by those customers who could drive out the most value. The focus has switched from growing volume to growing market share value. This has entailed understanding the value of each individual customer, devising a method of segmentation, and developing value-enhancing strategies to exploit the potential value of each segment. The customer-focused improvements have been supported by training engineers, in 'Flame Academies', to improve their technical and customer service skills.

Success

The organisation has been successfully restructured into one British Gas brand unit, with a long-term customer strategy guided by a five-year implementation plan. This single brand unit is consistent with a customer perception of a single entity, but now provides the consistency needed to support and protect this customer experience. This has involved investment in databases, systems and employees and the development of a new brand 'idea', 'Doing the Right Thing', reflecting what British Gas does and how it does it, and successfully communicating the change of direction and culture to employees, customers and stakeholders alike. A single management team, in one location, with end-to-end responsibility for the branded customer experience, now runs the company. Departments are responsible for customers, not products, and they are supported by a single employee reward and recognition scheme that is focused on contribution to customer strategy. The organisation implements a single strategy for each customer. Previously, it developed disparate product-based strategies. The customer solution offered is now customised and segmented, rather than being regarded as a mass-marketed commodity product; and the customer experience is brand-led and consistent. The company's view of the current and future customer has improved. Data provide more than a transactional tool; they show customer value, attitude and potential. A focus on customer product acquisition has given way to Europe's largest customer relationship management programme, facilitated by Siebel call management technology, with a focus on data-driven retention and development. The customers are no longer seen as the object of British Gas' activity; now, they are the starting point.

Measurable impact

The value and potential of every customer is recognised by means of data generated via transactions. The company has developed a segmentation and process strategy for every customer; it operates inbound through data-driven prompts, and through targeting and selection in outbound channels. Customers are provided with service experiences based on their needs and corresponding value. For example, price-sensitive customers are offered the opportunity to make further savings with online (rather than paper) billing, and those who want simplicity are offered a single gas and electricity bill. A high level of segmentation granularity is achieved by overlaying multiple data: attitudinal data, profile characteristics, life-stage and needs. In addition, core processes have been simplified with the adoption of the Siebel-based CRM project, which has led to increased effectiveness and improved customer experience.

Benefits

Figures for 2002–2003 showed a reduction in cost to serve of 4%, a reduction in customer acquisition costs of 2%, and an increase in customer product holding of 7.2%. Customer churn rates were halved for this period. Customers seem to perceive the improvement. In 2003,

British Gas was awarded the JD Power Award for the highest customer satisfaction from a gas supplier. The focus on 'Doing the Right Thing' has led to a cultural sea change generating much greater understanding on the part of employees of the need to change how things are done for the customer. Increased revenue has resulted from cross-sell opportunities; the cost to serve is falling with efficiency gains, and acquisition and sustaining costs are also falling.

Conclusions

The Centrica approach aims for long-term profit rather than short-term growth. The five-year-plan approach means that returns will not be fully realised until 2007. When the transformation plans were made public in 2003, the City reacted with a jump in share price, but 2004 has seen high levels of price-sensitive customer defection. Only time will tell if the Centrica path has been the correct one, but it is likely that the customers who have left are of lower value. A shrinking customer base is not necessarily a bad thing, if persuading them to stay would be excessively costly, and the company is maintaining its more valuable customers with a higher value product and service offering. The strategies outlined in this case will increase the lifetime value of the organisation's entire customer base.

Case Study 3
Eversheds

Area of business excellence

Eversheds intensively manages and promotes the relationship between its customers (or clients) and its frontline staff.

Background

Eversheds LLP is a limited liability partnership law firm, advising international business organisations and large-scale public sector organisations on all aspects of business and commercial law. Internally, it is structured around six practice groups: Commercial, Corporate, Human Resources, Litigation and Dispute Management, Real Estate, and Legal Services Group. It has a turnover of £297 million, employs 4500 staff and has approximately 10,000 current clients.

Aims and aspirations

The organisation has two key aims, one internally and one externally facing: to be a great place to work and to be the most client-centred international law firm. The key values of Eversheds are its focus on being client-centred, being a straightforward and down-to-earth organisation to deal with (both internally and externally), promotion of teamwork, promotion of mutual respect between staff members, accountability, and a focus on continuous improvement.

Success

Eversheds performs well in three key areas. It has developed a culture of embracing change, which helps it to develop its programme of continuous improvement and has enabled it to pioneer electronic service delivery methods in law. It values its people and their work-life balance, which helps it to retain them and allows development of its culture. Finally, it applies a business approach to legal practice, which puts it ahead of some industry members. Eversheds is recognised to be at the forefront of client relationship management. In 2004, it won the prestigious Managing Partners Forum 'Best CRM Strategy Award'. This is no mean feat, when one considers the systems needed to ensure good communications across 4500 heterogeneous staff, in 24 locations, across 15 countries. It also has more named specialist lawyers than any other law firm in the UK (*Chambers Legal Directory*, 2004). One of the key indicators of its success is the list of big corporate names on its client list, which include Du Pont, Unisys, Hewlett Packard and Volkswagen Group UK.

The development of frontline-client relationships

The aim of the initiative to manage frontline-client relationships is to deliver unbeatable levels of client service in the legal sector. The strategy formulated to achieve this is to determine a limited number of key attitudes or messages, to micromanage the delivery of those attitudes, and to monitor and reward performance against delivery of those attitudes. All staff were involved in a '*Vision and Values*' consultation exercise, and were directly involved in selecting the key messages, including being client centred. The message to everybody who works in the firm is that what they do matters; clients are impressed by the whole experience and not just the quality of the legal advice. Everyone is encouraged to work out what the delivery of being client-centred means for them in the job they do. This is not just about what you say and do; it is *how* you say and do it. Eversheds is now examining its team management processes, to ensure that they are aligned with the delivery of these attitudes and messages. Eversheds aims to create consistency of delivery of these attitudes and messages to all new clients equally. All clients are entitled to the same first-class service. From this common base, Eversheds aims to demonstrate to its most loyal clients that they are especially valued.

Measurable impact

In pursuance of this strategy, the key measurement methods Eversheds use are employee surveys, post-transaction client surveys investigating satisfaction, and independent review reports. Employees are rewarded and recognised for their delivery of the key attitudes and messages as recorded by these multiple channel measurement methods. Delivery of great client service is one of Eversheds' key performance indicators for its reward and recognition scheme. Measurement is followed by reward, to encourage and promote future improved performance.

Benefits

Independent review reports have revealed increasing client satisfaction. The effect on staff has not been quantified, although it should be revealed shortly, with a second employee survey. The practical outcome for staff is that they are prepared to be more consistent and accountable because standards are better communicated and because they are more empowered and rewarded for their actions. Staff now know exactly what is expected of them; previously, in a similar situation, they might have been afraid of a reprimand for taking an unexpected initiative. A great example of the type of relationship-building initiative Eversheds now encourages was demonstrated when a member of the reception team noted a client's disappointment that there were only Liquorice Allsorts available in reception, and an absence of the

Murray Mints he had enjoyed on a previous occasion. The staff member posted a letter to the client, enclosing a bag of Murray Mints, apologising for their absence in reception, and telling him that they had bought a bag of Murray Mints, which would be kept behind the counter, to ensure that they always had some available when he visited next. The competitive advantage Eversheds is exploiting in this approach lies in its recognition that customer-relationship marketing is not something that only occurs in the client-core personnel (in this case legal) meeting. The belief is that firms that concentrate on building B2B relationships solely between clients and legal advisers are missing out. Secretaries and reception teams play key roles and often have similar responsibility to business managers. Driving the coordination of a consistent level of attitude and message delivery through reward and recognition, at every level of an organisation, positions the organisation's service in a unique place in the market.

Conclusions

Geoff Harrison, Head of Client Relationship Management at Eversheds, claims that the firm chose a relationship-focused route because it believes in its importance. Eversheds' view is that it cannot be wrong to have people who want to deliver great service and to have clients who feel valued the minute they walk in the door. The firm is prepared to take the longer view, avoiding a short-term goal of instant profit. If it truly delivers great client service then it believes it will increase the depth of client relationships and the motivation of staff, creating a virtuous circle.

The key to this process is threefold. First, Eversheds values and recognises its people, encourages them to maintain a work-life balance, and pursues the measurement and reward of the delivery to clients of the correct attitudes and messages. Secondly, it has embraced a culture of change, which has facilitated and supported the development of relationship management. Finally, the firm recognises the need to take a business excellence approach to legal practice, something that puts it at the leading edge of the industry.

Case Study 4
National Blood Service

Area of business excellence

Management and internal communication of donor comments; complaints and compliments.

Background

The National Blood Service (NBS) is a unique UK organisation. The nature of the business is health, specifically, the saving and improving of patients' lives. Its direct customers are the hospitals it supplies *and* the blood donors it relies on for its supply. The key business activities are collection, processing, testing and distribution of blood and blood products. Blood and blood products are supplied, 24 hours a day, to hospitals in England and North Wales, from 15 blood centres. NBS supplies approximately 300 hospitals with supplies from 1.6 million donors. It had a turnover of £375 million in 2003/4 and employed approximately 6000 staff. The organisation is structured around nine directorates: (i) Clinical; (ii) Corporate and Workforce Development; (iii) Diagnostics, Development and Research; (iv) Finance; (v) IT and Facilities; (vi) Processing, Testing and Issue; (vii) Public and Customer Services; (viii) Services to Donors and (ix) Service Delivery.

Aims and aspirations

The core purpose of the NBS is to save and improve the lives of patients. Its mission is to deliver world-class services while building ever-stronger partnerships with donors and the healthcare community. The key values of the organisation involve valuing, trusting and encouraging people. NBS shows that it values people, by listening and communicating clearly, striving to meet all customer needs and by recognising the achievements of others. The organisation trusts its staff to work to the highest possible standards of safety and quality, to take responsibility for problem solving and to embrace continuous improvement. NBS also encourages its people to be creative and innovative, to work in teams to get things right, and to enjoy themselves and celebrate success. This trust in the employees is supported by the NBS Donor Plus Project, outlined below.

Success

The scientific work of NBS is acknowledged as world-class and leading edge. The last staff survey reveals that staff have a good understanding of equal opportunity issues and feel that NBS provides good quality products and service to hospitals. The news from 'customers' is also positive, in part. Donor contacts have doubled between 2002/3 and 2003/4, quadrupled since 2001/2, and complimentary comments have proportionately trebled, when comparing 2001/2 to 2003/4. Perhaps as a result of various improvements in complaint handling outlined below, donor satisfaction levels continued to rise through 2004.

Management and internal communication of donor complaints and compliments

NBS has implemented a number of new processes to improve the handling of donor complaints, with the strategic aim of maximising donor loyalty. Its complaints policy involves a commitment to using complaints as a means to secure donor loyalty and to help to improve the service provided to donors. NBS recognises that, if it can satisfy complainants, it is likely to convert them from dissatisfaction to greater loyalty.

The format of the donor response cards used to generate comment from donors is a potential key learning tool for any manager of consumer responses. The leaflet is entitled, 'Compliment and Complaints' and invites donors to submit feedback of a positive or negative nature. This creates a feedback mechanism that values complaints and compliments equally, and thus it is seen as fair and valuable by staff.

Work has been conducted in five areas on new processes that were introduced as a consequence of focusing on complaints and loyalty, and these are outlined below:

1. A Loyalty Recovery Checklist is issued to all employees responsible for responding to donor complaints as part of the NBS complaint-handling procedures. This asks employees to consider a number of questions when writing to donors. They cover letter construction, content, tone and likely outcome (the hoped-for satisfaction and return of the donor).
2. Since November 2004, members of the NBS Donor Strategy Group, comprising senior management members responsible for developing donor-facing strategic planning activities, have also been respons-ible for investigating a proportion of donor complaints, in order to give senior managers a greater understanding of donor perceptions and better awareness of the challenges faced by frontline staff.
3. The Donor Plus Project, established in January 2004, involves the trial of a documented framework that empowers staff to take actions (including incurring expenditure) to secure donor loyalty on a session, or to answer donor requests, as long as they can be sure that their action will not harm the recipients, the donor, or NBS. If they are not sure, they can seek advice via a number of channels. The project has resulted in staff being surprised at the simplicity of the guidelines. Before implementation, a number of issues were considered: legal implications, current expenditures as a result of donor complaints, and benchmarking with other organisations that had empowered staff.

This project aims to achieve five outputs:

- the creation and implementation of a framework to empower staff to meet donors' immediate needs;
- to take every opportunity to positively influence donor's loyalty and so maintain a loyal donor base;
- to work within current NBS policies and procedures to minimise risk to staff and donors;
- to put in place a tracking system for any financial expenditure;
- to track team performance, donor feedback and donor loyalty to measure the success of the scheme.

4. The Delivering Donor Loyalty programme was introduced in spring 2005 as a holistic programme of service excellence, focusing on enabling team managers and supervisors to support their staff better in providing a truly customer-focused service. Intended outputs include developing manager/supervisor understanding of service excellence, their role in its delivery, their performance capability and enthusiasm as a role model, and their ability to communicate the service excellence strategy to their teams. Developing their understanding of the drivers of donor loyalty is also included, as well as their demonstration of NBS values and management, coaching and monitoring of staff activity, in line with the organisation's mission. Managers/supervisors should also be able to brief their teams, reinforcing NBS values and providing daily focus, and also apply the decision-making principles reflected in the Donor Plus trial, in order to embrace the processes of service recovery. Finally, managers and supervisors are actively encouraged to develop a culture of rewarding and thanking their teams. Additionally, a service quality manual is currently under development to aid staff with its delivery.

5. In November 2004, the 'Analysis to Action' Group held its first meeting. Details of its purpose are highlighted under 'Measurable impact' below.

Measurable impact

The 'Analysis to Action' Group was set up to use a planning and performance structured agenda to make the best possible use of donor feedback to influence donor loyalty. The group is to meet every six weeks and is charged with producing improvements to place before the executive and board.

In addition to the five main process developments highlighted above, small-scale testing on initiatives is being carried out. For example, following adoption of a technique identified via benchmarking outside the industry, 549 Christmas cards were sent to complaining donors, 91 (17%) of whom returned to donate within the month.

A partial consequence of the better communication of donor complaints and compliments is seen in the most recent NBS staff survey, which reveals that staff believe that they have a clear understanding about expected standards of behaviour. As outlined above, the success of the Donor Plus Project is being monitored by tracking any changes in financial expenditure, team performance, and donor feedback and loyalty.

The key indicators for NBS are the percentage of complainant donors returning to donate, the relative volume of feedback by compliment, complaint and other (quantified overall by region and by collection team), the percentage of each complaint category (overall and by team), and the overall top box satisfaction results of individual collection teams. How NBS performs when persuading complainants to return and donate forms a measure in their newly developed, donor-facing, balanced scorecard, which will be deployed shortly. A team award system is also in development, which will reward various outcomes, including success in securing loyalty of complaining donors. Teams are also appraised on their ability to generate comment. Positive or negative, all comments are seen as valuable, and NBS wants to avoid a staff perception that generation of many compliments and few complaints is a desirable team target. The method of feeding back complimentary comment is at the discretion of team managers; all share them, usually in printed form, often with their own feedback, and they are used as motivational and learning tools for individuals and teams, with some managers awarding certificates for excellent feedback comments.

As suggested above, the response from 'customers' is also generally positive. Donor contacts up to 2003/4 have quadrupled since 2001/2. Complimentary comments have increased from around 13% in 2001/2 to 42% in 2003/04, and the trend is upwards; 54% of customer feedback in October 2004 was complimentary, and 'top box' donor satisfaction levels have risen consistently, from 36.9% in 2002/3 to 44.4% for the third quarter of 2004/5. The number of complaints received has almost doubled since the 1997/8 period, and complaints are at a higher level than at any time in the last seven years; but this must be placed in the context of much greater contact numbers. In 2001/2, over 85% of contacts were complaints, in 2004/5 this figure had fallen to less than 44%. Donor feedback has been actively sought over this period through promotion of the NBS 'Compliments and Complaints Leaflet'. As a consequence of improving contact handling, NBS has improved its rate of acknowledgement of complaints within two working days from 84% in 1997/8 to the targeted 98% for the three years since 2001/2. A total of 93% of complaints were cleared within 20 working days in 2003/4.

Benefits

The key benefits to NBS have been the rising 'top box' satisfaction scores, suggesting future loyalty, and the higher donor loyalty rates from complainants. Donor compliments have highlighted the excellent staff care, friendliness, improving efficiency and professionalism. However, other new initiatives are being implemented, and all the increases in loyalty cannot be attributed to current management improvements, but they are probably responsible for some of the success. At the end of 2004, at least 64% of complaining donors returned, and donor loyalty is increasing.

Conclusions

The focus on service recovery and loyalty is working for NBS in a situation where a potentially shrinking donor base is shrinking their supply market. Advanced management and communication of customer comment, positive or negative, is being used successfully to improve service levels, donor satisfaction and, ultimately, loyalty. Although the market is different from the majority of businesses, the key lessons from this case are universal: treat complaints and compliments as equally important; analyse them and learn from them, at every level of the organisation. Finally, empower all staff to view customer comment as an opportunity to make a positive difference, as quickly as possible.

Case Study 5
Shell

Area of business excellence

Shell has developed customer profitability analysis, and carries out segmentation of customers to identify the most appropriate method of service provision.

Background

Shell has been in operation since 1833 and is part of the Royal Dutch Petroleum Group. In 2004, Shell's 119,000 staff generated earnings of $6530 million. Shell operates in over 145 countries, providing products to several million customers on a daily basis.

The business supplies commercial businesses with fuel, lubricants and bitumen. The business is structured by business segmentation: consumer markets; industrial lubricants; commercial road transport and wholesale fuel business; and the bitumen market. Shell possesses a unique brand position in the market.

Aims and aspirations

The main aim of the organisation is to grow the profitability of the oil products business in the markets selected for operation. This is strived for with internally promoted group values of honesty, integrity and a respect for people. The group aims to be the world leader in energy and petrochemicals. Group priorities are the regaining of upstream strength and delivery of downstream profits. This involves a focus on improvement of performance across all activities and the creation of a culture of putting 'Enterprise First'.

Success

The organisation measures success in terms of its returns on investment, cash generation, and the total return to its shareholders. Its successes are created through high-level operational performance and project management. To date, key achievements have been recognised in the industry, and Shell is regarded as a pacesetter in refinery operations, with an innovative approach to market service in global fuels retailing. It is becoming a leading marketer of B2B fuels and lubricants. This has been achieved through focus on customer satisfaction performance improvements, health, safety, security and the environment, and cost reduction through the elimination of unproductive, over-complex procedures, supported by a focus on staff performance and a refined approach to managing talent. The focus has been on taking an end-to-end process, breaking that process into its constituent elements, and focusing on developing flawless execution of each element. Achievement of flawless execution at every stage has enabled Shell to drive up customer satisfaction.

The group produces high-quality, differentiated products in a notoriously commoditised industry. It has also had success at new product development and launch, as seen in products such as Optimax. One secret of this success is that Shell puts into practice its cultural value of 'respect for people', through offering training in leadership and supervisory skill development, and by holding workshops on maintenance of its staff's work-life balance. The last major staff survey revealed that, compared to industry norms, its staff valued Shell's emphasis on health and safety, team working opportunities, the value the company places on employees' individual contributions, the scope for personal development and growth, the clear direction given to them, and the respect shown to staff members. Staff also believe that Shell acts responsibly in relation to the environment and community, and the majority would recommend Shell as a good employer.

The development of customer profitability analysis

The organisation is focused on standardising and simplifying pricing and harmonising its product catalogue. Shell realised that allowing sales managers to strike individual unique deals with every customer creates complication and cost for back-office service operations. It also recognised that it was over-delivering to some customers. In many cases, the level of service provided was unnecessary, and some customers actually resented a superior level of service, because the interaction required with Shell's account manager involved too much of their precious time. These customers wanted a simpler (and less costly) service contract. Shell is now developing an initiative to generate true customer profitability analysis, to provide customer portfolio management, improved customer servicing and sales force effectiveness, with the ultimate goal of increasing profitability and reducing costs, both internally and for the customer. This strategy involves identifying the real causes of unprofitable business and attempting to make all customer relationships profitable by improving working capital management, reducing costs to serve, and increasing prices. Where this is impossible, the organisation ceases to do business with any customer causing them a loss, who cannot be, or refuses to be, switched to a profitable contract.

The initial setting of customer profitability business goals and strategy development was carried out at senior level, but its success and development rely on complete buy-in and involvement of employees. Account managers have to review their unprofitable customers on an ongoing basis and determine the appropriate action to be taken to make them profitable. This may involve transferring customers to a different segmented group, to receive a different level of service. Customers are currently banded Platinum, Gold, Silver or Bronze, depending on two combined factors: customer needs and customer value to Shell. Platinum customers are serviced by key account managers; Gold customers are serviced by field-based account managers; Silver by office-based account managers; Bronze by campaign executions.

Customer profitability calculation

Customer profitability is calculated as part of a monthly process, including the following customer specific costs, which are allocated at an individual customer level:

- Cost of the customer service centre (broken down at customer level by activity).
- Cost of the sales force (broken down by activity).
- Hospitality costs.
- Working capital costs (e.g. cost of credit, loans).

Account managers are provided with a model that allows them to view current performance at a named customer level, and calculate the impact on profitability of pulling various levers; e.g. changing price, growing customer profitable volumes, changing credit terms, or switching customers from a key account manager to a cheaper, office-based account manager.

The group still feels that there is some way to go in the development and refinement of customer profitability analysis within the organisation. It is anticipated that the profitability-focused actions carried out by account managers will become part of a sales and marketing plan, where progress will be measured. It is planned to change the way customer service centre costs are allocated to the different lines of business. Currently, these are set once a year, based on estimates of time spent in the preceding year on the different lines of business customers. It is hoped that future customer service centre costs will be allocated based on the actual costs of activities performed on the customers of each different line of business, using actual data provided each month. The segmentation banding is currently being reviewed to include differentiation of services offered by the customer service centre and supply. The customer service centre has to become accountable and be able to quantify the cost of the services it provides to customers. Achieving the required level of data generation and analysis is not a simple process.

Measurable impact

The key indicators tracked by the group are:

- Customer profitability (margins and returns on capital employed).
- Customer numbers: total, negative trading (those creating a loss), negative dormant (those who have been creating a loss but are now not traded with).
- Increases/decreases to credit terms: daily sales outstanding (DSO) versus plan. The organisation is focusing on reducing credit days. To achieve this, it has vastly reduced the number of different credit terms available. The aim of this process is to reduce the range of global systems, applications and products in data processing (enterprise resource planning (ERP) cost reduction), and to reduce payment terms to reduce working capital.
- Customer relationship management/customer service management under-/over-recovery.
- Customer service management cost breakdown (e.g. cost of ordering, price queries, master data changes, etc.).
- Customer relationship management under-/over-servicing.
- Number of customers in different profit bands by key account manager, field-based account manager, office-based account manager and the total.

The key items to be measured are customer contribution and return on capital employed for individual customers, recorded and analysed using S curves, profit cliffs, pie charts and bar charts. These new measures are then reconciled to actual costs on a monthly basis.

Benefits

The implementation of customer profitability analysis has resulted in improved customer satisfaction through improved customer service. Service issues have been highlighted by analysing customer information, identifying areas of concern and putting in place actions to improve service; for example, by moving customer orders to a cheaper channel, such as web-based, where this suits both parties. Historically, Shell, like most organisations, lost customers due to service problems such as incorrect invoicing and late deliveries. The information this analysis provides will enable the group to improve in this area and, hence, to reduce the number of dissatisfied customers leaving.

Account managers have never before had such powerful information regarding the true profitability of their customers. This information will allow them to allocate their time more effectively because they have visibility on the impact of changing credit terms, hospitality, loans etc. The customer service centre also has powerful information regarding what activities are driving costs, plus an accurate basis on which to allocate actual costs to the different lines of business.

Conclusions

Shell has achieved significant increases to customer profitability and large reductions to working capital. This was achieved through development of the group's culture and values and by showing respect for its people. On this foundation of positive morale, a culture of change has been developed, with an ongoing process of review of service delivery that has led to the identification of the most cost-effective channels. Shell's understanding of customer profitability analysis, although in continual development, is more advanced than in many organisations. Its segmentation of customer groups and development of procedures to make unprofitable customers profitable have been built on an understanding and identification of key, detailed cost-measurement criteria. Shell recognises that measuring customer profitability must not be treated as just another one-off initiative, but, instead, it becomes part of the ongoing monthly process that will provide a competitive advantage over those companies that do not measure it.

Bibliography

Aaker, D.A. (1996) *Building Strong Brands*. New York: Free Press.

Allworth, E. and Hesketh, B. (2000) Job requirements biodata as a predictor of performance in customer service roles. *International Journal of Selection and Assessment*, **8**(3), 137–47.

Arkin, A. and Allen, R. (2002) Satisfaction guaranteed. *People Management*, **8**(21), 40–2.

Ashby, F. and Pell, A. (2001) *Embracing Excellence*. Harlow, Essex: Prentice Hall.

Balle, M. (1995) *The Business Process Re-Engineering Action Kit* London: Kogan Page.

Bee, F. (1995) *Customer Care*. London: Institute of Personnel and Development.

Bell, C.R. and Zemke, R. (1992) *Managing Knock Your Socks off Service*. New York: Amacom.

Berger, P.D. and Nasr, N.I. (1998) Customer lifetime value: marketing models and applications. *Journal of Interactive Marketing*, **12**(1), 17–30.

Brown, S.A. (1995) *What Customers Value Most*. Ontario: John Wiley & Sons Canada Ltd.

Bruce, A. and Pepitone, J.S. (1999) *Motivating Employees*. New York: McGraw-Hill.

Buckingham, M. and Clifton, D.O. (2001) *Now, Discover Your Strengths*. New York: Free Press.

Burton, A.J. (1997) *Service Quality and Service Recovery*. Manchester: Doctoral Programme, Manchester Business School.

Butterfield, W.R. (1991) *Quality Service Pure and Simple*. Wisconsin: ASQC Quality Press.

Buttle, F. (1996) *Relationship Marketing*. London: Paul Chapman.

Buttle, F. (2004) *Customer Relationship Management*. Oxford: Elsevier, Butterworth-Heinemann.

Buttle, F. & Burton, J. (2002) Does service failure influence customer loyalty? *Journal of Consumer Behaviour*, **1**(3), 217–27.

Buttle, F. & Cox, J. (2004) *Mid-market CRM Customer Relationship Excellence in Mid-size Enterprises*. White Label Publishing.

Campbell, N.C.G. and Cunningham, M.T. (1983) Customer analysis for strategy development in industrial markets. *Strategic Management Journal*, **4**, 369–80.

Chang, R.Y. and Kelly, P.K. (1995) *Satisfying Internal Customers First*. London: Kogan Page.

Chun, R. (2003) *Customer Management Leadership Group Report*. Manchester, Manchester Business School.

Chun, R. (2003) *The Links between Employee Satisfaction and Customer Satisfaction*. Manchester, Manchester Business School.

Clark, B.H. (2003) Bad examples. *Marketing Management*, **2**(1).

Clark, R. (2004) Flexibility adds to the bottom line. *People Management*, **10**(12), 49.

Clark, R. (1995) *The Customer Loyalty Report*. Somerton: SJB Services.

Clemmer, J. (1992) *Firing on all Cylinders*. New York: Irwin Professional Publishing.

Cook, S. (1997) *Customer Care*. London: Kogan Page.

Coopers & Lybrand (1998) *Customer Value Strategy, the Marketing Strategy Approach that Creates Customer Value Both Ways*, Thought Leadership Series. Utrecht: Coopers & Lybrand NV.

Craven, R. (2002) *Customer is King: How to Exceed Their Expectations*. London: Virgin Books Ltd.

Cross, R. and Smith, J. (1995) *Customer Bonding, Pathway to Customer Loyalty*. Chicago: NTC Business Books.

Cunningham, M.T. and Homse, E. (1982) *An Interactive Approach to Marketing and Purchasing Strategy*. Chichester, John Wiley & Sons Ltd.

Currivan, D.B. (1999) The causal order of job satisfaction and organizational commitment in models of employee turnover. *Human Resource Management Review*, **9**(4), 495–524.

Curry, J. (1992) *Know Your Customers!* London: Kogan Page.

Czerny, A. (2004) Woolworth's aims to involve staff. *People Management*, **10**(13), 13.

Daetz, D., Barnard, B. and Norman, R. (1995) *Customer Integration*. New York: John Wiley and Sons Inc.

Daffy, C. (1996) *Once a Customer, Always a Customer*. Dublin: Oak Tree Press.

Davidow, W.H. and Uttal, B. (1989) *Total Customer Service, The Ultimate Weapon*. New York: Harper & Row.

Davies, G., Chun, R., Da Silva, R. and Roper, S. (2003) *Corporate Reputation and Competitiveness*. London: Routledge.

Doyle, P. and Saunders, J. (1985) Market segmentation and positioning in specialized industrial markets. *Journal of Marketing*, **49**, Spring.

Edwards, C. (2004) Called to account. *People Management*, **10**(15), 833–4.

Eyre, E.C. (1979) *Effective Communication Made Simple*. London: William Heinemann.

Financial Times (2004) Managing people: leader on the route to success. 2 September.

Fiocca, R. (1982) Account portfolio analysis for strategy development. *Industrial Marketing Management*, **11**, 53–62.

Foster, T.R.V. (1997) *101 Ways to Boost Customer Satisfaction*. London: Kogan Page.

Freemantle, D. (1992) *Incredible Customer Service*. London: McGraw-Hill.

Freemantle, D. (2004) *The BIZ: Little Things that make a Big Difference to Team Motivation and Leadership*. London: Nicholas Brearley.

Freeston, R. (2004) *Questionnaire for the Development of a Common Customer Metrics Framework*. CMLG Customer Metrics Survey.

Galford, R. and Drapeau, A.S. (2003) The enemies of trust. *Harvard Business Review*, February.

Garnett, J. (1989) *The Managers Responsibility for Communication*. London: The Industrial Society.

Garratt, R. (1994) *The Learning Organisation*. London: HarperCollins.

Gerson, R.F. (1992) *Keeping Customers for Life*. California: Crisp Publications Inc.

Gerstner, L. (2002) *Who Says Elephants Can't Dance?* London: HarperCollins.

Gober, M. (2003) *The Art of Giving Quality Service*. Camberley: Mary Gober International Limited.

Gordon, I.H. (1998) *Relationship Marketing*. Ontario, John Wiley & Sons Canada Ltd.

Grey, R. (2003) Brand benefits of loyalty initiatives. *Marketing UK*.

Griffin, J. (1995) *Customer Loyalty, How to earn it, How to keep it*. New York: Simon & Schuster.

Guest, D. and Conway, N. (2002) *Pressure at Work, and the Psychological Contract*. London: Chartered Institute of Personnel and Development.

Haeckel, S.H., Carbone, L.P. and Berry, L.L. (2003) How to lead the customer experience. *Marketing Management*, **12**(1).

Hansemark O.C. and Albinsson M. (2004) Customer satisfaction and retention: the experiences of individual employees. *Managing Service Quality*, **14**(1), 40–57.

Hellriegel, D., Slocum J.W. and Woodman R.W. (1995) *Organisational Behaviour*, 7th edition. West Publishing.

Herzberg, F. (2003) One more time: how do you motivate employees? *Harvard Business Review*, January.

Heskett, J.L., Jones, T.O., Loveman, G.W., Sasser, W.E.J. and Schlesinger, L.A. (1994) Putting the service profit chain to work. *Harvard Business Review*, **72**, 164–74.

Heskett, J.L., Sasser, W.E.J. and Schlesinger, L.A. (1997). *The Service Profit Chain: How Leading Companies Link Profit and Growth to Loyalty, Satisfaction and Value*. New York: Free Press.

Hill, N., Brierly, J. and MacDougall, R. (1999) *How to Measure Customer Satisfaction*. Aldershot: Gower.

Hope, K. (2004) Bonuses reward speed over service. *People Management*, **10**(16), 10.

Howe, R.J., Gaeddert, D. and Howe, M.A. (1993) *Quality on Trial*. London: McGraw-Hill.

Hudson-Davies, R. (1997) *Service Quality and its Consequences*. Manchester: Doctoral Programme, Manchester Business School.

Hussey, D. (1998) *How to Be Better at Managing Change*. London: Kogan Page.

IOMA (2003) *Back to Basics: How Well Are Your Customers treated by Frontline Staff?* Report on Customer Relationship Management, June.

Jenkinson, A. (1995) *Valuing Your Customers*. London: McGraw-Hill.

Johnson, H.T. and Kaplan, R.S. (1991) *Relevance Lost: the Rise and Fall of Accounting*. Boston, MA: Harvard Business School Press.

Johnston, R. (2003) *Delivering Service Excellence: The view from the Front-line*. Institute of Customer Service, Warwick, Warwick Business School.

Kang, J. (2003) *Latent Class Modelling*. Manchester, Manchester Business School.

Kaplan, R.S. and Narayanan V.G. (2001) *Customer Profitability Measurement and Management*. Harvard: Harvard Business School.

Kaye, B. and Jordan-Evans, S. (2002) *Love 'Em or Lose 'Em*. San Francisco: Berrett-Koehler.

Kennedy, C. (1996) *Managing with the Gurus*. London: Random House.

Kinlaw, D.C. (1992) *Continuous Improvement and Measurement for Total Quality*. San Diego: Pfeiffer.

Kotler, P. (1978) *Marketing Management: Analysis, Planning and Control*, 4th edition. Englewood Cliffs: Prentice Hall.

Krapfel, R.E. Jr., Salmond, S. and Spekman R.A. (1991) Strategic approach to managing buyer-seller relationships. *European Journal of Marketing*, **25**(9), 22–37.

Lawson, I. (1989) *Appraisal and Appraisal Interviewing*. London: The Industrial Society Press.

Leigh, A. and Maynard, M. (1994) *Perfect Communications, All You Need to Get it Right First Time*. London: Arrow Books Ltd.

Lencioni, P.M. (2002) Make your values mean something. *Harvard Business Review*, 1 July.

Levesque, P. (1995) *The Wow Factory: Creating a Customer Focus Revolution in Your Business*. Burr Ridge: Irwin Professional Publishing.

Levièvre-Finch, D. (1996) *Service Quality, Customer Satisfaction and Loyalty*. Manchester: Manchester Business School Doctoral Programme.

Lewis, P.S., Goodman, S.H. and Fandt, P.M. (1995) *Management Challenges in the 21st Century*. South-Western.

Lovelock, C., Vandermerwe, S. and Lewis, B. (1996) *Services Marketing, a European Perspective*. New Jersey: Prentice Hall.

MacDonald, J. and Tanner, S. (1998) *Successful Communication at Work*. London: Hodder & Stoughton Educational.

McKean, J. (2002) *Customers are People: The Human Touch*. Chichester: John Wiley & Sons Ltd.

Maddux, R.B. (1988) *Effective Performance Appraisals*. London: Kogan Page.

Martin, W.B. (1991) *Managing Quality Customer Service*. London: Kogan Page.

Martin, W.B. (1993) *Quality Customer Service for Front Line Staff*. London: Kogan Page.

McCarthy, D.C. (1997) *The Loyalty Link*. New York: John Wiley & Sons Inc.

Murphy, J.A. (1993) *Service Quality in Practice*. Dublin: Gill and Macmillan Ltd.

Murphy, J.A. (2001) *The Lifebelt: the Definitive Guide to Managing Customer Retention*. Chichester, John Wiley & Sons Ltd.

Murphy, J.A. (2004) *Customer Management Integration Framework*. Manchester, Manchester Business School.

Murphy, J.A. & Burton, J. (2005) Listen to your frontline staff – they listen to your customers. *Customer Management*, **13**(1), 22–6.

Neal, W. and Wurst, J. (2001) Advances in market segmentation, *Market Research*.

Neubert, M. and Cady, S. (2001) Program commitment: a multi-study longitudinal field investigation of its impact and antecedents. *Personnel Psychology*, **54**, 421–48.

Oliver, R.L. (1997) *Satisfaction, a Behavioral Perspective of the Consumer*. Singapore: McGraw-Hill.

Page, K. (1993) *Creating Customer Loyalty*. London: Kogan Page.

Pavich, R. (2003) Using alerting to boost customer loyalty and drive profitability. *Card News*, January.

Peccei, R. and Rosenthal, P. (2001) Delivering customer-orientated behaviour through empowerment: an empirical test of HRM assumptions. *Journal of Management Studies*, **38**(6), 831–58.

Peck, H., Payne, A., Christopher, M. and Clark, M. (1999) *Relationship Marketing, Strategy and Implementation*. Oxford: Butterworth-Heinemann, pp. 407–27.

Peel, M. (1987) *Customer Service, How to Achieve Total Customer Satisfaction*. London: Kogan Page.

Penrose, J.M., Rasberry, R.W. and Myers, R.J. (2004) *Business Communication for Managers: An Advanced Approach*. South-Western College Publishing.

People Management (2003) B & Q builds on winning HR, *People Management*, **29** May, p. 10

People Management (2004) Britannia focuses on attitude, not skills. *People Management*, **10** (11), p. 12.

People Management, (2004) Employees' ideas boost staff retention. *People Management*, **10** (11), p. 8.

Peppers, D. and Rogers, M. (1994) *The One-to-One Future*. London: Piatkus.

Rangan, V.K., Moriarty, R.T. and Swartz, G.S. (1992) Segmenting customers in mature industrial markets. *Journal of Marketing*, **56**(4), 72–82.

Reichheld, F.F. (1996) *The Loyalty Effect*. Boston: Bain & Co.

Reichheld, F.F. (2003) The one number you need to grow. *Harvard Business Review*, December.

Reichheld, F.F. and Sasser, W.E. Jr. (1990) Zero defections, quality comes to services. *Harvard Business Review*, September–October: 105–11.

Renshaw, R. (2004) FYI Secretaries: the missing link. London: *The Times Newspaper*.

Rice, C. (1997) *Understanding Customers*. Oxford: Butterworth-Heinemann.

Rickards, T. and Moger, S. (1999) *Handbook for Creative Team Leaders*. Aldershot: Gower.

Rogelberg, S.G., Barnes-Farrell, J.I. and Creamer, V. (1999) Customer service behaviour: the interaction of service predisposition and job characteristics. *Journal of Business Psychology*, **13**(3), 421–36.

Rucci, A.J., Kim, S.P. and Quinn, R.T. (1998). The employee–customer-profit chain at Sears. *Harvard Business Review*, January–February, 83–97.

Rust, R. and Zahorik, A.J. (1993). Customer satisfaction, customer retention, and market share. *Journal of Retailing*, **69**(2), 193–215.

Sarel, D. and Marmorstein, H. (1999) Managing the delayed service encounter: the role of employee action and customer prior experience. *International Journal of Bank Marketing*, June: 286–94.

Schneider, B. and Bowen, D.E. (1995) *Winning the Service Game*. Boston: Harvard Business School Press.

Scott, C.D. and Jaffe, D.T. (1991) *Empowerment*. London: Kogan Page.

Sergeant, A. and Frenkel, S. (2000) When do customer contact employees satisfy customers? *Journal of Service Research*, **3**(1), 18–34.

Shapiro, B.P., Rangan, K.V., Moriarty, R.T. and Ross, E.B. (1987) Manage customers for profits (not just sales). *Harvard Business Review*, September–October, 101–8.

Sheth, J.N. and Sharma, A. (1997) Supplier relationships, emerging issues and challenges. *Industrial Marketing Management*, **26**, 91–100.

Silvestro, R. and Cross, S. (2000) Applying the service profit chain in a retail environment. *International Journal of Service Industry Management*, **11**(3), 244–68.

Smedly, M. (2004) Training platform. *People Management*, **10**(16), 36–7.

Smethurst, S. (2004) The culture of care. *People Management*, **10**(11), 41–3.

Smith, W. (1956) Product differentiation and marketing segmentation as alternative strategies. *Journal of Marketing*, **21**, 3–8.

Smola, K.W. and Sutton, C.D. (2002) Generational differences: revisiting generational work values for the new millennium, *Journal of Organizational Behavior*, **23**, 363–82.

Sparrow, P.R. (2004) *Growing and Sustaining a Customer-Based Culture.* Manchester: Manchester Business School, Literature Review.

Sparrow, P.R. and Cooper, C.I. (2003) *The Employment Relationship: Key Challenges for HR.* London: Butterworth-Heinemann.

Spekman, R. (1981) Segmenting buyers in different types of organisations. *Industrial Marketing Management*, **10**, 43–8.

Storbacka, K. (2000) Customer profitability, analysis and design issues. In J. Sheth and A. Parvatiyar (eds), *Handbook of Relationship Marketing.* London: Sage, pp. 565–84.

Sunday Times (2002) The 100 best companies to work for. 24 March. London.

Swailes, S. (2002) Organizational commitment: a critique of the construct and measures. *International Journal of Management Review*, **4**(2), 155–78.

Swanson, R.C. (1995) *The Quality Improvement Handbook.* London: Kogan Page.

Szwarc, P. (2005) Researching customer satisfaction and loyalty (market research in practice). London: Kogan Page.

Turnbull, P.W. and Zolkiewski, J.M. (1997) Profitability in customer portfolio planning. In D. Ford (ed.), *Understanding Business Markets*, 2nd Edition. London: The Dryden Press.

UNISYS (1995) *The Age of the Customer.* Research Report.

Vandenbosch, M. and Dawar, N. (2002) Beyond better products: capturing value in customer retention. *MIT Sloan Management Review*, Summer.

Vandermerwe, S. (1996) *The Eleventh Commandment.* Chichester: John Wiley & Sons Ltd.

Vilares, M.J. and Simões Coelho, P. (2003) The employee–customer satisfaction chain in the ECSI model. *European Journal of Marketing*, **37**(11/12): 1703–22.

Wellemin, J. (1999) *Successful Customer Care.* London: Hodder & Stoughton Educational.

Whitely, P. (2002) *Motivation.* Minnesota: Capstone Publishing.

Wilkie, W.L. (1994) *Consumer Behaviour.* New York: John Wiley & Sons Inc.

Woodruff, R.B. and Gardial, S.F. (1996) *Know your Customer, New Approaches to Understanding Customer Value and Satisfaction.* Cambridge, MA: Blackwell Publishers.

Yi, Y. (1990). A critical review of consumer satisfaction. In V.A. Zeithaml (ed.), *Review of Marketing.* Chicago: American Marketing Association.

Yorke, D.A. (1984) Market profit centres: fiction or an emerging reality? *Management Accounting*, February, 21–7.

Yorke, D.A. and Droussiotis, G. (1994) The use of customer portfolio theory: an empirical survey. *Journal of Business and Industrial Marketing*, **9**(3), 6–18.

Zeithaml, V.A., Berry, L.L. and Parasuraman, A. (1996) The behavioral consequences of service quality. *Journal of Marketing*, **60**: 31–46.

Zenger, J.H. and Folkman, J. (2004) *The Handbook for Leaders: 24 Lessons for Extraordinary Leadership*. New York: McGraw-Hill.

Zolkiewski, J. and Turnbull, P. (1999) *A Review of Customer Relationships Planning: Does Customer Profitability and Portfolio Analysis Provide the Key to Successful Relationship Management?* Manchester: MSM Working Paper Series.

Index

Index compiled by Annette Musker